SHROPSHIRE BLUE

A SHROPSHIRE LAD IN THE RAF

VOLUME 2

ON THE BUFFET

RON POWELL

Cover design by Martin Butler

To my wife, Geraldine,

for all those

uneaten breakfasts

and so much more

Table of Contents

Introduction

Those that have read the first volume of Shropshire Blue, Preparation For Flight, will know that my journey into Royal Air Force flying training had been longer and more circuitous than most.

The standard route was to enter straight from school or university. But although my sole ambition while growing up in rural Shropshire had been to join the RAF as a pilot, when I left school at 18, they wouldn't take me. So I joined as an engineering apprentice, a Trenchard Brat, and spent three years at RAF Halton, training to become an airframe and propulsion technician - and growing up.

From Halton, I went to RAF Scampton, the home of half the Vulcan nuclear bomber force. It was the height of the Cold War and I did more growing up as a tiny but necessary cog in NATO's efforts to prevent nuclear Armageddon.

Throughout, I'd maintained the ambition to be a pilot, and when I re-applied after two years at Scampton, I was successful. Six months later, in August 1979, I completed officer training. This volume takes up the story as I embark on my pilot training at the relatively old age of 24½ years.

As I warned in Volume One, despite the aid of diaries and scrap books, memory can be slippery and unreliable, as well as partial and self-serving. So, once again, what follows is my story, my truth.

Perhaps the title, On The Buffet, deserves some explanation.

When the smooth airflow over an aircraft's wings becomes turbulent and breaks away, it buffets against the airframe. This buffeting can be the last warning a pilot gets before their aircraft falls from the sky in a potentially lethal condition known as a stall. So, in aviation terms, someone nearing disaster can be referred to as being *on the buffet*.

Most of my three years in flying training were spent in this condition, never far from failing to make the grade, or from crashing out in more dramatic style, as the following episode demonstrates.

Great pillars of cloud bubble up, dwarfing me as I sit beneath the domed canopy of my red and white jet. Blindingly white, the clouds seem to be closing in, blocking the way ahead.

Resplendent in Top Gun flying kit – dark visor down - this first solo flight around the Vale of York should be a moment of triumph. After all, it's another significant step on the road to achieving my ambition of becoming a Royal Air Force pilot.

And yet, as with many keenly anticipated experiences, the reality is proving more complicated.

What pleasure there is in weaving my Jet Provost among the clouds is over-written with anxiety. I'm far from the shining light of my flying training course, taking longer to learn new skills than most – although, not all. During my short flying career to date, three fellow students have been suspended from training, or in our parlance, *chopped*.

I drop the left wing and search for a feature I recognise. The action betrays my biggest concern, failing to find my way back to the airfield.

With the ejection seat to my right empty, there's no-one to criticise my flying, but also no-one to take control and sort things out if they go wrong. And most importantly, no-one to prompt me if I head off in the wrong direction at three miles a minute.

Oh, stop being such a wimp! Even if the forecast bad weather seems to be arriving early, I can't go back to the circuit after 20 minutes. I have to press on.

But where am I?

Bugger! Cloud has slid in below to obscure the ground. No problem. I know roughly where I am and how to work out a heading for base. I could even swallow my pride and ask air traffic control to help. But among the many things I have yet to learn is how to fly in cloud.

If I can't find a gap in which to descend, I'm toast.

Sweat prickles my upper lip, vying with a trickle of snot I can't wipe away without lowering my oxygen mask. As usual, I wrinkle my nose and sniff. Such irritants have long shattered any notion that military flying might be glamorous.

Threading my way between the towering walls of white, I search in vain for a glimpse of the ground. Time passes and my pulse begins to race. But then, the clouds part to reveal shadowy fields and dark, leafless, woods. I heave a sigh and spiral down.

In my haste, I omit a set of routine but vital actions.

Below cloud, it's still a beautiful late winter's morning. And of course, now I'm down here, there seems to be plenty of blue sky above me. Too late to climb and rejoin the planned route though, so I ease the rate of descent and level when the altimeter indicates 2,000 feet.

Thank goodness. Ahead, something I recognise. The distinctive twin towers of York Minster stand tall – perhaps taller than I remember, but what the heck, at least I know where I am. Now to find the airfield. I arc round to the east of the city.

When I spot the long runway at RAF Elvington, I call the air traffic control tower. The controller relays a pressure setting of 968 millibars. With this dialled into a little window on the face of the altimeter, the instrument will display my height above the runway. But I should have done it before I descended.

A pressure of 968 is unusually low for the UK, an indication of the depth of the approaching depression. And because of my omission, I'm still flying on the standard pressure setting of 1013 we use in the upper air, a difference of 45 millibars.

I grasp a knurled knob at the base of the altimeter and start winding from 1013 to 968. As I do so, the hundreds needle rotates rapidly anti-clockwise, sweeping down 30 feet for each millibar reduction in pressure. Soon, it's completed one revolution, wiping off 1,000 feet. And still I wind the numbers back. When the little window finally displays 968. I simply stare.

It can't be!

The unusual view of the Minster suddenly makes sense, as does the proximity of some of the buildings and electricity pylons. When I thought I was flying around York at 2,000 feet, I was actually at about 650, within a few hundred feet of those obstructions.

Hoping no-one has seen me, I open the throttle and climb to 1,000 feet abeam the airfield. I then eat up the rest of my 45 minutes flying circuits, and letting my pulse return to normal.

As after every solo flight, I report to my instructor. He raises a quizzical eyebrow when I tell him I returned early because of the weather. But he doesn't quiz me further and I omit to mention that I'd descended with the wrong pressure setting on my altimeter, or that I'd flown around York at 650 feet.

In my room that night, I wonder whether members of the public will have made low-flying or noise complaints. More importantly, I question whether I'm cut out for this life.

If I manage to make it through the syllabus to the point where I'm allowed to fly solo in cloud, a similar mistake could see me flying into high ground. I could kill not only myself, but innocent people on the ground.

The next morning, no complaints have been received and I decide to put the episode behind me. After all, it isn't the first time I've had reason to question the wisdom of persisting in my quest to become a military pilot.

And it won't be the last.

Chapter 1 – An Unexpected Hurdle

'Eyes left!' the drill instructor barks.

The approaching flight of 30 recruits snap their heads and eyes to the left and the corporal throws up a smart salute.

For a split second, I wonder who they're saluting. But I soon recover and return the salute, lowering my right arm only when the last file of three airmen has passed.

A few moments later, the corporal bawls, 'Eyes front!'

I listen to the rhythmic beat of their footsteps and his occasional shouts of, 'Left, right, left, right,' fading into the distance.

How things have changed?

Five years and ten months earlier, I'd have been one of the marching airmen, turning my head and eyes left to acknowledge the officer, a holder of the Queen's commission. Now, it was me, Flying Officer Ron Powell, being saluted, and at the very base where it had all started: RAF Swinderby, the RAF School of Recruit Training in Lincolnshire. The salute was the clearest sign yet that my career had entered a new stage.

My previous life as an airman had left its mark, though.

As the flight had approached, I'd wondered if the drill instructor could be the stocky, pugnacious, Corporal Piggy Tonner, the man who'd terrorised me during my first six weeks in the RAF. If it had been, I'd have been tempted to hide behind the nearest tree until he'd passed.

Rank wasn't everything!

I was 24 years of age, one of nine young men fresh from officer training at either Henlow or Cranwell. We'd met in the Officers' Mess bar the previous evening, Sunday 2nd September 1979.

We came from a mix of backgrounds, although unusually, four of us were ex-Halton apprentices; one from an entry senior to mine, the 121st ; one, from my junior entry, the 124th; and one, Steve Atherton, from my own 123rd Entry. Steve and I had been corporals on the same Vulcan squadron at Scampton, and all of us had recently graduated from Henlow. The other five comprised a recent school leaver, an ex-policeman, two graduates and someone who'd left a civilian job to follow his dream.

We were at Swinderby to begin our RAF pilot training, or, more accurately, to see if we had what it took to begin pilot training. The unexpected shift in emphasis had left us feeling more than a little apprehensive.

You see, we'd expected to start our flying on the Jet Provost, the RAF's basic training aircraft, at one of its three basic flying training units. But the failure rate on the Jet Provost was too high, especially among those with little or no flying experience. And because training on jets is expensive, the cost of these failures was raising concern at the highest levels.

The solution was to form a new unit, the Flying Selection Squadron, its task to take students with less than 25 hours of previous flying training and winkle out those deemed unlikely to succeed. It was to be done on a successor to the Tiger Moth biplane, the De Havilland Chipmunk T10. This piston-engined monoplane was much cheaper to operate than the Jet Provost.

Neither my teenage Chipmunk flights nor my gliding counted as flying training, so here I sat with the eight other members of Number 1 Flying Selection Course. We knew we had only 14 hours in the air to convince our instructors that we had the potential to succeed on the Jet Provost. If we failed, our promising new careers would be over before they'd started.

It sounds brutal, and it was. Four of our peers had just departed after a few weeks as guinea pigs, used to work up the instructors and validate the flying selection syllabus. Had their course been *live*, we were told two of the four would have failed - a 50% chop rate. At least one of the two, another friend from my apprentice entry at Halton, would indeed go on to be chopped at an early stage of his Jet Provost course.

So, as the nine of us sipped our beer, we couldn't help wondering whether the chop rate on our course would be as high, and if so, which of us would fail to make the grade?

The first Monday was taken up with arrival admin and the collection of flying kit and a large pile of study material, including the Chipmunk Pilot Notes. This hard-backed folder was one in a series of Air Publications that exist for every aircraft operated by the RAF. They contain nearly all a pilot needs to know about his aircraft and how to operate it.

Another publication was the Flight Reference Cards, known as FRCs. They comprised a series of small, laminated, cardboard pages about three inches across the top and eight inches deep. Through two holes punched in the top corners of each page, we passed tie grips to form a book that could be flipped open to whichever page was required.

The cards listed the actions, known as checks, to be carried out from the moment we walked toward our Chipmunk on the pan, until we walked away again after flight; ie, the Engine Starting, Take Off or Landing checks. FRC pages with red borders contained the checks to be carried out in an emergency, anything from Radio or Electrical Failures to Engine Fires and Forced Landings.

So that they could be taken out quickly in the air, the FRCs were slotted into a knee pocket of our olive green flying suits. Not that they'd come out very often. The checks on each and every card had to be committed to memory, and to be chanted as we carried them out. Only in the case of an emergency would we be encouraged to pull out the cards to confirm we'd carried out the right actions, and then only if there was time.

The feat of memory seemed pretty intimidating, although, as we were to find out, the Chipmunk FRCs are slim compared to those of larger and more complex aircraft.

There were tricks to help you, and because RAF flying at the time was a solely male preserve, these tended to be rude. For instance, the prompt for the Chipmunk landing checks was My Friend Fred Has Hairy Balls: Mixture, rich – Fuel, sufficient – Flaps, as required – Harness, tight and locked – Hood, closed and latched – Brakes, off.

Some were longer and ruder, but I found them less useful. I tended to remember the rude phrases easily enough, but not the checks they were meant to prompt. This forced me to learn purely by rote, a feat I seemed to manage.

Of course, I never flew with my fellow students, so I never knew how they coped with learning their checks. It wasn't until I became a flying instructor that I discovered how difficult some people found it, and that some who could remember checks under normal circumstances, forgot them when the pressure was on, such as during tests or emergencies.

But I've jumped ahead a dozen years, so back to Swinderby.

On normal flying training courses, students had time to come to grips with the study material and learn checks and procedures during a period of ground-based training known as groundschool. Depending on the complexity of the aircraft, this could last several weeks and comprise a mixture of theory in the classroom and practical exercises utilising anything from life-size cardboard instrument panels to dynamic flight simulators.

Flying selection allowed no such luxuries. There was no groundschool, and although we could sit in a Chipmunk in the hangar and practice our checks, there was little time. Our first flight was to be on our second day, and subsequent flights were to be at the rate of one or two a day, depending on instructor availability and the weather.

In fact, the British weather was the sole reason six weeks

had been allowed to complete the course. With the forecast for early September looking good, we expected to rattle through the 14 hours and finish in a much shorter timescale.

The conduct of selection flights was also vastly different from flying training. For instance, if we reached basic flying training, we'd have an hour in the air to learn and consolidate each new skill. Following first solo at about the 14 hour point, we'd spend several more hours circling the airfield, learning to take off and land consistently, before moving on to more complex skills, such as aerobatics, navigation and coping with increasingly dire emergencies.

Here at Swinderby, we were to complete all these basic and advanced exercises within 14 hours. The instructors demonstrated a skill and we attempted to replicate it, while they assessed our performance.

Unsurprisingly, it had been decided that only instructors with long experience of RAF flying training could judge whether we were likely to succeed on the Jet Provost, or had deficiencies so great that failure was the likely outcome. So when they formed the Squadron, they populated it with men of vast experience. To us, they also seemed to be men of vast age.

Some were probably no older than their late 30s or early 40s, but most were in their 50s, positively ancient to us relative youngsters, and my instructor for my first eight sorties, Tom Scott, was 63.

Tom enjoyed playing on his age, one of his more memorable lines being, 'You better pay attention to everything I tell you, Ron, because I've got a dickey heart. One day you might have to bring the aircraft back without me!'

This gave an added frisson to those first eight hours, not least because my performance often seemed to drive him close to the heart attack we both dreaded. It also added to my nervousness as I prepared for my first flight on Tuesday 4th September 1979.

Of course, it was a marvellous moment stepping out onto

the flight line for the first time dressed in an olive green flying suit and silver helmet. But any illusion of fighter pilot chic was swept away by the parachute dangling beneath my bottom. It caused a waddling gait that had the Senior Aircraftman waiting for me by the Chipmunk's wing root smiling behind his hand.

Huffing and puffing by the time I reached him, I climbed onto the wing, stepped into the front cockpit and, with his help, strapped into the seat harness. And there I sat, breathing in the heady perfume I vaguely remembered from my air cadet days – oil, sweat, fear and vomit.

The oxygen mask dangling from my helmet emitted the same cocktail of odours, plus a whiff of rubber I always found unpleasant. To add insult to injury, the Chipmunk had no oxygen system, so the mask was worn solely because of its integral microphone. I used to delay clamping it to my face for as long as possible.

From the back seat, Tom did his best to put me at ease. But the words coming over the intercom into the earpieces of my helmet seemed hopelessly distorted. My befuddled brain struggled to make sense of any of it.

He'd already explained that my intelligence would halve when I climbed onto the aircraft wing, halve again when I strapped in, again when the engine started, again when we moved, etc, etc; so that by the time we were airborne, I was likely to be little more than a gibbering idiot.

It certainly felt that way, and this same sense of idiocy was replicated to a greater or lesser degree every time I flew a new aircraft type. Years later, when I became a flying instructor myself, I tried to remember Tom's analogy and temper my impatience as my students struggled to strap in next to me.

As I strained to make sense of Tom's words through the static and engine noise, he taught me how to do some of the checks, start the Gypsy Major engine – with an ear-splitting bang from a starter cartridge – and taxy, using the rudder pedals and brakes to weave the high nose from side to side so that you could look out for obstacles ahead of you.

All too soon we were at the end of the runway. Tom told me to follow through on the controls for the take off, which meant lightly touching the rudder pedals, throttle and control column in the front cockpit, so that I could feel the movements he was making on the same, inter-connected, controls in the back. Cleared to take off, he began talking as the aircraft rolled forward.

'Smoothly open the throttle and keep straight with coarse use of rudder, reducing your inputs as the speed builds and feeding on left rudder to counter the swing to the right because of engine torque. A quick check of the engine, then move the control column forward to raise the tailwheel and, at 45 knots, ease the control column back with the lightest of pressure to get airborne. And relax.'

I took my hands off the controls but, as we'd been told, left my feet resting lightly on the rudder pedals.

'And that's all there is to it, Ron. Any questions?'

As Tom had predicted, my higher brain functions had by now completely deserted me. The take off had been a complete blur, and I really needed him to go over the whole process again.

But of course I replied, 'No, sir.'

It was RAF tradition for students to call their instructors sir, not only in the air, but on the ground, unless they said we could to use their first names when out of uniform, which some junior officers – those below the rank of squadron leader - did.

Anyway, on this first sortie, Tom showed me the local area around Swinderby, while also teaching me how to use the flying controls; moving the control column backward and forward to make the Chipmunk's nose pitch up and down; easing it from side to side to make the aircraft roll; and pushing the rudder pedals to yaw – swing - the nose from side to side, the left pedal yawing the nose left and vice versa.

Then on to the engine controls, opening the throttle to go

faster and closing it to slow down, countering with rudder the tendency for the nose to swing due to the increase or decrease in engine torque. I learnt that you could make rough power settings by listening to the sound of the engine as you moved the throttle, before confirming the setting on the instruments.

He also introduced me to the checks you needed to carry out periodically during a flight, the FEEL checks: Fuel, sufficient and balanced; Engine, temperatures and pressures within limits; Electrics operating correctly; and Location, that is, where you were, where that was relative to your base and where you'd go if something went wrong.

I then went on to practice using the engine and flying controls together to make – or try to make - the aircraft fly at a certain speed in a certain direction, climb, descend and turn. I seem to remember we even flew a few basic aerobatic manoeuvres before we returned to the airfield, landed, taxied back in and shut down.

It was a tremendous amount to cram into one sortie, although Tom made clear that, apart from some of the checks, he didn't expect me to assimilate it all and reproduce it perfectly next trip. Just as well, but I had to make progress. There would be little time for re-teaching because subsequent trips would introduce new skills.

My diary describes that first flight simply as, *Magic,* while a letter to my girlfriend, Geraldine, back in Shropshire, also indicates how much I enjoyed it.

So why, despite the pressure, had it been such an uplifting experience?

Well, for a start, Tom Scott was very good at getting me to relax, quite a feat when the stakes seemed so high. I'd also felt no hint of air sickness, banishing the anxiety caused by my one flight in a Vulcan, during which I'd been violently ill, an experience that had led me to question the wisdom of trying to become a pilot. And then, perhaps my glider and Chipmunk flying as a teenager in the Air

Training Corps had given me a tiny head start when it came to learning the basics.

But mostly, my enjoyment was down to the euphoria of flying. It's hard to explain, partly because the experience is so personal, and partly because it's composed of so many elements. Many, though, are the same no matter what the stage of your flying career.

There is the ritual of strapping yourself into a smelly cockpit that vibrates and rattles as you start the engine, taxy and take off. Then there are the sensations in the air, sometimes of speed, sometimes of floating motionless in a bubble, surrounded by the vastness of the sky and the clouds. There are the flutterings in your stomach as you manoeuvre or pass through areas of turbulence, a feeling that can be magnified many times as you progress to the more dynamic areas of flight, like aerobatics and spinning, manoeuvres that add the sensations of positive and negative g.

And then there is just being in the air, clouds forming and shape-shifting around you, their crisp white edges lined with silver or gold, below you the ground, alive with natural or manmade contours and patterns. And throughout, there's an amazing palette of colours that change constantly with the weather and the light.

The aviation psychologists reckon military aircrew need at least one inspirational moment a month to motivate them for the prodigious effort necessary to achieve success in the cockpit. Over my career, I saw many wondrous sights, but in truth, the motivator for me could be as simple as flying above hills bathed in shafts of sunlight, or climbing above cloud to see a glistening carpet of white.

I can't pretend I always noticed such things, especially in the darker days of my flying career. But for me, these were still some way ahead. For others, though, they came all too quickly.

That evening, Steve Atherton left the course.

On his very first trip, he'd been violently ill from the moment his Chipmunk took off until several hours later. I found it all too easy to imagine how the combination of nerves, discomfort, unpleasant smells and unfamiliar motion could create a toxic and ultimately debilitating mix. But Steve's reaction must have been particularly extreme.

Although we didn't know it then, when someone doing well in flying training was continually plagued by airsickness, efforts could be made to de-sensitise them, with some going as far as being sent to the School of Aviation Medicine to be put through a bespoke course designed to build up their tolerance, culminating in flights in a Hawk jet.

And some that had never suffered with airsickness could find it becoming a problem at later stages of their career, when least expected. I went through my Hercules training with a pilot who'd found the eccentric underlying motion of the Nimrod maritime reconnaissance aircraft – Dutch roll I think – so vomit-inducing that he was ill for days after each sortie. It had necessitated a change of aircraft, at which point the problem had gone away again.

But it was far too early for my friend Steve to merit such effort and expense, and it sounded as if the experience had been so awful that he didn't want to see the inside of a Chipmunk again anyway. So, in a mutual decision between him and the RAF, he went off to try his hand at something else.

His departure was a tremendous shock, on several levels.

For a start, it didn't seem to bode well for the rest of us. Despite the possibility – probability - of several of us failing in due course, we hadn't expected to lose someone quite so early.

And I couldn't help thinking back to the section of the commissioning letter Steve and I had received as ex-airmen. This stated that we could be returned to non-commissioned service if we failed training. Would going off to try something else mean Steve going back to Scampton as a corporal airframe and engine fitter?

It was sometime later that I discovered he was sent to the Officers and Aircrew Selection Centre at Biggin Hill to have his future decided. In Steve's recollection, after little more than a peremptory interview, and with little advice to guide him, he went off to train as a Supply Officer.

At the time, I found this surprising. It seemed a waste of several years training and experience as an aircraft technician, surely an ideal lead in to becoming an Engineering Officer. Perhaps there'd been no vacancies, or no appetite to educate him to degree level, a pre-requisite for the Engineer Branch. But surely he should have been made aware of the possibility.

By the time I commanded the Officers and Aircrew Selection Centre in the early Noughties, we put considerable effort into making sure officers turning up for re-selection received help to secure the choice of branch that best suited them. That said, it was still a numbers game, and they could only go to branches in which there were vacancies, and for which they had the aptitude.

In Steve's case, he succeeded in his Supply Branch training and retired as a wing commander. We still meet at apprentice entry reunions.

I completed one flight a day for the next three days, all of them passing without comment in my diary, so I assume they went reasonably well. I also played squash and a game of football against Swinderby's RAF Regiment Section, fit young NCOs who taught the ground defence syllabus to airman recruits. We lost seven goals to six.

After flying on Friday I travelled home to Shropshire. By now, I usually stayed with Geraldine and her parents in a spare room of the head gardener's house tucked into the corner of the walled garden of the Earl of Plymouth's estate a couple of miles to the north of Ludlow. But on this occasion, she and her family were on holiday, so I suspect I spent the weekend in my family's terraced council house.

Although my mother's depression had led to periods in hospital during my childhood, the move to her father's old house had led to an improvement, and I don't remember her being ill throughout my flying training. Dad was still working as a dustman for the local council, a tough job for a man in his late 50s with a weak ankle – the result of an injury more than 30 years earlier, during his Army days. And my younger brother, Brian, worked in a local newsagent, something he did for the next 30 years.

Of my friends, Simon was now a policeman in north Shropshire, while Nick and Andy had stayed in Ludlow to work at McConnell's agricultural machinery factory. Like Simon, Nick was already married and Andy was shortly to marry. I was to be his best man, a task that would see me complete a hat-trick, performing the duty for all my best friends.

Even when working on Vulcans, I'd often found it hard to explain to friends and family what I was doing. This was partly because it was so different from life in Ludlow, and partly because I dreaded sounding as if I was boasting, especially when relating the more unusual and exciting aspects of Service life. Now I'd begun flying, it became even more of a problem.

No matter how matter-of-factly I recounted my experiences of turning upside down among the clouds, I feared it would sound boastful. It was even more difficult to explain that, glamorous as it may sound, the pressure to learn checks and procedures and produce the goods during those fleeting hours in the air could be unbearable.

As my career progressed and my life became even more exciting, or at least interesting, I tended to shy away from saying much about what I did. Although there is a contradiction in that I'm now writing this series of books, I think that in the main I've tried to skate over my adventures rather than elaborate and overplay them. In my experience, most Servicemen and women are the same, having a natural tendency to downplay or understate their achievements – unless relating war stories to colleagues or someone that shows a genuine interest, in which case the floodgates can open.

That's why those who've served in the military so distrust people who shout that they've done this or that, usually with the Special Services. I once heard that the number of people in the US who claim to have been Navy Seals is ten times the number that have actually served with that unit since it formed. This is probably true for our own Special Air Service, Special Boat Service or any other *elite* organisation.

Not that I'm claiming involvement with any elite, beyond the RAF of course!

Anyway, the upshot was that I began to feel more distant from life in Ludlow. It was only the wish to see friends and family, and especially Geraldine, that kept me returning every weekend it was physically possible to do so.

Back at Swinderby, I was also coming to terms with being a junior officer. This meant more than just being saluted. For the first time I was to live in a *proper* Officers' Mess, able to enjoy the privileges that entailed.

Or most of them.

RAF Swinderby was a base with relatively few officers, just those in charge of recruit training, plus others running the sections on the Station that supported that task. No more than a dozen officers tended to live in the Mess, the remainder living with their families in Married Quarters.

Most of those living in the Mess were unmarried and known as Singlies. The remainder were married, but *living in* was their solution to a dilemma all married officers faced: whether to move their families every time they were posted to a new station, causing disruption to their spouse's employment and their children's education; or to buy a house and put down roots somewhere to provide the family with stability.

The latter option meant living in the Mess during the week and seeing family only at weekends. Those who chose this way of life were known as bean-stealers, because the cost of their food and accommodation was reduced in recognition that they were paying for another home elsewhere.

It wasn't something I gave a lot of thought to at that time, although perhaps I should have. I married less than a year later. Just for the record, Geraldine chose to follow the flag, meaning she had 15 houses in our first 25 years of marriage, and that our children both had four schools before they were seven years of age, and several more thereafter.

Anyway, with the arrival of the Flying Selection Squadron, the small Mess community at Swinderby suddenly found itself inundated with several flying instructors, most of whom were bean-stealers, plus up to nine young officers every six weeks. The influx overwhelmed the facilities, meaning that the more junior Mess members - me and my fellow course members - were forced to double-up and live two to a room.

Having lived in rooms of up to 20 airmen for much of the last six years, I found this no great hardship, especially as the Mess employed the modern equivalent of the officer's batman, civilian staff, known as Batties, who cleaned our rooms and would even polish our shoes and do our laundry, the latter for a small fee. Most Batties were women, and often the wives of airmen serving on the Station.

Something I hadn't considered much before being commissioned was how I should treat subordinates. The model offered at Henlow was to remain aloof – haughty even – never deviating from addressing subordinates by rank and surname, and passing no more time with them than was necessary for the business at hand.

But from my time as an airman, I knew there were many more models, the norm being a formal relationship at work and a more relaxed one socially, but always with the officer setting the pace and the tone of any relaxation. After all, he or she was the one who had to lead subordinates, sometimes making them do things they didn't want to do, even on occasion having to discipline them or order them into harm's way.

I'd seen plenty of examples of officers failing to strike the right balance, some tending to be overly starchy, others too familiar. Young officers especially tended toward over-familiarity in a quest for popularity, usually with the stronger *characters* in a group of airmen. It was a tactic that might impress the few, but it tended to alienate the many, or at least make them feel uncomfortable. It was also bad for discipline, as someone invariably over-stepped the mark, creating situations which, while merely embarrassing for the officer, could be career threatening for the airman, especially if violence was involved. Over-familiarity with subordinates of the opposite sex was even more fraught with danger.

Later in my career, a senior officer in the United States Air Force told me he hadn't had a non-professional conversation with someone of the opposite sex or from an ethnic minority for years. He judged it too easy to say something innocent, which, in the cold light of day at an employment or harassment tribunal, could be seen as inappropriate. While I understood what he was saying, I found it sad. And yet, as I write this, I fear that we're approaching a similar situation in all walks of life.

Back at Swinderby, within the confines of Service etiquette and the need to maintain some air of authority, I just wanted to carry on being friendly and civil with everyone.

There was another complication, however. I already knew that some airmen disliked officers and would go out of their way to avoid them, or to make any unavoidable interaction as brief as possible. It wasn't necessarily the individual officer such airmen disliked, but their rank. A few such characters had given me a rough time when I applied for a commission, questioning why I on Earth I wanted to become a Zob – one of the politer slang terms for an officer.

I experienced a variation on this soon after I arrived at Swinderby.

The first time I went into the hangar holding our Chipmunks, I bumped into a corporal with whom I'd worked on Vulcans at Scampton. We greeted one another cordially and were chatting fairly naturally when some of his fellow airmen arrived, at which point I noticed him becoming uncomfortable.

I think he feared some sort of ridicule for being seen to be friendly with an officer, even if that officer was an old mate. Afterwards, we continued to find opportunities to chat freely, but only when others weren't around.

It was an early sign that my intention to be open and friendly wasn't always going to be as easy as it sounded. But the need to maintain the street cred of those I spoke to certainly wasn't something I'd considered before!

When I returned to Swinderby after my weekend in Ludlow, I'd picked up a snuffle.

About the only piece of aviation medicine advice we'd been given by this stage was that to fly with a cold risked causing lasting damage to our ears and sinus cavities. It would be several weeks before we were given the science behind it, but we were armed with a simple procedure to see whether we should fly.

Sitting in the crewroom, we were told to close our mouths, pinch our noses and blow gently. If our ears popped, we were fit to fly. If they didn't, we weren't. The procedure is called *clearing your ears*. We were taught to use the same procedure if we felt a pressure build-up when we flew, usually during descents.

On that Monday morning, my ears wouldn't pop and I was grounded. The cold didn't develop though, so I resumed flying on Wednesday, completing Exercises 5 and 6. Flying twice a day left even less time to assimilate each lesson but it would be the norm for the rest of the course.

By the end of Exercise 6, I seemed to be doing reasonably well in most areas. I could fly straight and level, climb, descend and turn, and I enjoyed aerobatics, even if I did loop and roll the aircraft with more enthusiasm than skill.

But there were areas in which I struggled, like keeping straight on take off. I tended to over-correct on the rudder pedals, making the aircraft weave evermore wildly to left and right as it gained speed.

Sometimes we made it into the air just before I clipped the grass to one side of the runway or the other. But usually, Tom had to take control before we hit one of the ten-inch high lights spaced along each side of the runway; or to stop us scaring drivers with a low pass over the A46, a busy road that paralleled the main runway. And occasionally, he had to prevent us pirouetting all the way round in what is known as a ground-loop, a real danger in any tailwheel aircraft.

I won't give his name, but later in my career, I was present when a wing commander on the staff of the RAF Central Flying School returned to the Ops Room to admit that he'd just ground-looped a Chipmunk. It was a salutary lesson that aviation can bite you on the bum at any stage of your career.

At Swinderby, my landings were little better than my take-offs, worse in fact, as I had a tendency to make the Chipmunk porpoise just above the ground, before bouncing along the runway, the bounces becoming ever higher, the contacts with the runway evermore violent. Without correction, or Tom's intervention, the result would have been, at best, juddering to a halt with a damaged propeller, at worst, a spectacular crash from a nose-dive.

Both the bouncing and my over correction with the rudders on take-off are examples of pilot induced oscillations (PIOs), caused when the recognition that an action is required and the action itself are out of phase.

In the case of my landings, before we struck the ground, I'd recognise the need to pull up. But, by the time I pulled back on the control column, we'd already bounced and my actions merely made us climb higher. To stop the climb, I knew I needed to push the control column forward, but by the time I'd done it, we were already on the way down, and destined for an even heavier bounce; which I could only avert by pulling the control column back, by which time we were already going up - and so on, until I was bouncing so violently that a crash was inevitable – unless...

Tom drummed in that the only way to stop a landing PIO was to force myself to hold the control column just back from centre and open the throttle, accepting that we may bounce one more time before the power bit and we climbed away from the ground in what we termed an overshoot.

And of course, on the few occasions I managed to get us on the runway without bouncing too extravagantly, we'd weave from side to side as I struggled to bring us to a halt on the tarmac, rather than the grass.

Sometimes, I wondered how Tom could just sit there, seemingly unperturbed while I attempted to kill us both. When I became an instructor myself, I learnt to give my students some leeway before taking control, but I'm not sure I let any of them explore the boundaries of safety as much as Tom let me in those early Chipmunk flights.

I completed two flights on each of Thursday and Friday. The second on Thursday was my last with Tom Scott, the first on Friday – Exercise 9 – the first of many tests in my flying career. To succeed on this occasion I had to demonstrate that I could start, taxy, take off, climb to a sensible height, fly steep turns, stalls and aerobatics, return to the airfield and land to an acceptable standard.

I honestly can't remember anything about the flight, but I must have passed because I carried on with the syllabus.

We lost a second course member though, taking our failure rate to near 25%.

By his own admission, the 18-year old school-leaver, John, had never really come to grips with the demands of the course. Eventually, he went off for re-selection. I don't remember seeing him again, but I think he became an Administrative Officer.

My second flight that Friday was with my new instructor, Mike Dutton, a lovely man I was to meet off and on for the next 25 years. The only new skill I remember being added at this stage was navigation. Mike taught me how to draw up a map with a triangular route, add headings and times based on the forecast wind on the day, and make corrections in the air using a technique known as mental dead reckoning.

After landing, I just wanted to go home to Geraldine, but there was one other duty to perform.

Like most stations at that time, RAF Swinderby hosted a Battle of Britain Reception as close as possible to the anniversary of the Battle on 15th September. It was a way of thanking local MPs, mayors, and others in the community who helped or supported the Station. The format was fairly standard.

Guests would arrive, be introduced to the Station Commander and escorted to one of several small groups of officers and their partners waiting in the Officers' Mess Anteroom. As drinks and canapés were circulated by the Mess staff, we'd make polite conversation until the national anthem was played about an hour or so later. Guests would then depart and on many stations this would be the signal for a party to begin.

I can't remember whether Swinderby had a party because as soon as I could get away I drove to Shropshire.

The next Monday, the weather grounded us, but on both Tuesday and Wednesday I flew twice. The second flight on Wednesday was Exercise 14, the final test of the Flying

Selection course. I flew it with a man we students had elevated to mythic status: Pete Thorn.

Pete had flown as a fighter pilot with both the Fleet Air Arm and the RAF, and in his spare time he entertained hundreds of thousands, probably millions, of spectators by flying Spitfires at the many air displays held throughout each summer. He was also a career flight lieutenant, having never climbed the greasy pole to reach higher rank.

One of his favourite lines was that his shoulders sloped because they'd borne the weight of all the people who'd climbed over him to get to the top. But the truth was he didn't want promotion, preferring to fly an aircraft rather than a desk, a fate that was inevitable if you became a senior officer.

I was privileged to serve alongside him for two and a half years in the late 80s, and to meet him periodically until his death in 2011. During that period, I had many reasons to be grateful to him, but never more so than after that final test in September 1979. Although my diary states that my performance was *Awful*, Pete rated it a pass.

Much to my relief, I was going to proceed to the next stage of flying training on the Jet Provost.

Given the importance of flying selection, the end of the course was all a bit anti-climactic, with no graduation ceremony or certificate. A late proposal that we should finish with a 5-minute solo floundered because authorisation didn't arrive until after we'd left Swinderby. In my case, I can't help thinking it was just as well, because I'm not sure I ever mastered taking off or landing the Chipmunk consistently enough for someone to send me solo!

The only milestone was an interview with the Squadron boss, during which he said, *well done, but now the hard work starts*, a fairly standard speech I'd hear many more times in my career.

By the Thursday evening, the remaining six had all

passed the course and we decided to go into Lincoln to celebrate. After watching the James Bond film Moonraker and having a meal, we visited a nightclub called Cinderella Rockafeller's.

We were joined by a senior officer who lived in the Officers' Mess: the Station Dentist.

He was a squadron leader in his late thirties who seemed to embrace our arrival as an opportunity to revisit his mis-spent youth or, and I think this was nearer the mark, to enjoy the mis-spent youth he never had - because he was too busy studying to become a dentist.

Whatever the reason, he spent many evenings, not only keeping up with us, but leading us astray and providing top cover when things went awry, as they often did.

He was one of those dentists - perhaps an early example - who tried to calm his patients with hypnosis. One night, yielding to our pestering for a demonstration, he hypnotised John. I seem to remember it being something of a non-event, not least because John was so naïve and gullible that he seemed to spend much of his time in a trance, hypnotised or not.

A more vivid memory is of the dentist standing on the grass outside the Officers' Mess and attempting to chip a golf ball through the bar window into a cardboard box held by – you've guessed it - John. The Station Commander was driving past just behind him as the chip shot missed the open window and broke an adjacent pane of glass.

All I can say is it was a good job it was the squadron leader who did it and not one of us!

And my final memory provided evidence that the dentist's youth had been rather sheltered. For our visit to Cinderella Rockafeller's, although one of, if not the oldest man in the club, he was determined to strut his funky stuff.

Disappointment came early.

Having walked onto the dance floor to be rebuffed by the first girl he asked to dance, he returned to our table looking more crestfallen and disillusioned than the situation seemed to merit. He related what had happened.

'When I asked her to dance, she said, "No thanks, I'm going for a shit!"'

I don't think he'd met girls like this in his youth!

Such is the complexity of the flying training pipeline that individual students rarely move between courses without a wait of anything between several weeks and several months. The next course on my horizon was five weeks away, so I had to find what was termed a holding post. Ideally, it should be something of benefit to the next stage of my training, but also my development as an officer.

I can't remember the details of the process, but after a few telephone calls to a flight lieutenant at HQ Support Command with the title of P2(Air), it was decided that I should take a week's leave and then report to RAF Shawbury, the helicopter training school in north Shropshire, 40 miles north of Ludlow.

The first Saturday of my leave was Andy's stag night, the second his wedding.

Stag nights in those days tended to be simple affairs, a tour of the pubs in your local town rather than a weekend in Prague or Las Vegas. I recently spoke to Andy about his. He remembers setting out with the intention of not drinking too much, and finishing by falling backwards into unconsciousness having failed to grasp a door handle in his parent's house. His only other vague memory was of walking along the top of a high wall and falling headfirst into a garden when a fence panel gave way.

Ah, simple pleasures!

I can't remember anything, so who knows what state I was in. It was fortunate the wedding wasn't the day after the stag night or Best Man and Groom may not have turned up.

The night after the wedding, I warned in to the Mess at RAF Shawbury.

Chapter 2 – A Short Introduction to Helicopters

RAF Shawbury's primary role was – and still is - to train the RAF's helicopter pilots. I expected to spend four weeks working on one of the Helicopter Training Squadrons, and having the odd flight in their Gazelle and Wessex helicopters.

But on my first Monday morning, I was directed to the hangar occupied by the Central Flying School Helicopter Squadron, a detachment of the oldest flying school in the world, its task to train a small number of pilots from front-line helicopter squadrons as instructors.

I think my hosts were as surprised at my arrival as I was. They didn't seem to know what to do with me, and I spent much of the first few days conducting a stock-take of stationery supplies, before ordering anything from paper-clips to sheet upon plastic sheet of letters and numbers in various sizes, fonts and colours for use in the production of overhead projector transparencies.

If the foregoing sentence is gobbledegook to you, all I can say is that overhead projectors were as important then as computerised presentation tools such as Powerpoint are now. In a time-consuming process, slides were prepared by painstakingly transferring the letters or numbers onto transparent acetate sheets. These slides were then placed, one at a time, on the overhead projector, which cast the image onto a screen.

The RAF used them for almost every brief and presentation. Hence the importance of renewing stocks.

Not sure it was a job for a flying officer though!

On the Thursday, I hosted a visit by a class of primary school children. I still have several of their illustrated 'thank you' letters in a scrap book. And I spent most of Friday helping to decorate the Officers' Mess for an Autumn Ball with a Halloween theme. I remember much use of camouflage netting and paper to turn rooms into caverns, and corridors into dark passages embellished with spiders' webs and dangling creep-crawlies to brush against.

With the addition of subdued lighting, it all looked very professional. But having many years later been in charge of a building that burned down, I dread to think what would have happened if it had caught fire. Perhaps the health and safety regulations that now limit such ad hoc decoration aren't so daft after all.

Geraldine travelled up for the Ball and both of us were amazed at the quantity and quality of the food, and the magnificent way in which it was presented. Discounting my graduation from Henlow, it was the first of many enjoyable events we attended in various Officers' Messes over the next 25 years.

After a week in which I'd seen very little of the flying on the unit, my second Monday offered the opportunity to sit in the back of a Gazelle helicopter while a student instructor practiced teaching a member of staff an exercise called Straight and Level Two: how to keep straight and level as you accelerate and decelerate.

It sounds innocuous enough, but the flight included the first, although not the last occasion during my flying career when I thought I was going to die.

After a briefing about the conduct of the sortie from take off to landing, we walked out of the hangar onto the flight line, where our red and white Gazelle sat among a row of similar machines. To my eyes, they were delightful, the helicopter equivalent of a sports car.

Behind a curving perspex crew compartment, a red fuselage tapered back to a small vertical tail rotor enclosed within a flared white fin. Above the fuselage just behind the crew, a single jet engine powered rotor blades that rotated a few feet above their heads. And the helicopter sat no more than 18 inches above the ground, not on wheels, but on two metal skids, like chunky skis.

The pilots stepped into their seats at the front of the

bubble, and I strapped in the back. It was like sitting in a goldfish bowl with only the metal floor and rear wall of the cockpit preventing true all round visibility.

All was routine as we lifted off and climbed to the local operating area to the north of Shawbury. Here, the student instructor practised teaching his captain the exercise he'd briefed. I sat back and enjoyed the view of the world drifting by. After about 45 minutes, we set heading to return to the airfield.

When we were overhead Shawbury's relief landing ground, Tern Hill, the captain gave his student a simulated engine fire. I'd been given these by my instructors on the Chipmunk, so I sat back to watch how a much more experienced pilot handled the situation in a helicopter.

To my eyes and ears, it was all very slickly done, check list actions tumbling from the would-be instructor's mouth as his hands flashed round the cockpit flicking switches and pulling levers. In the process, he simulated shutting the engine down by cutting the power to the rotor blades, leaving them to rotate in the airflow, producing enough lift for us to glide down.

All was calm in the cockpit and I was enjoying the ride – until, while still way above the grass of the airfield, the pilot pulled back on the control column to arrest the rate of descent.

My heart leapt.

Surely, we were far too high. We were running out of speed fast and it seemed inevitable that we'd drop to the ground like a runaway lift.

But all remained calm down the front. The student pushed the nose forward again, but this time until we seemed to be looking vertically down at the grass. Pressed back into my seat, eyes wide open, I could see nothing but green below me. We picked up speed, arrowing down. Just as a crash seemed inevitable, the nose came up and we sped along, skids inches above the grass. I breathed again.

Then I realised there were no wheels!

My relief evaporated. Surely, the metal skids would dig into the ground and we'd tumble end over end across the airfield. I was about to cry out when we touched down, slid smoothly across the grass and came to a halt.

Sweat prickled my upper lip. My heart pounded. In front of me, the student completed the after landing checks, and the captain praised his handling of the practice emergency.

By the time they'd lifted off and carried out another couple of these emergency landings, I was fully in control and able to appreciate the skill of the manoeuvre to reduce the rate descent, followed by the final plunge and roundout to skid across the grass.

I can only think that both pilots assumed I had more flying experience than I had, or that I'd been on the unit long enough to have seen it all before. I didn't tell them that nothing could have been further from the truth.

I can't claim that the menial tasks I spent the rest of the month performing did much for my development as an officer, but I did gain an insight into the amount of effort required to succeed as an RAF pilot. The highlights, and the biggest eye-openers, were a couple of flights in a Westland Wessex.

While the Gazelle was used for basic training, the much bulkier Wessex - a camouflaged workhorse of the RAF helicopter fleet - was used for advanced training, where the emphasis changed from merely being able to fly the aircraft, to operating it in ever more demanding scenarios. If the student pilots succeeded, they'd gain their wings and move on to the Operational Conversion Unit for the helicopter type they were to fly on the front line.

But even flying the Wessex was a challenge for some.

For a start, it was much larger and more complicated than the Gazelle, with two engines instead of one, and many more systems that could malfunction. It also had the thickest set of FRCs that had to be learnt by rote, card after card of checks that provided a formidable test of memory, especially when the pressure was on.

My first flight was with a student pilot just coming to grips with hovering the Wessex. He soon had the hang of lifting it into the hover. But maintaining a stable position above the ground was a different matter altogether. The problem was that when the Wessex hovered, it had a distinct lean to the right.

And so, of course, did its occupants.

This made the view to the front - of buildings, trees, the horizon, everything - look *wrong*. The student's natural inclination, with which I sympathised, was to put things back to normal, using the controls to set the helicopter, and himself, upright. But with this done, the helicopter would drift left, a movement he had to counter – leaving us all leaning to the right again.

Each time we hovered, I sensed him gritting his teeth in an attempt to ignore the lean. But after a few seconds, he'd put us upright again, and we'd drift left. We all knew that if he couldn't maintain a stable hover, his flying training would be over. After all, nobody wanted to jump in or out of a drifting helicopter, and lifting or dropping a suspended load would be impossible.

I was told it could take several sorties before some students could hover for long periods without drifting, and that some never mastered the skill and were chopped. By the end of this sortie, the student had improved markedly, and I know he mastered the skill in the end.

My second Wessex sortie was with a more advanced student who was being taught to fly in and out of clearings in woodland to the north of Shawbury. It showed clearly why being able to maintain a stable hover was essential. So tightly did the trees ring some of the clearings that a drift in any direction would have been disastrous.

The exercise also brought home the importance of another aspect of helicopter operations: crew co-operation. The student pilot had to learn to work with a second pilot –

in this case, his instructor - and a crewman, the NCO down the back responsible for the freight and/or passengers.

On this flight, the crewman was also a student, accompanied by his own instructor. He was seeking a one-winged aircrew brevet bearing an L for Loadmaster.

As we descended into ever-tighter clearings, not only did the student pilot have to trust his own judgement and make precise control movements to prevent the rotor blades hitting the trees, but he also had to learn to trust and act on the judgement of the non-handling pilot and the crewman.

The crewman was especially important. Only he could assess dangers in the blind spots behind and below the helicopter. He had to give something akin to a running commentary, reassuring the pilot when things were going well, and giving concise instructions to avoid obstacles when they weren't. Without this, it would have been all too easy for the tail rotor to slice through foliage, or for the unsighted pilot to land on an area of boggy ground, a hidden slope or a cattle trough.

I was never quite sure how close the whirling rotor blades were to the trees, but it often looked to be no more than inches.

I was tremendously impressed.

But looking back, the true highlight of my time at Shawbury was not professional, but domestic.

On the night of Friday 12th October, I proposed to Geraldine.

I was incredibly nervous, so much so that I chickened out of proposing early in the evening when I'd driven her to a beauty spot overlooking the lights of Ludlow. Instead, full of trepidation, I went down on bended knee in the living room of her parent's house at the end of the night.

There were two main reasons for my hesitation.

Firstly, we'd never discussed marriage, which meant I had no idea what she'd think of my proposal. And secondly, at a time when most people seemed to be co-habiting before tying the knot, or at least spending most of their time together over several years, we'd seen one another for two and a half years of weekends, and short weekends at that.

Marriage seemed such a risk, especially as she'd have to leave her friends and family to live on some RAF station in the middle of nowhere. I wanted to make her happy, not miserable.

I was prepared to take the risk. But would she be?

To my intense relief, she said yes.

I'd had such a conventional upbringing that I felt I had to ask her father if I could marry his youngest daughter. And, once again, I had no idea what he would think of the idea. What if he expected her to stay at home to look after him and his wife in their old age?

And just what would we do if he said no?

Luckily, the matter didn't arise because he too said yes. Geraldine and I drove straight to Shrewsbury to buy a ring.

I obviously have no idea how my life would have differed if I'd failed to pluck up the courage to propose to Geraldine, or if she'd said no. But I do know that although I may not always have said and acted as if it was the case, she has been the single most important thing in my life.

In whatever guise, wife, mother or friend, I can't imagine life without her.

Chapter 3 – Aviation Medicine Training

'Eject! Eject! Eject!'

Before I'd even heard the word repeated, I pulled the yellow and black handle between my legs with both hands.

Click, whiiirr, ping.

I waited, listening to the sounds of the ejection sequence running its course. Then silence. It seemed endless, but still I waited, until... Finally I could stand it no longer. Perhaps I hadn't pulled the handle hard enough. I looked down.

Bang!

My chin was forced into my chest as I shot upwards.

'Ouch!'

Hearing laughter, I opened my eyes and looked down on 16 fellow course members, a doctor – our aviation medicine instructor - and a couple of safety equipment fitters. I rubbed my neck, an action that evoked another peal of laughter as they walked across the car park toward me.

I was strapped into an ejection seat at the top of a 20-foot crane-like jib rising near vertical from the back of a fancy trailer.

The safety equipment fitters turned a big red wheel attached to the jib to wind me down. The rest formed a semi-circle and waited until I reached the base of the rig, unstrapped and stepped away from the seat, still rubbing my neck.

'What did I tell you?' the instructor said with a knowing smile and shake of the head.

He turned to face the group as I walked over to join them. 'I say again, it's only a smidge over half a second, but when you're on the rig, it seems like a lifetime. Be patient, and *don't*, I repeat, *don't* look down.'

He pointed at me and the ginger-haired man standing next to me. 'Or you'll end up like those two.'

Both Keith Whittaker - the ex-policeman who'd been on my Swinderby course - and I played along, grimacing and massaging our necks. The others smirked. How could anyone be so stupid, especially me, as I'd already seen Keith look down just as he'd been shot up the jib?

By the end of the afternoon, another eight members of the course were rubbing their necks.

It was a powerful demonstration of the way time slows at moments of stress and danger. Despite all the warnings, the half-second pause between pulling the ejection seat handle and the seat firing had been so stretched in our minds that we'd been unable to resist looking down.

If I ever had to eject from a Jet Provost Mk3 in a real emergency, that half-second would allow the thick perspex canopy above me to be blasted away before my seat fired me clear of the stricken airframe. And if I looked down then, the damage to my neck would be much worse, as the kick from the ejection seat would be five times that of the rig in the car park.

The practical followed several hours of theory on ejection seats completed in one of the classrooms of the Aviation Medicine Training Centre (AMTC) at RAF North Luffenham. It was situated in Rutland, a small, rural, county in east-central England.

We were on a four-day aviation medicine course, the aim of which was to prepare us for our basic flying training by giving us an insight into the effects of flight on our bodies. It would also introduce us to the flying equipment we'd be wearing in the Jet Provost and its safety equipment. Like all RAF aircrew, I'd visit the Centre several more times during my career, either for periodic refresher courses, or every time I transferred to a new aircraft type.

Just to finish on the subject of ejection, AMTC's teaching aimed to minimise the number of spinal injuries aircrew received when blasted from their cockpits. One way was to encourage them to reach up for and pull down on the upper handle of the seat, rather than the lower one. This had the twin effect of pulling a blind over the eyes to protect them from flying debris, and straightening the back, making it more likely that the force of the ejection would pass through a straight rather than a curved spine.

The practice rig lacked an upper handle, but the prevalence of stiff necks demonstrated its effectiveness in highlighting the need for the correct posture when ejecting.

All 17 members of Number 43 Basic Flying Training Course had upheld RAF tradition by meeting in the North Luffenham Officers' Mess bar on the evening of Monday 29th October 1979.

Six of us were reuniting a few weeks after completing flying selection at Swinderby. The other 11, who I assumed had bypassed Swinderby because they had at least 25 hours of flying training under their belts, included a few faces I recognised from Henlow. The remainder were new to me, a mixture of school-leavers and graduates who'd completed their officer training at the RAF College, Cranwell, in Lincolnshire.

There was no real hurry to get to know one another. After North Luffenham, we anticipated spending the next year together at a flying training base in Yorkshire. Or should that be, we hoped to spend the next year together?

As was also traditional when setting out on an RAF course, we couldn't help wondering how many would survive the year or, to put it another way, how many would be chopped at some stage. It was probably best that we didn't know the answer, which was five, a 30% failure rate; and even I didn't finish with them, although my absence would be for a reason other than failure. But that's a story for later.

On that first night, we were in high spirits, and that set the tone. Over the few days and nights at North Luffenham, we bonded as a group in the classroom, but also in the Mess bar and the local pubs, where we consumed copious quantities of the local beer, Ruddles County bitter.

I found the aviation medicine training fascinating, if somewhat daunting, because the pass mark for many of the written and practical tests was 100%. It was hard to argue with the rationale for such high standards when, in many cases, our very survival would depend on reproducing what we'd been taught without error. But it was still a shock.

My most vivid memories are of the practical sessions, during which the theory was driven home on, or in, torture devices of varying sophistication. I've already mentioned one, the ejection seat rig.

Another was an enclosed black box on a short, horizontal, rotating arm. As the 17 of us filed into the small room in which it sat, I thought it looked like a toddler's fairground roundabout, albeit with space for only one large toddler.

The first course member stepped forward, strapped into the box and donned a headset with a boom microphone. The lid was closed. After a substantial pause, the arm began to rotate very slowly in a flat circular orbit. Over several minutes, during which the box rotated faster and faster, the passenger was talked through a series of exercises by the instructor/doctor.

One by one, my fellow course members entered the box and went through a similar routine, the only major difference being the duration of the pause before the box began to rotate. Then it was my turn. I strapped in. The lid snapped shut. Inside the box, it was totally black. A red spot appeared ahead of me and a little way up in the *dark sky*.

'Use the control column to put the spot on the horizon,' the doctor commanded.

I moved the spot down until it was right in front of me and told him I'd done it.

'Good. Now tell me when you sense movement.'

The light went out and I waited in the dark. It seemed like more than a minute before I sensed that I was rotating and told the doctor – and the 16 others standing outside. The sound of muffled laughter confirmed that like those that had gone before, I'd probably been moving for much of the time I'd been silent.

The red light reappeared, now high in the *sky*.

'Put the light on the horizon again,' the disembodied voice ordered.

I moved the light down with the control column until it was where I imagined the horizon to be and told the doctor. Having witnessed the reaction of those preceding me, I waited in some trepidation for the next instruction.

'Good. Now put your right ear on your right shoulder.'

I don't think I'd tilted my head far before the world began to tumble.

'Whoooa!'

It was like the wildest aerobatics I'd ever experienced. Much more violent than anything I'd done in a Chipmunk. That tiny box was looping, rolling and spinning all over the room. It had to be. It must have smashed my new friends and the doctor into a bloodied jumble of body parts.

The lid opened and I squinted into the light.

'Okay, Ron, you can get out now,' the doctor said.

Easier said than done. Despite the visual cues to the contrary, my body was still adamant I was spinning wildly. Slowly, the sensations began to settle, but I remained unsteady on my feet as I swayed over to join the group.

Only when the final course member had climbed out of the box and tottered over to us did the instructor put his aviation medicine hat on to explain what we'd just experienced.

'Your inner ear has what is known as a vestibular system,' he began. 'It's made up of three small semicircular canals oriented in different planes: fore and aft, side to side and up and down. The canals contain viscous fluid and are lined with hairs. When, for whatever reason, your head moves, the fluid in the canals is displaced, which bends the hairs, like the tide bending seaweed.

'The movement of the hairs in each of the canals is transmitted to your brain, along with messages from other parts of the body, most notably your eyes. The brain interprets the information to form a picture of what's happening and, if necessary, activates your muscles and joints to help you regain or maintain balance.

'As an aside,' he said, 'the reason your balance is affected when you drink to excess is that alcohol lessens the viscosity of the fluid in the canals, making it flow more easily, and giving you exaggerated sensations of movement. In some instances it can feel as if the world's spinning even when you're standing still or lying down, especially when you have your eyes closed.

'But back to the box. When we put you in the dark and make you rely only on your vestibular system for situational awareness, you discover that some strange things can happen. For a start, when we moved you so steadily that the fluid in the canals didn't deflect the hairs, you all missed the motion, and for some considerable time.

'And then, when you finally sensed that the box was moving and we accelerated it, your vestibular system interpreted the acceleration as a pitch upward, like an aircraft going into a climb. So, when the light appeared, you felt you had to push it forward to put it on the horizon, as if you were regaining *level flight*. But the light was already on the horizon and you'd actually pushed it down. Unsurprisingly, the effect is known as Pitch-up.

'And the final dramatic experience when you felt as if you were tumbling in a washing machine was caused by no more than your brain's interpretation of the rotation of the box and the movement of the fluid in the various canals when you tilted your head, again in the absence of visual clues. The box didn't deviate one jot from its flat circular orbit, but you all believed it had.

'So,' he said, building up to his conclusion. 'I hope we've proved that you can't always trust what your body is telling you, especially when you can't see anything. And believe me, flying in cloud, even during the day, can be remarkably similar to being in that box, only enveloped in grey cotton wool rather than a black cocoon.

'The bottom line is that whenever you're in cloud or poor visibility, you have to rely on your aircraft instruments, *not* your vestibular system.'

I had no way of knowing it at the time, but I'd experience sensations like those in the box almost every time I flew in cloud. Sometimes it was no more than a sensation of leaning slightly to one side, known as The Leans. But sometimes the disorientation was more dramatic.

As part of a three-aircraft formation, I once flew a Bulldog across the Low Countries and English Channel to Manston in Kent. All bar the first and last 500 feet were flown in thick cloud, and for the majority of the flight I felt as if my aircraft was at 90 degrees of left bank and about to slice down on the Bulldog hanging onto my left wing. It took real determination to trust my instruments rather than my vestibular system.

I remember that example because it involved a long sea crossing, but there were many other instances where succumbing to disorientation could have caused a dangerous, even life-threatening situation had not my training, including the experience of the box, come to my aid. Unfortunately, others were not so lucky.

Within four years of my North Luffenham course, disorientation had been a factor in the death of three members of my various flying training courses: Paul Bishop died in a Jet Provost Mk5a near Leuchars in Scotland in January 1981; Bill Edward in a Canberra T17 in Gibraltar in August 1983; and Byron Clew in a Harrier Mk3 near Goose Green in the Falklands in November of the same year.

Bill was almost certainly killed by the Pitch-up effect.

A year after our graduation from multi-engine training, he took off into low cloud in his Canberra. A short while later, he dived out of the cloudbase and into the ground. Both he and his navigator died.

It seems that as his aircraft accelerated in cloud, he thought it was pitching up. To counter this, he pushed the nose forward, thinking he was ensuring a steady climb, when he was actually pushing his Canberra's nose forward until they were diving toward the ground. If he realised his mistake before he speared out of the cloudbase, there was too little time and height for him to recover, or for him and his navigator to eject.

The fact that Bill and many others have been lost due to disorientation of one form or another might seem to undermine the effectiveness of aviation medicine training. But I've always wondered how many more of us would have died if we hadn't been exposed to devices such as the disorientation rig.

Before we could undertake the final practical, we needed to pick up our flying kit, including flying helmets and oxygen masks, not as simple a task as it sounds.

In the case of the helmet, my head was measured by a couple of safety equipment fitters, one of whom scuttled away. He returned, carrying by its handle an old-fashioned brown suitcase, only in the shape of an 18-inch cube. He eased its two latches to the side, the locks snapped up and he opened the lid. Inside, encased in foam rubber was an RAF flying helmet with a tough, olive-green, exterior and a padded interior faced in cream kid leather.

Amazed at its weight - about four and a half pounds - I took it from the case and rolled it on, pulling it down over my ears. As instructed, I positioned the front rim an inch or so above my eyebrows, just out of sight when I moved my eyes to look up.

The safety equipment fitters then pulled – none too gently - on strings protruding from holes on each side. These tightened a cradle of cords and pads inside the dome of the helmet. When I felt them encasing my skull, I gave a thumbs-up. The fitters then knotted and trimmed the strings and covered the knots with tape.

Next, they directed my hands to small toggles on each side of the helmet. When I eased these forward, internal kid leather pads clamped tightly around my ears. Suddenly, sounds were muffled to the point where I could hear little beyond the blood whooshing through my veins.

But it also felt as if my head was in a vice and my eyes were bulging, Gollum-like. The fitters shouted to assure me this was exactly as it should be, and the discomfort would soon pass as everything *rode up with wear*. I wasn't so sure. After all, they couldn't feel how tight it really was.

Nonetheless, I carried on following their instructions, reaching up to the top front of the helmet to ease up a black cloth cover and operate catches near my temples to lower two visors, one after the other. The inner, clear, visor had to be down at all stages of flight to protect my eyes from the buffeting airflow in an ejection, but also from daggers of perspex in the event of a birdstrike, not to mention blood, bone and feathers.

The outer visor was dark, making the aviator sunglasses I'd also been given surplus to requirements. It was more than a year before I used them for their intended purpose, when I wore headsets rather than helmets, first on the Jetstream and then the Hercules. And it was several years more until the film, Top Gun, made them a much-sought-after fashion accessory.

The next item to be fitted was an oxygen mask with an integral microphone. Again, there was much measuring, followed in my case by a fair amount of head scratching from the fitters.

The problem seemed to be that I have a long face and a prominent nose. Most of the masks they tried seemed to leak where the rubber seals were meant to hug my face. The mask they eventually settled on was another very snug fit. It didn't allow any leaks, but seemed intent on crushing the bridge of my nose. Again, they said this was only to be expected and the pressure would ease with wear.

That evening, I put on the full kit and admired myself in my wardrobe mirror.

Over an olive green roll neck shirt, long johns and long woollen socks, I wore a fire retardant olive green flying suit, black boots and thin, white, chamois leather flying gloves. The addition of the helmet - visors down - and the oxygen mask meant very little skin was on show, reducing the risk of injury in the case of ejection, birdstrike or cockpit fire.

Although the chamois leather gloves were wondrously tight fitting, they reduced sensitivity, so we'd been told to practice lowering the visors, clipping on the oxygen mask and switching its microphone on and off while wearing them.

By the time we'd spent an hour or so in front of our mirrors, we were in need of a break, so we adjourned to a pub to dissect our experiences. Among the things we agreed was the need to add flying clothing to the kit insurance we'd taken out to cover loss or damage to our dress uniforms and Mess kits. The helmet alone was worth £500, which seemed a lot of money in 1979.

Clad in the full kit again next morning, we followed a squadron leader doctor into a large cylindrical decompression chamber, like those used by deep sea divers. Once inside, we sat in numbered seats lining the walls. We all seemed to be waggling our bulky helmets and oxygen masks, so I guessed I wasn't the only one feeling uncomfortable.

Such had been the build-up to this event that we were also nervous, a feeling the faces staring in at the portholes did nothing to dispel. As the others did the same, I plugged into an oxygen regulator and checked that a little dolls eye indicator alternated between white and black as I breathed. The doctor, looking totally at ease in his blue uniform, green cloth flying helmet and oxygen mask, checked his radio then spoke to the control team.

'Take her up to eight thousand.'

Slowly, the pressure in the chamber was reduced as if we were in an aircraft climbing from sea level to 8,000 feet. The doctor set out to re-iterate some of the main points from a lesson given in the classroom the previous day.

'As you know,' he began, 'when an aircraft climbs, the

air pressure reduces, and when it descends, it increases again. As long as the cavities and tubes in your body remain unblocked, gases can flow in and out of them to keep the pressure the same on the inside as outside.'

He looked round to acknowledge the nods of understanding.

'The cavities and tubes of most interest to you as aviators are the eustachean tubes in the ear and the sinus cavities in the skull. If these become blocked for any reason, gas can't escape as you climb, or enter as you descend, leading to pressure differences that can cause severe pain, even tissue damage. In the case of the sinuses, the pain is most likely to be above your eyes, but it could also be in your cheeks.'

He pointed to these areas on his own face, before continuing.

'In the case of the eustachean tubes, the pain will be in your ears. And you don't need me to tell you that any damage to your hearing could be life changing, and certainly career-ending.'

In the previous day's lesson, we'd also been told that one of the main reasons sinus cavities and eustachean tubes become blocked is inflammation of the surrounding tissue due to colds or viruses. Those of us who'd completed flying selection at Swinderby had already been warned never to fly with a cold, and taught how to check if we were fit to fly - squeeze the nose, close the mouth and blow gently to see if your ears pop.

We'd all been especially diligent ensuring our ears popped before stepping into the chamber that morning, because the next event was to be an extreme test of our tubes and cavities.

'So here we are at eight thousand feet,' the doctor continued, after acknowledging a message from the control desk. 'It's the sort of height at which the cabins of aircraft with pressurisation systems are maintained when they're actually flying much higher.

'So what would it be like if you were flying a pressurised aircraft, or sitting there as a passenger on the way to Majorca at, say twenty five thousand feet, when there's a sudden, explosive, decompression?'

With a theatrical, 'Well let's find out,' he gave a thumbs-up to one of the windows and began a ten second countdown.

At zero, there was a whooshing thump and I found myself sitting in thick mist at a chamber altitude of 25,000 feet. The only body cavity I noticed was my stomach. The gaseous remains of the previous night's Ruddles County expanded until they had to escape. Not to put too fine a point on it, I let out an almighty fart.

The mist wasn't the result of that, but rather the air in the chamber cooling to its dew point and forming cloud because of the rapid reduction in pressure. As the cloud cleared, I looked around. I could tell by the mischievous glint in their eyes that some of my fellow course members had also coughed in their rompers.

'Knowing what you lot were up to last night,' the doctor said, 'all I can say is it's a good job we're wearing oxygen masks. I think we'll sit here and let them purge the system a bit before we move on.'

'Now,' he said, making use of the delay, 'if any of your cavities were blocked because you were flying with a cold, a decompression like that could cause quite a bit of damage.

'But there's more. From the time aviators started using oxygen systems to climb into the thinner air at high altitudes, there have been instances of aircraft falling out of the sky for no apparent reason. Many crashed, killing the occupants. But some pilots woke and managed to recover before they hit the ground.

'They thought they may have lost consciousness or, for some reason, been unable to think straight. And in most instances, they realised they'd either failed to switch on their oxygen, or to notice a problem with it.

'And at the crash sites, investigators often discovered oxygen systems that were switched off or damaged, and/or bodies displaying signs of low oxygen levels, or hypoxia. Thankfully, such accidents are less prevalent today, but they still happen.

'So why don't pilots notice the low oxygen levels?' he continued. 'And why are they a problem anyway? After all, we know people can run around on the top of Everest without supplemental oxygen – and that's at twenty nine thousand feet for heaven's sake.'

Twenty eight years later, I was to find out much more about this on a medical research expedition to Everest, but back in the chamber, the doctor continued.

'Well, as we heard yesterday, the mountaineers have climbed up to that height over several days, weeks even. They've acclimatised.

'You on the other hand, have suddenly been lifted from sea level and dumped at twenty five thousand feet. The air beyond your mask is less than half as rich in oxygen as it was a few seconds ago. What's going to happen if you try to survive on that amount?'

Again there was a theatrical pause before he continued. 'Okay, let's find out. Number 1, take off your mask.'

Under the gaze of everyone in the chamber and those peering through the portholes opposite him, Number 1 unclipped his oxygen mask and let it fall, picked up a clipboard and pencil and began writing answers to problems set by the doctor.

Only a short time after removing his mask, I could tell that the guinea pig was beginning to struggle. The movement of his pencil became increasingly hesitant, as did his answers to questions about his well-being. After about 90 seconds, his speech began to slur and he was told to refit his mask and give a thumbs-up when he felt restored.

And so it progressed, one after another, my colleagues removed their oxygen masks and suffered the effects of hypoxia.

It came to my turn. I lowered my mask.

'Write down the sequence of numbers obtained by subtracting thirteen from one thousand and seven,' the doctor instructed.

Now, I'd have found the arithmetic difficult in the oxygen-rich atmosphere of a classroom, but in the chamber, I was soon struggling to get below 981. When he directed me to draw an elephant, I found it hard to remember what one looked like. And as I doodled, I began to feel woozy. It wasn't an unpleasant feeling, and even in the artificial setting of the chamber, the thought of closing my eyes and going to sleep was very tempting.

'Number 12!'

I could tell it wasn't the first time the speaker had tried to get my attention.

'Put your mask on, Number 12!'

Once my mask was fitted and I'd taken a few whiffs of oxygen, I recovered very quickly, but with a residual tingly feeling that lasted a little longer. I looked down at the paper. It hadn't taken long for me to start writing like a five year old, and the bit of elephant I'd drawn was very strange. More worryingly, though, I also knew I wouldn't have refitted my mask if not prompted to do so. The consequences in an aircraft didn't bear thinking about.

Once we'd all had our experience of hypoxia, the doctor drew his lesson.

'So what happened to you?' he began. 'Well, fairly quickly, your brain started to suffer from the shortage of oxygen. Because you were expecting it, most of you probably noticed the deterioration in your mental abilities. But perhaps the timescale was a bit of a surprise.'

We all nodded.

'Yes,' the doctor continued. 'And within about ninety seconds, it was time to put your masks back on. If you hadn't, you'd have been unconscious within about another thirty seconds. And then, if you didn't get more oxygen, either through your mask or a descent, brain damage and death would follow.

'So what does it mean in practice? Well, if you fly a pressurised aircraft and suffer a catastrophic decompression, I suggest that you're going to notice and get onto emergency oxygen fairly quickly. In your case of course, because the JP Mk 3 isn't pressurised, the hypoxia is more likely to result from you failing to switch on your oxygen, or failing to spot a leak. The important thing is, no matter how it occurs, you must recognise that something isn't right.

'And even in the chamber here, you've seen how the symptoms creep up on you. Imagine how much more difficult it would be if you weren't expecting it, and other things were distracting you, such as flying an aircraft, or navigating, or dealing with an emergency.

'So, the message is, if at any time you notice unusual symptoms - confusion, lethargy, inexplicable euphoria or drowsiness - suspect hypoxia and check your oxygen.'

I had occasion to put this lesson into practise only once during my flying career. And it wasn't due to lack of oxygen, but a g-induced loss of consciousness, from which I woke up confused and with that tingly feeling. The circumstances are a story for another time, but I recognised the symptoms and, having remembered the session in the chamber several years earlier, checked my oxygen.

Back in the chamber, there was one final exercise. The descent.

'Remember, if you feel any pain, put your hand up,' the doctor said before asking the controller to bring the chamber back to seal level.

'As we descend,' he continued, 'the pressure is going to increase and air should flow into your tubes and cavities. If, for some reason, swollen tissue has blocked your sinuses or eustachian tubes, the pressure won't be able to equalise and you're likely to feel pain, maybe even suffer damage. Even without inflammation, I can see that some of you have already had to clear your ears.'

I was one. I'd felt the pressure build up, so I'd pinched the bridge of my nose and blown gently until my ears popped and the pressure was relieved.

'That's because,' the doctor continued, 'the ability to equalise pressure varies from individual to individual, depending on your anatomy. When you've been flying for a while, some of you will probably find that you can clear your ears merely by swallowing, or waggling your lower jaw from side to side in a yawning motion. Some of you may even be able to do it now.'

There were a few nods.

Unfortunately, I was to discover that I'd always have to clear my ears frequently during a descent. Worse, on occasion, I'd have difficulty clearing them even when there'd been no indication of a problem on the ground. It meant that whereas some of my colleagues seemed able to fly with a full-blown cold, I couldn't risk getting airborne with even the slightest snuffle.

It wasn't until I had sight of my medical documents many years later that I discovered my nasal and eustachean tubes were so narrow and twisted that I should never have been selected for aircrew. I had no inkling of this as the chamber at North Luffenham stabilised at sea level, the heavy metal door opened and we filed out.

With our masks and helmets removed, we pointed at one another and smiled.

Each of us bore a deep red groove where our oxygen masks had clamped to our faces. The marks made us look ten years older. In a matter of minutes, they faded, restoring our youthful looks.

A few months later, we were to discover that after an hour flying in the Jet Provost, many of us would *feel* as if we'd aged 10 years, an effect that took longer to shake off.

Chapter 4 – Welcome to Linton

After lunch on Sunday 4th November, I left Ludlow to drive to RAF Linton-on-Ouse, a few miles north-west of the mediaeval-walled city of York. It was a journey of 175 miles, much of it on minor roads, and it always took at least 4 hours. This meant that when I made it home for the weekend, I spent almost as much time on the road as I did with Geraldine.

I hoped my latest car, a second-hand Wolsely 1300, would prove more reliable than some of its predecessors.

I warned in to the Officers' Mess and found my room on the upper floor of a modern, two-storey annex tacked onto the side of a traditional Mess. It was larger than any room I'd had to myself as an airman, and better furnished, with a bed, table-cum desk, upright chair, armchair, wardrobe and chest of drawers. It also had a washbasin, a luxury that saved me having to pad down to the central ablutions to clean my teeth.

On the bed - which, in another deviation from my airman service would be made for me each morning by the Mess batting staff - was a set of printed Joining Instructions for No 1 Flying Training School. I opened them and began to read.

You have been appointed Course Leader with immediate effect.

I re-read the words. They rather took the wind out of my sails. After all, some of the university graduates on my course were flight lieutenants, a rank above mine. I doubt I'd ever considered who might lead the course, but if I had, I'd have assumed it would be one of them. But the truth was that they'd jumped the ranks of acting pilot officer, pilot officer and flying officer within months of joining the Service only because they were graduates. This led to them being universally and disparagingly known as Green Shielders.

The name derived from a loyalty scheme of the time

favoured by shops and petrol stations. The more money a customer spent, the more Green Shield Stamps they were given to stick in books that could be exchanged for goods from a catalogue. The inference was that the graduates had obtained their rank from a catalogue in exchange for stamps.

What particularly galled more experienced flight lieutenants, including many of our flying instructors, was that no-one could tell the difference between them and the Green Shielders. Or so they thought.

In fact – but don't tell them I said so - our instructors were so much older and more careworn than the youthful and shop-new Green Shielders that there was rarely much difficulty in telling one from the other. And to be fair to the Green Shielders, they'd merely benefited from what the RAF saw as a vital recruiting tool.

To compete for quality graduates, they felt they had to offer a high starting salary, and because pay in the services is linked to rank, the only way to do this was to award accelerated promotion. Thus, in one bound, the Green Shielders became flight lieutenants and received the salary that went with that rank.

By contrast, the accelerated promotion to flying officer gained by me and other ex-airman raised no animosity at all. We were seen as having earned our stripes.

So, I'd probably been chosen as course leader ahead of the Green Shielders through a combination of their relative lack of experience and my strong report from initial officer training. But whatever the reason, there it was in black and white.

As course leader, the letter continued, *you have certain responsibilities. You will smooth the path of your course through its training, being responsible for their discipline, dress, punctuality and conduct.*

My heart sank with each word. Although a great bunch, I assessed only a handful of those with whom I'd spent the week at North Luffenham as being in any way responsible.

The rest could best be described as free-spirited, like a basket of puppies. The likelihood of getting them to turn up at the right place at the right time and behave seemed infinitesimal. I was pretty sure I'd end up as nothing more than a whipping boy for their frequent misdemeanours.

The only ray of light was hidden in a paragraph on page 3: *Course Leaders are appointed on a rotational basis...* As far as I was concerned, the sooner I was rotated out of the position the better. When I'd finished the ream of paperwork, I re-read the bits that outlined my responsibilities as course leader.

You are to ensure your Course comply with Officers' Mess Rules, Officers' Confidential Orders, Station Routine Orders and Station Standing Orders. You are responsible for their tidiness and for ensuring that any barrack damages are reported immediately. Each month, you will submit a report...

And so on and so on.

After the week at North Luffenham, several of us had been home for the weekend, but others had travelled directly to Linton. They'd spent the weekend settling in and exploring the local area. When we met up in the bar later that Sunday evening, I found them in good spirits, relating tales of wild nights in York.

It seemed they'd met a group of young women, some of whom seemed to know more about the training we were about to undertake than they did. A few had accompanied them back to the Mess, and surprised everyone with their knowledge of its layout.

One of our younger course members was particularly enthusiastic. 'They really seemed to know their way around,' he gushed.

The consensus was that it augured well for the social life of the course.

My diary has only one word for Monday 5th November

1979 – the sixth anniversary of the day I joined the RAF: *Mayhem*.

I'm not sure exactly why I chose that word, but there's no doubt that the day contained few pauses for breath.

As laid out in the Joining Instructions, it began with a series of briefings from, in descending order of rank, the Station Commander, the Chief Flying Instructor, Chief Ground Instructor, General Service Training Officer and several others who were to supervise or support our training. Their words followed a predictable pattern.

Welcome to Linton. You are about to embark on the first stage of a tremendously demanding series of courses leading to the award of your pilot badge. Give it all you've got, but don't be afraid to come and see me if you need help. My door is always open.

Only one briefing stands out, that from the Station Security Officer, a flight lieutenant policeman.

Moving up to the lectern, he began by outlining the major threats to us and the Station. At the time, these were the Irish Republican Army and the Warsaw Pact.

'Both organisations,' he said, 'are active in intelligence gathering, the IRA to facilitate the planting of bombs, the Warsaw Pact to increase their knowledge, not only of our military installations and equipment, but also of you as individual pilots.'

The last words were a surprise, but they were something I was to hear many more times in my career.

'Sitting here, you may think that's a bit far-fetched,' he continued, 'but if you're successful in reaching a squadron, you'll be one of a relatively small number of front line pilots. So you're bound to be of interest to a potential enemy. And the sooner they start gathering information on you, the better. They've probably started already.'

He'd really gained our attention now.

'And as they're building their profile of you,' he continued, 'what if weaknesses come to light, things they can exploit - debt, infidelity, or something more unusual, like homosexuality.'

At the time, homosexuals were widely viewed with disgust, and nowhere more so than in the military. It was taken for granted that they could be blackmailed into almost anything if threatened with exposure.

'One of the Soviet's favourite ploys is the honey trap, the offer of sex. This could lead you to reveal secrets, or leave you open to blackmail, especially if you're being unfaithful to someone.'

If we wondered where he was going with all this, we were about to find out.

'Now, you'll find that certain young ladies in York can spot an aircrew watch at a range of 100 yards,' he continued, looking around the group. 'And some will probably know more about the Station and the training you're about to undertake than you do yourselves.'

The audience now divided into two groups: those who'd regaled us with stories of their night on the town, and those who'd listened. The former were trying to look inconspicuous, the latter to contain their mirth.

'Aha,' the Security Officer said with a sparkle in his eyes. 'I can see that some of you have already met them.'

Rather than being concerned, he seemed to be enjoying the discomfort of our fellow course members as much as we were.

'Now, I'm not going to stand here and tell you they're all Soviet spies,' he said, 'but you should at least be aware that some of them tend to be handed down from course to course.'

I looked at the young man who'd been most enthusiastic about the girls they'd met. His cheeks were the colour of beetroot.

The Security Officer showed no mercy. 'The next time you meet them, you might just like to think about some of what I've said.'

When the laughter had subsided, he delivered his final flourish. 'So, gentlemen, just be aware that, as of today, you are a target. Be on your guard.'

The punch line had hardly been necessary. We'd received his message loud and clear.

Now, I'm treading in very hot water here, because several of my course colleagues and countless other student pilots married partners they met in the fair city of York. So I have to make it plain that not all the City's young women were out to snare a pilot, let alone turn them into traitors.

In reality, although there were some like those described by the security officer, the vast majority of the young women that became girlfriends – and later wives – seemed to be setting out on their own vocational careers, often as nurses or teachers. And it seems that the character traits required for success in such a career are similar to those required for success in the military, including a single-minded determination to succeed. So it's hardly surprising that there was mutual attraction.

Or maybe I'm being too philosophical and both groups just like to party!

I hope I've said enough to stop me being cold-shouldered at the next reunion – once every five years – but I suspect I may have more explaining to do.

None of the other briefings were anywhere near as entertaining, but they all in one way or another made a point that I hadn't considered before. The whole infrastructure of the Station and its 1,500 or so personnel were there to get us, the 90-odd student pilots in residence at any one time, into the air.

And of course the same was – and is - true on any RAF flying station. Everyone is there to ensure that the aircrew and aircraft are as well prepared as possible when they fly. That was my raison d'être when, as a junior technician and corporal at Scampton, I'd worked on the airframes and engines of the base's Vulcans. But now, I'd be the one in the cockpit and everyone would be pulling for me.

Perhaps it was this sense of being at the top of the food chain that had led some aircrew I'd met in the past to seem arrogant. And I can't pretend I didn't meet others in the future who were similarly full of themselves. But in my experience, most aircrew fulfil their role with a sense of, if not humility, at least a desire not to screw up and let the side down.

If all these people are working for me, surely I have to give of my best.

That was certainly how I felt at Linton, and everywhere else I served. I won't pretend such thoughts were always at the front of my mind, the day to day pressures of flying usually occupied that spot, but they were in the background as an added incentive to succeed.

Not that it always felt as if some of those in supporting roles were holding up their end of the bargain. In some cases, just the opposite. A few seemed determined to be obstructive, to the point that you sometimes wondered whose side they were on.

The Supply Branch tended to come in for most criticism. Cases where they refused to issue something like a new aircrew watch, because *they only had one in stock and someone might need it,* may be largely apocryphal, but everyone had similar stories of Suppliers failing to supply much-needed items for reasons that defied logic, and enjoying themselves in the process. In retaliation, we called them storemen, or even worse, blanket stackers, and said we'd use their proper title only when they stopped storing and started supplying.

And Station Headquarters, the home of a unit's administrators, was fairly universally known as Handbrake House for its perceived tendency to hinder rather than enhance progress; while anyone else deemed to be obstructive could be dubbed a member of the Flying Prevention Branch.

Films depicting how poor support for aircrew could lead to accidents were a regular feature of periodic flight safety days and all courses of training. One from the 1970s starred sitcom actor, Richard O'Sullivan – Man About The House and Robin's Nest – playing a Harrier pilot so distracted by the failings of those around him that he taxies onto the runway in front of a Phantom jet fighter in the final stages of landing.

Another much older but no less effective film was Frustration. It featured a Gloster Javelin pilot and navigator flying one of the high-tailed, delta-wing, fighters to the Far East. En route, they suffer a litany of poor support that culminates in a needless ejection and the loss of their jet.

I particularly liked one line from this film, delivered by the pilot in a cut-glass accent, 'To cap it all, the Mess had run out of my favourite beer.'

Of course, in their defence, the supporting trades would say that aircrew are merely prima donnas who expect pampering and resent any attempt to make them conform and follow essential admin procedures.

Undoubtedly, there is truth on both sides.

The day to day reality at Linton was that we rarely felt pampered. The pressures of training were such that we were more likely to feel put-upon, harassed even. We were given an inkling of what to expect on that first morning when we walked into one of four large hangars ringing the south-eastern arc of the airfield.

On the way there, the air had been alive with Jet Provosts, taking off and departing, returning and landing or circling the airfield. This, I realised, was the backdrop to my new life. And in about a month, I'd be up there, learning to fly one of those red and white jets.

Unsurprisingly, with all the air activity, the hangar was empty. So, footsteps echoing around the cavernous space, we made our way across to a central door and turned right to pass a suite of offices and briefing rooms belonging to D Flight of No 2 Squadron. It would be our home when we reached the flying phase of the course. The other side of the central door was C Flight, its students several months ahead of us.

We were ushered into a narrow briefing room and directed to seats at the rear. Ahead of us sat ten or so flight lieutenants in green flying suits. To the right, windows overlooked the airfield and I found it hard not to be distracted at the sight and sound of Jet Provosts taking off or landing on the distant runway, or taxying past on their way to or from the dispersal area.

The flight lieutenants were our flying instructors, most in their early 30s, some older. At the front, facing us, his elbow on a spindly wooden lectern, was our new squadron commander.

He was tall and thin, with dark hair and a hawkish intensity. Appraising us from under furrowed brows, he reminded me of the schoolmaster in the cartoon version of Pink Floyd's single, Another Brick In The Wall. Much of what he said about hard work and dedication was a reiteration of words we'd heard from the station executives earlier in the morning. But then he set out to provide more detail on what we could expect over the course of our time on 2 Squadron and beyond.

'After full-time groundschool for the rest of November,' he began, 'the pattern for December and January will be mornings in groundschool and afternoons flying with us, or vice versa.'

He waved a hand toward the flying instructors, a few of whom turned to offer a smile.

'You switch to full-time flying from February' he continued. 'Progress will depend on factors such as weather and instructor availability, but those of you that aren't suspended for lack of ability, or *effort*,' - the word was followed by a pause and an intimidating stare – 'should have completed your one hundred hours of Basic Flying Training on the JP3 by the end of July.'

JP was the universally accepted abbreviation for the Jet Provost, and we were to fly the JP Mk3A.

'From the outset,' he continued with a delivery that never veered from the businesslike, 'we will be aiming to turn you into fast jet pilots. And make no mistake,' – that stare again – 'anyone who shows the potential to fill a fast jet cockpit *will* be sent down this route, *whatever their personal preference.*'

This might be bad news to a couple of my fellow course members who hankered after flying helicopters, but the rest of us would be more than happy. We all wanted to fly fast jets. I wanted to be a Harrier pilot, even though I had little idea of what the job really entailed. It just seemed the most iconic of the options on offer. The problem was that only the pick of the crop got to fly it. But hey, why not aim high.

'Those reaching the end of the course but falling below the standard for fast jets,' the squadron leader continued, 'might, if places are available, be fed into the helicopter or multi-engine streams. That decision will be made approaching the one hundred hour point.'

My focus was solely on that first 100 hours, but he went on to give us an idea of the process beyond that.

'Those selected fast jet will fly another sixty hours here on the JP5,' – a sleeker, pressurised, cousin of the JP3 – 'before moving on to the Hawk at Valley,' - on Anglesey – 'and then tactical weapons training at either Chivenor' - in Devon – 'or Brawdy' – in south west Wales.

'As a generalisation,' he continued, 'those just failing to reach the standard for fast jets are likely to be sent down the helicopter route. They'll complete just another couple of hours here, before moving to Shawbury for basic training on the Gazelle, and advanced training to the award of wings on the Wessex.

'Those below the standard for fast jets or helicopters *might* be able to go down the multi-engine route, completing a further twenty five hours here, before moving on to earn their wings on the Jetstream at Finningly,' – a flying training base near Doncaster that also trained navigators and airmen aircrew.

'However,' the squadron commander's tone became grave,' you should be aware that there have been no multi-engine slots for the last few courses. Finningley has instead taken students suspended from fast jet and helicopter training, because, to be brutally honest, they're likely to be of a higher standard than those with a mere multi-engine recommendation.'

He now looked and sounded positively funereal. 'I'm afraid this has meant that those suitable only for multis have had to return to OASC for reselection. And while some managed to secure places in navigator training, some had to accept reselection to ground branches.'

So you could pass basic flying training and still be chopped!

Hard rules to say the least. And I feared that if it happened to me, I might face an added complication. Although Steve Atherton had managed to retain his commission, there was still the possibility that I might revert to being a corporal airframe and engine fitter. Oh well, a bridge to be crossed later, if it came to it.

'So,' the squadron commander said, leaning forward to add weight to what we guessed was his final message, 'to guarantee at least a shot at gaining your wings, I suggest you put maximum effort into achieving the fast jet standard.'

Phew! Pilot training was becoming more daunting by the minute. I was still prepared to meet the challenge head on, but I can't pretend my heart hadn't sunk a little.

If there'd been any vestige of complacency left, it was swept away by the final speaker of the morning, our flight commander, John Dignan, a slim, moustachioed officer in his early 30s, universally known as Dingdong.

Fixing us with a steely stare, he began, 'When you come to the squadron to fly in about a month's time, you must be prepared, with as much knowledge of checks and procedures as possible. You'll find that we can be sympathetic to those that struggle through no fault of their own, but there'll be absolutely no sympathy for anyone that turns up unprepared. Lack of effort will *not* be tolerated! Any questions?'

Millions!

Exactly what does prepared mean? How do I ensure I'm prepared? What checks and procedures do I need to know before I've been anywhere near a Jet Provost? What am I doing here?

Of course, that morning, nobody asked a question. I guess we all assumed things would become clearer with time. And to be fair, they did. Groundschool housed a dummy ejection seat into which we could practice strapping in, a cockpit in which we could practice checks and a rudimentary cockpit trainer for later in the syllabus. Then there were visits to the squadron to look round aircraft in the hangar and to find out exactly what we were expected to know when we turned up to fly for the first time.

The final event of the morning, a visit to stores, was another chastening experience. There we picked up our JP3A FRCs and Pilot Notes - much bulkier than those for the Chipmunk – and a stack of Student Study Guides and Groundschool Notes on a bewildering array of subjects: Aerodynamics, Aircraft Systems, Flight Instruments, Avionics, Aircraft Operations, Meteorology, Aircraft Navigation, Morse Code and Combat Survival, as well as pure academic subjects such as Mathematics and Physics.

And overlaid on all this was the need, as course leader, for me to be far enough ahead of the game to get, not only myself, but the rest of the course to the right place at the right time.

Oh well, nobody said it would be easy.

After a hurried lunch, we reported to Cheshire Hall, a complex housing a lecture theatre and classrooms where we were to spend much of the next three months.

Our groundschool instructors were drawn from a small

group of education officers and aircrew on ground appointments. But they delivered only about half our lessons, maybe less. The remainder were designated self-study, which meant sitting in a classroom reading up on the relevant subject in our Student Study Guides.

Tests came thick and fast. We had a maths test on each of our first five days, and tests on other subjects at a similar rate until mid-January, when the pace slowed for the final two weeks of formal groundschool. A small number of tests linked to specific points in the flying syllabus slipped into the following weeks and months, events such as our first medium, high or low level navigation sorties, or our first airways crossing.

Just as during aviation medicine training, many of the tests had a 100% pass mark. I don't think anyone really expected us to be infallible, but when we did get a question wrong, because it might have a direct bearing on our future survival, we had to sit with an instructor and convince him that we knew the right answer.

Most, if not all the written tests comprised questions in the style known as multiple choice, meaning we had to tick a box against one of four possible answers to each question. It was the educational orthodoxy at the time. Perhaps it still is. But I remain to be convinced that ticking boxes offers as good a check of understanding as narrative answers.

We called them multiple guess.

Just as during my other RAF training to date, I found most of the subjects fascinating, and enjoyable. Not that some didn't seem a hard slog, in my case, Maths and Morse Code – the latter required because we had to be able to decode the three-letter Morse transmissions by which individual airfield landing aids and airways navigation beacons were identified.

I spent most weekday evenings closeted in my room studying, which paid dividends in terms of results. I made only one mistake in all the exams in November, and not many more in subsequent months. It didn't do much for my street cred, especially as it meant less visits to the pub than some of my contemporaries. But I felt I had to cram as much reading as possible into the week, because weekends were for Geraldine.

I think I also had a premonition that I was going to find the flying phase of the course hard-going, so a reputation for hard work would do me no harm.

Not that it was all work and no play. A fair proportion of each self-study period was given over to the playing of charades. I have a piece of paper in a scrap book with some of the books, films, plays and TV programmes I acted out in front of the rest of the course. It's an eclectic mix, anything from Abelard and Heloise to One Million Years BC. I can't help wondering how I performed two others on the list: Everything You Always Wanted To Know About Sex But Were Afraid To Ask, and Muffin The Mule.

There was also plenty of sport. I represented the station at volleyball, and sometimes the football team, which meant weekly practices and games, but my diary also mentions regular sessions of 5-a-side football, squash, badminton and basketball.

As the name of the subject suggests, Combat Survival aimed to teach us techniques that would help us survive a wide a range of more or less dire scenarios.

For instance, a lesson on the Monday of our third week had covered the theory of surviving an ejection over the sea, or any other large body of water. The next morning, we found ourselves lined up along the side of a local swimming pool, preparing to put theory into practice. Also in attendance were several physical training instructors – PTIs - and the station combat survival and rescue officer, a navigator I was to fly with on the Hercules a few years later.

Apart from bare feet, we were dressed as we would have been in the air - in kit reserved solely for such exercises. So I stood there in an ill-fitting flying suit, flying helmet, oxygen mask, chamois leather gloves and a life preserver - a dark green waistcoat, buttoned at the front, with a salami-like pouch running up the right side of my chest around my neck and down the left side.

The garment was a miracle of design, positively brimming with survival aids.

For a start, a sharp pull on a beaded black handle under the left pouch would release high pressure carbon dioxide to inflate a large dayglo orange float, known as a stole. This would burst from the pouch to keep my head and shoulders out of the water, even if I was unconscious. A manual inflation valve on the right lobe of the orange stole would allow me to add or remove air if necessary – and if I was conscious.

In darkness or reduced visibility, when the vibrant colour of the stole couldn't be seen by would-be rescuers, the right lobe was topped with a light, while two canvas grab handles between the lobes held a whistle, to be blown six times every minute, in the hope of hearing three blasts from the cavalry.

Pockets on either side of the waistcoat contained more location and survival aids of varying sophistication: a first-aid kit, survival leaflets and a razor-blade - which we joked was for slashing our wrists when the cold and seasickness all became too much; a heliograph - a small mirror to be flashed at approaching aircraft or ships; a set of eight mini-flares - vivid red fireworks that could be shot 160 feet into the air from a pen-like gun James Bond would have been happy to own; and a radio beacon that could beam a homing signal on a distress frequency monitored by rescue organisations and many ships and aircraft.

For the moment though, standing by the side of the pool, all these treasures were hidden. In fact most of the life preserver was hidden behind a yellow plastic box about 15 inches square and eight inches deep I held in front of my chest. When I flew, it would be in the base of my ejection seat, topped by a thin cushion on which I'd sit.

The yellow box was my personal survival pack, and it

contained more survival aids, including a one-man dinghy. After ejection, when the ejection seat fell away to leave me dangling beneath my parachute, I had to release two fasteners on the parachute harness, allowing the dinghy box to drop away and sway below me on 15 feet of cord connected to the life preserver.

Standing by the pool holding the cumbersome object, I could well understand why you'd want to release it, rather than have it clattering against the back of your legs as you swayed beneath your parachute.

The combat survival officer shouted to get our attention. Then, voice echoing around the pool, he set the scene.

'You've just ejected at about two thousand feet over the sea. The ejection seat has dropped away and the parachute's opened. One by one, I want you to climb on the springboard, go through the post-ejection actions we talked about in the classroom, jump into the water, escape from under the parachute, swim away and go through your dinghy drills.

'Any questions?'

The only thing that came as a surprise was mention of escape from under a parachute. We'd talked about it the day before, but hadn't expected to see the PTIs draping yards of silk canopy across the water.

By the time I clambered onto the springboard and laid the yellow box down in front of me, several of my coursemates were bobbing about in their dinghies at the far end of the pool, while one was still trying to climb into his and another, just a few yards away was flailing under yards of parachute silk. The chlorine-laden air rang with shouts of instruction and encouragement over a background of splashing.

'Okay, Ron, go ahead,' the instructor boomed above the din.

'Check canopy,' I shouted, my voice muffled by my oxygen mask.

I looked up to check that my imaginary parachute had

deployed properly. About all I could do if it hadn't was pull frantically on the cords and wriggle.

The instructor let me off the hook. 'Canopy's good,' he shouted.

'Discard oxygen mask.'

I unclipped the mask to stop it filling with water and drowning me.

'Inflate life preserver.'

I pulled the black beaded handle. With a loud whoosh, the orange stole sprang from my chest and appeared in my eye-line, while the rear portion pushed against my neck and helmet.

Although I'd seen those ahead of me deploy their life preservers, I was still surprised at the solidity and bulk of the stole. I now understood why you might want to deflate it a little in the confines of a dinghy, and why the black-handled knife attached to the left knee of my flying suit might have to be used to stab it to death if it inflated in the cockpit.

Sticking up vertically from the left lobe like a black pencil was the six-inch aerial of the emergency locator beacon in the lower left pocket of the vest.

'Activate beacon,' I shouted, pulling a little toggle beneath the pocket.

A live beacon would emit a reassuring chirrup as the beacon transmitted its SOS message.

'Check lanyard connected.'

I reached down to ensure the fastener attaching the yellow plastic box to my life preserver was secure.

'And release PSP.'

I pretended to release the fasteners to either side of my bottom and kicked the yellow personal survival pack into the water with a splash. The person ahead of me had escaped the parachute and was swimming away.

'Unlock parachute QRF.'

Now I pretended to turn through 90 degrees a quick release fastener that would have been nestled against my stomach. In the real case I'd have held it until I saw - or at night, heard - the dinghy box hit the water. Only then would I press the fastener to let the parachute fly away so that it didn't drag me through the waves and water-board me.

Unfortunately, over the years several people descending at night or in cloud released their parachutes early, having mistaken the crashing of the sea for the sound of the box hitting the water. While some had been low enough to survive the resulting fall, others had died after plummeting hundreds of feet. As a result, the procedure was amended to advise pressing the fastener only when you entered the water.

Now though, I complied with the teaching of the time and pretended to squeeze the fastener as if the box had just hit the water. Then I leapt from the springboard.

I'm not a bad swimmer, but I wasn't used to jumping into water fully clothed, and certainly not in a bulky helmet weighing several pounds. So, as the orange stole raised me to the surface, I was a bit out of my comfort zone. Then, as if there was no wind to whisk it away, the PTIs dropped the wet parachute over me.

It wasn't totally black beneath the fabric, and it didn't cling to my face so tightly that I couldn't breathe, but it did add another layer of strangeness to an already unfamiliar situation.

A couple of my new friends were barely able to swim 25 metres, and I knew they'd been anticipating these drills with trepidation. How they'd fare under the parachute I dreaded to think, especially when one of the keys to escaping it with minimum fuss was to stay calm.

It was no use flapping around randomly in the hope that you'd work your way to the edge of the canopy. This could merely leave you trussed up in yards of wet silk and parachute cord. I had to find one of the seams and feed it over my head – so that the silk bunched behind me, not in front of my face. At the worst, I'd reach the centre of the parachute and have to work my way along another seam to the edge, but I'd still be clear in a matter of minutes, seconds even.

I listened for the tell-tale laughter from the poolside that would indicate I was heading for the centre. Hearing none, I carried on pulling at my chosen seam and was soon free of the silk.

Thankful that I wasn't wearing boots, I swam, dragging the yellow box on its fifteen feet of cord toward the middle of the pool, where I trod water and reeled it in. With the box in front of me, I located a cloth handle on one edge and pulled. The plastic pack split and a black shape burst out. In no more than a few seconds, a dinghy floated in front of me like a mis-shaped lorry tyre, five feet long and three, tapering to two feet wide.

I turned it until I was at the thin end, reached for two grab handles along the side and, heaved myself in, face first, filling the dinghy with water in the process. After taking a few seconds to compose myself, I felt around for a cloth bag on a length of cord and threw it over the rear. This was the drogue, designed to provide at least some stability in a swell or current, a bit like a small anchor.

Next, I heaved myself round onto my front, fearing all the time that I'd capsize as the dinghy wobbled beneath me.

In the warmth of the swimming pool, the several inches of water in which I was sitting seemed the main concern. But in the sea, the most immediate threat would be developing hypothermia because my upper body was exposed to the elements. So I reached down and pulled a dayglo orange canopy up over my back and shoulders, then over the helmet. From above my head, the two sides of the canopy sloped down to my feet.

Before I pulled the sides together, I searched for and found another length of cord, on the end of which was my goodie bag, full of treasures like water and chocolate, another first aid kit and sea sickness tablets. I pulled this inside the canopy and closed the Velcro fastening until I was cocooned. The little plastic window in front of my face steamed up immediately, and I realised how heavily I was breathing.

This was hard work, but there was much more to do.

I reached down to my right, found a longish tube running from the floor, lifted it to my lips, turned a valve at the end and blew in several puffs of air. The idea was to inflate the floor just enough to insulate me from the cold sea, but not enough to make the dinghy fly away on the breeze, or make a capsize more likely.

Again, I felt around, this time to find a bag attached to the floor toward my feet by a short length of cord. I opened the canopy a little and used the bag to bale out the water in which I was sitting. This gave me a few moments to look about.

I was surrounded by black and orange dinghies, bobbing around and nestling against one another. A couple of the PTIs had joined us in the water.

If I'd been in the North Sea, I'd probably have been shivering, but there in the pool I was overheating. I wasn't allowed to remove my gloves and helmet, so I opened the canopy further to let some air in.

'Cover up!' shouted the combat survival instructor prowling the side.

Then the dinghy next to mine reared into the air and rolled over. The smiling face of a PTI appeared beside it.

Bugger!

In anything other than a calm sea, we'd been told we could expect to be swamped or capsized fairly regularly. And apparently, aviation history was full of pilots who should have survived, but who died of hyperthermia bobbing alongside their upturned dinghies because they'd lacked the determination to re-board.

From the amount of screaming and splashing around me, I suspected my determination was about to be tested. In preparation, I hunched up and cracked open the Velcro fastening a bit. As if on cue, a PTI appeared at the foot of my dinghy. I flinched, but he did nothing more than yell at me to cover up and carry on with my drills.

Reluctantly, I closed the Velcro until I was just able to continue baling. When the water that remained was pooled round my bottom, I found another inflation tube and blew until the canopy began to look like an orange puffer jacket. I'd just started to mop up the rest of the water with the sponge from my goody bag, when the dinghy heaved around me.

Even though I'd known it was coming, I found being plunged upside down under water in a dark rubber coffin very unpleasant. To complicate matters, I was enmeshed by inflation tubes and cords. And who knew Velcro could be such a tenacious fastener?

Trying not to panic as my helmet filled with water, I used my arms to burst out of the canopy and, coughing and spluttering, bobbed to the surface. There I was greeted with expletive-laden encouragement to right and re-board my dinghy and start again.

By the time I'd become more or less cosy for the second time, I was shattered. Thankfully, the next shout seemed to indicate that we weren't to be capsized again.

'You hear a helicopter.'

This was the cue to fire off my mini-flares. With great difficulty, I felt my way to a pocket beneath the stoles of the life preserver, opened it and took out the mini-flare pouch. I couldn't think how to do more without being able to see the pouch, so I pushed it through the Velcro. Only then did I remove the firing pistol, screw it into a flare, draw it out and point it skyward. As I pretended to fire one flare after another, I ruminated on how difficult – impossible - this and many of the other operations I'd performed would be with fingers numbed with cold.

'The helicopter's coming into the hover over you,' the combat survival instructor shouted.

Again, this was a cue, this time to ease my head and shoulders free of the canopy and untangle myself from the various cords criss-crossing my legs.

'The winchman's above you.'

I located and held up the fastener still tethering my life preserver to the dinghy. The winchman would secure me by placing a strop over my head and shoulders to nestle under my arms. Only then would he disconnect the fastener and signal for both of us to be winched up into the helicopter.

At the time, rescuers from some other nations lifted people from the water by the grab handles between the stoles of the life-jacket. But if an RAF winchman had reached for these, I'd have been very concerned. They were used only to lift bodies.

I was to complete many more dinghy drills during my RAF career, a couple in the sea, complete with parachute drags and live helicopter winching. But few are more memorable than that first one. It felt like another milestone, another building block on the way to becoming, not just a pilot, but a military pilot.

There were other reminders that we were in the military.

At 11.30pm a couple of days after the dinghy drill, the sirens sounded to announce a station exercise. Like most I should think, I was snuggled up in bed, close to, if not actually asleep. So I roused myself, pulled on my uniform, gathered up the rest of my course and reported to 2 Squadron.

I soon discovered that exercises at Linton had a strategic backdrop similar to those at Scampton, that is, mounting tension between NATO and the Warsaw Pact, leading to war. But they lacked the visceral sense of menace I'd felt when working on Vulcan bombers preparing to unleash nuclear Armageddon if the need arose.

I'm sure Linton would have had several war roles, including finishing the training of student pilots close to the end of their courses. But gone were the Battle of Britain days when someone with few hours could be fast-tracked into combat, or new airframes produced in a matter of days. Modern aircraft were – are - just too complex to build in short order, or to operate with little or no experience. So, after no more than a few weeks in groundschool, no-one was going to continue our training, especially in the face of nuclear exchanges.

About the only thing we were good for was guard duty, but I don't remember doing much of that. Instead, we spent the night sitting in the crewroom becoming acquainted with an unwelcome feature of our time on 2 Squadron: the cry from the instructor's crewroom of, '*Student for a job!*' followed by some more or less menial errand.

The exercise finished at 1.30 the next afternoon. Its main purpose had been to test the station's ability to get everyone into work within a stipulated period, usually a couple of hours. Those living in messes and barrack blocks were woken by sirens and messages relayed through the Tannoy system, which included speakers in every building, if not every room on the unit. Those in married quarters were roused by the sirens of RAF fire engines and police cars; and those in private accommodation by telephone, having been dialled as part of an elaborate cascade plan, each person woken phoning others down the chain.

I suspect the Station Commander was none-too impressed. We suffered two similar exercises a few weeks later, the first from 5am to 2pm, the second from 5.30am to 3pm. I can say with confidence that they did nothing for my preparedness for war beyond allowing me to experience sleep deprivation.

The Tannoy system wasn't used only to announce exercises. On occasion, its speakers would crackle into life with warnings of crises, such as aircraft emergencies or fires in buildings. But more often than not, they transmitted news of upcoming events, like VIP visits.

The voice booming out of the speaker usually belonged to the Station Warrant Officer, the SWO.

With his chiselled jaw, neatly trimmed moustache, immaculate appearance and upright military bearing,

Warrant Officer Jack Holt was an NCO of the old school. Marching around the unit, pace stick under his arm, he was master of all he surveyed, reminding me of a bulkier version of the swaggering SWO in the 1969 movie, Battle of Britain.

If he spotted anyone falling short of the standard he expected, they'd be called over and told in no uncertain terms how they'd failed to measure up and what he expected them to do about it. He was particularly hot on the paying of compliments, which in the Services is a reference to saluting, not telling someone they have a lovely smile!

He was as likely to admonish an officer as an airman, although he wasn't totally blind to the rank of his victims.

An airman who incurred his displeasure could expect a call of 'You there!' to be followed by a thorough dressing down, delivered at full volume. This served, not only to punish the unfortunate victim, but to act as a deterrent to anyone else within earshot.

In the case of an officer, the bellow of, 'Sir!' or 'Ma'am!', would be followed by a smart salute and a slightly more deferential, 'I wonder if I might have a word.' The *word* would be politer and less public, but the message to the officer would be the same as that to the airman. *Sort yourself out*!

We suspected that our instructors feared Jack as much as we did, and that he was one of the reasons the cry of *'Student for a job!'* was heard so often. Rather than risk being pulled up by him for something like untidy hair or unpolished flying boots, they had us run their errands.

Anyway, at about 9am one morning, as if shouting orders on the parade ground, the SWO's voice boomed from every speaker on the Station, including the one in our classroom.

'Stand by for broadcast. Stand by for broadcast. The Parliamentary Under-Secretary of State for Defence for the Royal Air Force, Mr Geoffrey Pattie MP, and the Air Member for Personnel, Air Marshal Sir John Gingell, KCB

CBE, will visit Royal Air Force Linton-on-Ouse today, Wednesday 28th November 1979, arriving at 1145 hours and departing at 1600 hours. All personnel are to be meticulous in the paying of compliments. I say again…'

And the SWO would go through the whole message again, by which time one or more of us would be mimicking his delivery, substituting profane names for the real ones and finishing with the line, *all personnel are to be ridiculous in the paying of compliments*, while throwing up joke salutes in the manner of a Monty Python sketch.

Jack would have had our guts for garters.

As an aside, I discovered a softer side to his nature one Friday evening when I'd set out for Ludlow. My car had taken me no further than the local village before conking out. As I stood there in civvies, head under the bonnet searching for clues, a car pulled up and out stepped the SWO.

'Good evening, Mr Holt,' I acknowledged, trying not to show any fear.

'Good evening, young sir,' he replied in a fatherly tone. 'What seems to be the problem?'

I'd like to be able to say that even though I wore no marks of rank, Warrant Officer Holt recognised my inherent breeding and officer qualities when he addressed me as *young sir*. But the truth is that his deference to my rank resulted from nothing more than our mutual understanding of Service rank etiquette.

Warrant officers hold the highest non-commissioned rank, having been awarded the monarch's *warrant*. This means other airmen must call them Sir. But because officers hold the monarch's *commission*, warrant officers must address them as Sir, while officers generally address warrant officers as Mr.

So, if you're still with me, you'll realise that my use of Mr in addressing Jack Holt had told him I was an officer.

To cut a long story short, he fixed the problem with my

car and saved my weekend with Geraldine. It was typical of men like him, disciplinarians when required, but with many more strings to their bow.

I held him in the greatest respect.

Getting back to the VIP visit, soon after 12.30 on the day of Jack Holt's long-winded Tannoy broadcast, I found myself in the Officers' Mess sitting next to Air Marshal Sir John Gingell KCB CBE, at what was termed a Top Table Lunch.

Such hosting was something all officers had to do on occasion, and I would sit next to many more senior guests as my career progressed. But for me, this was a first. In such grand company, I felt every inch the ex-corporal son of a dustman.

I'm sure the Air Marshal could tell immediately that I'd been commissioned from the lower decks, but he was charm itself and I have no memories of any awkwardness in our conversation. This may have been because we both had experience of Scampton and the Vulcan, although Sir John had been ten years ahead of me, commanding a squadron of the delta-wing bombers when they were armed with Blue Steel missiles and provided the UK's strategic nuclear deterrent.

On retiring from the RAF, Sir John became a member of the Royal Household as Gentleman Usher of the Black Rod. I saw him on television several times, having the door of the House of Commons slammed in his face during the State Opening of Parliament, then banging on the door to summon the MPs and lead them to the House of Lords.

Sir John held the post, which included responsibility for many aspects of the security and day to day running of the Palace of Westminster, for seven years.

That day at Linton, he and the Under-Secretary of State were on the unit partly because a BBC Television crew was in the process of filming a major new series about RAF flying training. It went out under the title, *Fighter Pilot*.

The RAF hoped *Fighter Pilot* would raise its profile in the way the series *Sailor* - with its chart-topping theme song, Sailing - had promoted the Royal Navy. To that end, they'd given the BBC unprecedented access to RAF selection and training. The director had even been trained up to first solo standard on the JP to give him a deeper insight into the process.

Filming began in 1978. The idea was to follow six young men from selection at OASC, through officer and pilot training to a front line, fast-jet, cockpit. The film crew were regular visitors to Linton and had shot miles of aerial footage.

I think politicians and senior officers had expected the programmes to highlight, not only the professionalism of RAF flying, but also the fun and − a word they wouldn't have used − the glamour, making it a valuable recruiting tool. The rest of the RAF was looking forward to a realistic portrayal of the Service, again highlighting the professionalism, but including some good flying sequences.

When the eight programmes aired in September/October 1981, they were a great disappointment. Not only did they fail to fire the public's imagination in the way Sailor had, but they also infuriated the senior officers and politicians who'd commissioned them and the RAF's rank and file in equal measure.

There were several reasons.

At a late stage, the director in which the RAF hierarchy had set such great store was replaced, probably because of a disagreement within the BBC over editorial direction. Certainly, the series that emerged from the cutting room included precious little of the flying he'd seemed so keen to portray, and even less glamour.

Instead, and in a way that would be all-too-familiar to fans of modern reality television, it gave a warts and all portrayal of the six students, highlighting their character strengths and weaknesses; a less than flattering picture of those in authority over them; and an all-too-vivid idea of the difficulty and stress of RAF flying training.

Even the title of the series became something of a joke. Only one of the six subjects, a blunt-talking ex-milkman, succeeded in reaching a fast jet cockpit, but not as a fighter pilot. He became a Buccaneer bomber pilot. I met him many times over the years, and I think it fair to say that he regretted his participation in the series, certainly in the years immediately following its broadcast, when he came in for much criticism. He and the other participants were seen by the majority of the RAF as shallow, self-centred and lacking in officer qualities, while those in charge of them at all levels seemed cold and out of touch.

Nowhere does this come across more clearly than in the portrayal of the visit of Air Marshal Gingell and Geoffrey Pattie.

After the lunch, the Station Commander and his executives took them to a crewroom in one of the hangars to be filmed answering questions from a cross-section of the Unit's students, including the subjects of *Fighter Pilot*. The exchange can be seen in Episode Six of the series.

I don't know how many questions the students asked that afternoon, but those that made the programme were about the day to day difficulties of life as a trainee pilot, including the lack of leave, the continuous pressure and the mounting fatigue.

The VIPs answer as best they can, but seem genuinely bemused. In discussion afterwards, they express astonishment at the narrow focus of the concerns aired, describing them as *mundane and peripheral*. They'd expected enthusiastic quests for knowledge about the aircraft types the students aspired to fly, and what the flying would be like on the front line.

The scene captures two sets of people on totally different wavelengths, one group somewhat naïve and self-absorbed, the other aloof and out of touch. When the scene was aired, there was little sympathy for either group, but most vitriol was reserved for the would-be fighter pilots. They were seen as little more than self-centred whingers.

And I have to say that, at the time, the majority of us, their fellow students, tended to agree. We felt that no matter how real the concerns, they shouldn't have been raised in such an open forum.

Where was their stiff upper lip?

But in hindsight, when watching *Fighter Pilot* again decades later, I have more sympathy. Over the months following the VIP visit, I was to find that I too became so focused on surviving the day to day demands of my training that anything beyond Linton was pie in the sky.

Chapter 5 – Learning the Basics

I had my first flight in a Jet Provost TMk3A on Saturday the 1st of December 1979. It was a 30-minute sortie to familiarise me, not only with the JP, but the whole ritual - rigmarole - surrounding flying as a pilot in the RAF.

Of course, I'd already completed a similar ritual several times when flying the Chipmunk at Swinderby, but this seemed different, more grown up – a meatier aircraft and more complex flying equipment and procedures. And strange as it may sound, it's the rituals that have left the strongest memories, more so than the flight itself, which is a bit of a blur.

As with every flight at Linton, this one began with a briefing from an instructor in a small (about ten feet x ten), windowless, room with magnolia walls and two upright plastic chairs. I sat in one, while the instructor stood to the side of a wall-mounted white-board, briefing me on every aspect of our next hour or so together. Every now and then he paused to write key points on the board in coloured pen – black, green, blue, or red for airmanship points.

The instructor was my flight commander, Dingdong. By this time, we'd learnt that he had a lighter side than that on display at the briefing on our first morning. He was also a man of many parts with major achievements in the world of rallying, representing the RAF 14 times in international rallies, winning the RAF rally championship seven times and the trophy for the highest placed serviceman in the RAC Rally on one of the four occasions he competed in that world-famous event.

But he could also be very intense, and I found being trapped under his earnest gaze in a space little bigger than a broom cupboard intimidating. I was also uncomfortably hot.

Obeying the mantra, *Dress to Survive*, I was wrapped up as if the flight would end with an ejection and a long period lying out in the open awaiting rescue, unable to move because of injuries inflicted by the ejection and/or parachute landing.

So, beneath my flying suit and high-laced black leather flying boots, I wore thick woollen socks, a thin, cotton, long-sleeve vest and long johns, a thick fleece polo-neck long-sleeve vest and long johns and a green woolly jumper. Over my knees, ready to be put on when we left the briefing room, was a green flying jacket, the successor of the iconic fleecy leather number favoured by Second World War bomber aircrew.

And of course, because many of the people in the building were dressed in normal office attire, the heating was on full-bore. In fact, whatever the outside temperature, from the 1st of October until the 30th of April, the heating in all Service establishments was always on full-bore.

So there I sat, cooking. And despite Dingdong's best attempts to put me at ease, I was incredibly nervous, much more so than at Swinderby. At the time, I hoped it was a reaction to the weeks of hype leading up to this flight. But my nervousness never really improved, if anything, getting worse as the course progressed and the pressure ratcheted up.

On this occasion, after 30 minutes or so of pre-flight briefing, we walked the short distance to the squadron operations room, where we stood before the ops desk alongside other instructors and students preparing to fly. From our perspective, the desk was more like a five-foot wooden wall, its top sloping down toward us for about 18 inches, before dropping away vertically to the floor. Under clear plastic on this sloping surface were sheets of paper bearing all number of flying-related rules, regulations and procedures.

On a slightly raised platform on the other side of the wall, there really was a desk, behind which sat, or more usually, prowled, the duty instructor, the man responsible for supervising the ops room and running the flying programme. Alongside him was a duty student, responsible for doing the duty instructor's bidding and keeping the various displays up to date.

As I was to find later in my career, constructing a flying programme - deciding which aircraft will fly when, with what crew and on what exercise - is as much an art as a science, especially when factors such as poor weather and problems with aircraft conspire to throw it into turmoil. It's probably all done on computer now, but for most of my career, no matter where you served, the programme was constructed on a large, black, wall-mounted board behind the ops desk.

The board was divided into a grid of columns and rows. Each column was about six inches wide, and represented an hour of the day from seven in the morning until six in the evening. At the left hand side of each row was the serial number of a Jet Provost that had been allocated to the Squadron for that day.

Populating the grid were tens of white magnetic tiles, the majority six inches – one hour – wide. Each tile represented an individual flight, the left edge being placed beneath the planned take-off time. Written on each was the name of the crew - instructor and student, or solo student – and the exercise they were to fly. When a flight was completed, a cross was drawn on the tile.

Dingdong pointed out our three inch – 30 minute – plaque. It was in the row alongside serial number, XM405, and bore the script, Dignan/Powell Ex 1.

From a thin fabric sheath to the side of my right knee, I took out a small wax - chinagraph - pencil attached by a short length of cord and wrote XM405 on a rectangular plastic sheet slotted into a pouch above my right knee. The arrangement is known as a kneepad. By the end of the sortie, the plastic sheet would be covered in information of one sort of another. There was a similar kneepad above my left knee. Beneath its plastic sheet was a small map of the local flying area.

The walls of the ops room and the desk top were covered in reams of written information, maps and diagrams, while slots in the front of the desk contained several thick volumes of flying procedures and orders. Hidden amongst all this was the information we needed to conduct our flight.

But where?

Dingdong led me through, showing me what to check, and the order in which to do it. This included the weather at Linton and its diversion airfield – usually another flying training base nearby; the state of the airfield services at both, and their runways in use – which I wrote on my kneepad; the Notices to Airmen – NOTAMs – detailing unusual activities or hazards in the local flying area; and finally, whether there were any Royal Flights, and if so, the timings and routes they were to follow.

To flash into protected airspace around any danger or prohibited zone would lead to a bollocking at the very least, but flying into the time-sensitive bubble of protected airspace surrounding a Royal Flight was a crime so heinous we suspected a night in The Tower and a public beheading might be on the cards. So Royal Flights were best avoided.

Having checked all the relevant information, we moved over to the extreme right of the ops desk to fill in the authorisations sheets. Dingdong leaned over and entered our names, aircraft serial number and the exercise we were to complete, before initialling several boxes, including one to show we knew about the Royal Flight, if there was one that day. There usually was. The Royal Family seemed to spend most days criss-crossing the UK, often by helicopter.

With the flight authorised, we walked on to flying clothing. Here I selected a green life preserver waistcoat from a rack, checked a date on the back to ensure it wasn't due servicing, and made sure it was in good condition and all its pockets were closed. Squeezing it on over my flying jacket, I buttoned it down the front and pulled two straps by my waist to tighten it.

I was beginning to feel like a Michelin man.

Next, I picked up my flying helmet and oxygen mask, again checking the dates they were due servicing and that they looked to be in good condition. Stored inside the helmet were two loops of thick blue/grey webbing about an inch wide, incorporating a metal ring. These were my leg restraints. I crouched to put one loop over my right flying boot and pulled it up until it sat just beneath my knee, the metal ring on the inside of my leg. I tightened the loop and repeated the procedure for my left leg.

For the moment, the leg restraints were an encumbrance, rattling against one another when I walked, but when I eventually strapped into my ejection seat, two lengths of cord attached to the cockpit floor at the base of the seat would loop through the rings and into slots in the front of the seat. On ejection, the cords would pull my lower legs back from the rudder pedals and against the seat, preventing them from hitting the canopy arch or flailing around in the airflow as I shot out of the aircraft.

Finally, I put on my chamois leather flying gloves. If nothing else had done so, their pristine whiteness marked me out as every inch the new boy.

I then followed Dingdong to the abode of the groundcrew, engineering ops. Here, I had a pleasant surprise. Standing behind a desk similar to that in squadron ops was an old colleague, Mac McGavin. Mac had been a Vulcan crew chief on 35 Squadron at Scampton. He was now the flight sergeant in charge of the flight line at Linton.

His greetings of, 'Hello, young sir, off to poke holes in the sky, are we?' would raise my spirits every time I entered his empire. Our relationship would also do much for my street cred among the groundcrew, giving us something to chat about when, infrequently, the opportunity arose.

Mac was also the cause of the only occasion I can remember becoming angry in my capacity as Course Leader.

Sometime after that first meeting, I and my course were walking to some event or other, when I saw Mac approaching on the other side of the road. Now, I mentioned in the previous volume of this memoir that some airmen will do almost anything to avoid saluting an officer, from kneeling down to tie a bootlace, to veering off to divert around them. And some NCOs of Mac's age and seniority could seem especially reluctant to salute newbie officers young enough to be their sons.

But Mac threw up an immaculate salute, which I returned, only to see one of my peers saluting in the jokey manner we adopted when messing about to one of the SWO's Tannoy broadcasts.

If ever there was a case of over-stepping the mark, in my eyes, that was it. I'm not sure Mac noticed, but I made sure the young officer – no names, no pack drill – realised the enormity of his insult. To his credit, the miscreant was suitably contrite.

Anyway, that morning in eng ops, Mac and I both knew it was no time for small talk. We'd catch up on another occasion. Dingdong and I leaned over a black, hard-covered, folder Mac had placed on the sloping front of the desk. It was a Form 700, full of ring-bound sheets detailing the complete servicing history of Jet Provost TMk 3, XM405.

Every aircraft in the RAF had a Form 700. I'd used them every working day at Scampton. But that had been from the groundcrew perspective. Now, Dingdong showed me how to view the folder with a pilot's eye, checking the aircraft's major components weren't overdue servicing; that fuel, oil and oxygen had all been replenished, and to what level; that the most recent servicing – a daily, before flight or turnround - had been carried out; and that we were aware of any problems with the aircraft and how these might limit the conduct of our flight.

Finally, having checked that the engineering supervisor – Mac - had signed to say he was content, Dingdong initialled the 700 to accept the aircraft, and we stepped onto the flight line.

At this point, for a while at least, my trepidation gave way to excitement.

On a vast concrete pan stretching across the whole frontage of Linton's four hangars sat a line of tens of red and white JPs, Mks 3A and 5A. Many were attended by a couple of groundcrew. Most had at least an olive-green battery trolley – a piece of ground equipment about the size of a chunky wheelbarrow - near the left wingtip. Several were being replenished from fuel bowsers and gas bottles, or serviced with hydraulic rigs. Numerous vehicles – tractors, trucks and vans – traversed the pan, some towing the aforementioned battery carts, hydraulic rigs and gas bottles.

At one end of this flight line, aircraft taxied out; at the other, they taxied in to be replenished, serviced and made ready to go again. And, of course, the air resonated with the noise of all this activity, and the roar of jets flying above us.

Still carrying our helmets and keeping our eyes and ears open, I followed Dingdong into this maelstrom of sound and movement. The first task was to find XM405. On the JP and most other aircraft types, such numbers tend to be written in smallish black letters on the rear fuselage. They can be difficult to spot, so to help with identification, most also have larger fleet numbers painted on the nose and tailfin. Even so, tales of people strapping into the wrong aircraft are legion. Some even manage to get airborne without the mistake being discovered. I've witnessed the former several times, although the latter only once.

Having spotted XM405 toward the end of the line, we strode across the pan toward it.

The Jet Provost TMk3A is a single-engine, low wing, basic jet training aircraft in which instructor and student sit side by side on ejection seats. Looking solidly functional rather than elegant, XM405 sat a couple of feet above the ground on landing gear consisting of three sturdy undercarriage legs, one beneath the rounded nose and one beneath the lower surface of each wing. The black mainwheel tyres were about two feet in diameter, the nosewheel tyre about half that.

From front to back, the aircraft measured 32 feet 5 inches. Apart from a matt black portion in front of the cockpit to reduce glare, the top half of the fuselage was brilliant white, the bottom pillar-box red. At the rear, a rectangular white tailfin rose to 10 feet 2 inches above the ground. To either side of the rear fuselage below this, a small grey tailplane stuck out. Wings of the same colour extended out from low on the fuselage just behind the cockpit. The wingspan was 36 feet 11 inches and both wings and tailplanes were straight, rather than swept back.

On the tips of the wings were two red, torpedo-shaped, fuel tanks. These, plus another three tanks in each wing, held a total of 281 gallons of fuel, ready to feed an Armstrong Siddeley Mk 102 Viper jet engine, sitting directly behind the cockpit.

I could picture the engine, not just from lessons in groundschool, but because it had been the first jet engine I'd removed and refitted during my apprentice training at Halton.

Encased within a sturdy metal tube just over five feet long and two feet in diameter, the Viper's seven-stage compressor and single turbine could rotate at up to 13,800 revs per minute and produce up to 2,700 lbs of thrust. This allowed the JP3 to barrel along at up to 270 knots (310 miles per hour), although, more usually, we flew around at 180 knots (207mph).

Air entered the engine through a rectangular intake to each side of the fuselage at the wing root beneath the cockpit, and exhaust gases were funnelled from the rear of the engine along a hollow metal tube within the fuselage – the jet pipe – to roar out from a circular opening beneath the tailfin.

Air bled from the engine compressor fed the cockpit heating, windscreen de-misting and rain and ice clearance ducts. There were no windscreen wipers. An engine-driven pump supplied hydraulic fluid under pressure to operate the undercarriage, wheel brakes, flaps and airbrakes. The engine also drove a generator which, supported by two batteries, supplied the aircraft with electrical power. A third battery could supply power in an emergency.

To save the batteries on the ground before engine start, electrical power was trickled into the aircraft nose via a thick black cable snaking from one of the green battery trolleys parked by the left wingtip.

On this first trip, Dingdong taught me what to look for as we approached our JP, basically that it looked okay, with no visible signs of damage, such as panels hanging off, damaged aerials or flat tyres; and that there were no obvious hazards or obstructions to prevent us starting up and taxying away.

On my next flight, I'd have to demonstrate that I'd learnt these checks, before I was taught the next set, and so on, learning a new set of checks on every flight. By the time I reached Exercise 14, my first solo, I'd have to be able to perform all the checks without reference to the Flight Reference Cards, including many of the emergency checks.

This time, after nodding at our groundcrew, a young airman clad in grey overalls, I followed Dingdong as he walked round the aircraft doing the external checks. Content, he waved me round to the left wing root, while he walked round to the right. Here, we donned our flying helmets before climbing onto our respective wings at the trailing edge, walking a few steps along black strips and looking down into the cockpit at our Martin Baker Mk 4PA ejection seats.

Now, the Mk 4 ejection seat was basically a cannon. To use it, I'd have to pull either of two black and yellow cord handles, one at the front of the seat between my knees, called the seat pan, the other at the top of the seat above my head, called the face screen.

At the time, the favoured option was the face screen handle. As the name suggests, if I pulled it down, it would draw a thick cloth screen over my face, giving added protection against the buffeting airflow and any debris that might be flying around. Its use also ensured a better posture. But unfortunately, it could also take longer to reach, especially in high g situations, and this could have been a factor in some fatalities. So a few years later pilots were encouraged to use the seat pan handle when time was of the essence.

But whichever handle was pulled, the canopy would blow off and 0.6 seconds later, the seat gun would shoot me upward at 180 feet per second, or 122 miles per hour. On the ejection rig at North Luffenham, a kick up the pants much less forceful had been enough to leave me and half my course-mates with sore necks. So it should come as no surprise that those using seats like the Mk 4 in anger often ended up in hospital with spinal injuries. Sometimes, these were severe enough to end their careers, or at least their time as fast jet pilots, the health risks from another ejection being just too great.

Thankfully, modern seats provide a more progressive acceleration, lessening the risk of spinal injury.

As the Mk 4 seat began to rise, it would pull out my intercom and oxygen connections and activate an emergency oxygen bottle, while the leg restraints would draw my legs in until rivets holding them to the cockpit floor sheared. Half a second later, a small parachute would deploy and pull out a larger drogue chute to stabilise my flight and slow me down.

If I was above 10,000 feet, a pressure-sensitive unit would delay my separation from the seat so that I could breathe its emergency oxygen as I descended. On reaching 10,000 feet, or in the case of an ejection below this height, 1¼ seconds after the seat had sensed a deceleration to a safe speed, it and its leg restraint cords would drop away, and my parachute would open.

If, after the initial ejection, some or all of these automatic operations failed, I could pull a handle on the left hand side of the seat to initiate a manual separation, then pull my own parachute D-ring.

It goes without saying that neither Dingdong nor I wanted our ejection seats to blast off before we strapped in. So, before leaning over or stepping into the cockpit, he reinforced a lesson that had been drummed into us in groundschool - checking that pins were inserted in both face screen and seat pan firing handles, the canopy jettison firing unit and both manual separation handles.

There are many tragic examples of seats firing or being fired inadvertently because people have missed these checks, or because of some problem with the seat. One of the most recent involved a member of the Red Arrows, Flight Lieutenant Sean Cunningham, killed in November 2011 when his seat fired on the ground because of a fault with the seat-pan firing mechanism.

If such stories weren't enough to bring home the dangers, fight safety posters by Scarfe and others showed the bloody aftermath of such accidents.

But, on the other side of the coin, there are also instances of pilots forgetting to remove the safety pins before flight, rendering their seats useless. Again, as if the thought of someone hurtling toward the ground vainly tugging at the handle of a seat that was never going to fire wasn't enough, there were flight safety posters to drive that message home.

On a happier note, there were also stories of people managing to cheat death when a seat fired accidentally. One of the more famous is of a tradesman working in the cockpit of a Hunter jet. He heard the tell-tale sound of the ejection sequence starting and somehow managed to squeeze himself down by the rudder pedals underneath the instrument panel. The seat blasted out, leaving him untouched, apart from a bit of singing.

During the subsequent investigation, it proved impossible for him to squeeze into the same space. The only explanation seemed to be that the surge of adrenalin his body received when he heard the sound of the seat preparing to fire had not only allowed him to react incredibly fast, but also to shrink.

As a result of this story and others like it, most tradesmen, me included, hated working on and around ejection seats. Now though, I was going to sit on one every time I flew, hoping all the time that I didn't do something stupid and set it off at the wrong time, and that it worked as advertised if I needed it.

I could even use the seat on the ground, as long as the aircraft was doing more than 90 knots – just over 100 mph. If I tried to eject at lower speed, the parachute wouldn't have time to open and slow my descent before I hit the ground. The resulting injuries were likely to be fatal.

This meant that if there was some sort of emergency necessitating abandoning the aircraft on the ground at less than 90 knots, I'd have to brake to a halt, unstrap and get out under my own steam, taking care not to trigger the seat if there was insufficient time to refit the safety pins.

Inevitably, there was a story of someone misunderstanding the nuances of this.

Sitting at the end of the runway before take off, an instructor told his student he had an engine fire – what we called a practice emergency. He expected the student to pretend to shut down the engine and unstrap, then say that in the real case he'd step out onto the wing, jump clear of the burning wreck and run away.

Instead, he released the brakes and opened the throttle. When the startled instructor asked what on earth he was doing, the student explained that he was accelerating to 90 knots so he could eject. The slight matter that it was a practice – and that he'd be relying for his acceleration on a flaming engine a couple of feet behind him - seemed to have slipped his mind.

If nothing else, the story illustrates that faced with a choice, some people will always go for the wrong option. Or maybe the student just wanted the tie the ejection seat manufacturers, Martin Baker, present to everyone who survives the use of their product.

And before I leave the subject of ejections, just a couple of examples of how acquaintances of mine earned their Martin Baker ties.

The first was on Tornado GR1s at a time when the swing-wing jet bomber was fairly new in service. When low flying in Canada, he was forced to eject, suffering severe injuries when he and his seat hit the ground. Emergency surgery included a partial reconstruction of his face and the fitment of a pin running from buttock to knee to hold together a shattered thigh-bone.

Unsurprisingly, the presence of the pin debarred him from flying aircraft fitted with ejection seats.

Surely most people would have left it at that, but not my friend. Several years later, he pushed to have the pin removed so that he could get his bang-seat category back. After some initial resistance, the medical authorities agreed. But when they came to perform the operation, they had to ring Canada to find out whether the pin had a left or a right-handed thread!

Pin removed, he became a flying instructor on the Tucano, the training aircraft that replaced the JP, and went on to fly aircraft fitted with ejection seats as a squadron commander, chief flying instructor and station commander.

The other acquaintance had been flying a Hunter during the final stage of his flying training. For reasons I can't remember, he found himself in a dive from which he was unable to recover. He ejected at something over 600 knots – 690 miles per hour.

At the time, I think it was the fastest ejection that had been survived in the UK. But it left him with terrible injuries, photographs of which never failed to gain gasps of horror, even from those seeing them for the third or fourth time.

The buffeting airflow had so bruised his face that it

resembled a red and bloated soccer ball, his eyes mere slits. He was blind for a long time afterwards.

But he too recovered, and after a spell on helicopters, returned to ejection seats, becoming a squadron commander and chief flying instructor on the Tucano.

Anyway, back to the 1st December 1979. Having checked the cockpit was safe, Dingdong and I stepped in and lowered our backsides onto our ejection seat cushions. The airman appeared on the wing alongside Dingdong to help us strap in.

I'd practised strapping into the seat in groundschool so many times that it should have been easy. But now of course, attempting to do it under the eyes of my flight commander and a tradesman, Tom Scott's theory came into play. My IQ had already halved several times - walking to the aircraft, climbing onto it, donning my helmet, etc, etc. Strapping in suddenly seemed an impossible task.

First, I reached down to locate and operate a handle like a car handbrake to adjust the height of the seat. Then I leaned forward and reached under the instrument panel to adjust the rudder pedals until I was content I'd be able to apply full rudder with each foot.

Sitting up, I fumbled for the fastener at bottom left of my life preserver and connected it to the dinghy pack in the base of the seat. Next, vision restricted by life preserver pouches and dangling oxygen mask, I searched for two lap straps that, with the later addition of shoulder straps, would secure me to both my parachute and the ejection seat. I threaded the straps through loops and forced their metal ends into the lower slots of a quick release fastener. This I positioned centrally over my stomach, below the life preserver pouches, making sure the parachute D-ring sat snugly above my left hip where I could reach and pull it should the need arise.

Now I reached down to the base of the seat and located the leg restraint cords. By the time I'd threaded them through the rings on my legs and clipped them back into the seat, I was in quite a lather. And of course, when I looked across, Dingdong was already fully strapped in, smiling and drumming his fingers on the top of the instrument panel, adding to my feelings of inadequacy.

I raised my right hand and struck eye contact with the young airman, who passed me my right shoulder harness – consisting of an inner and outer strap. I pulled these down over the right side of my chest under the life preserver pouch, passed them through another loop and plugged the end into the top right slot of the quick release fastener.

Having repeated the operation for the left shoulder harness, I tightened the inner and outer straps, both lap straps and another strap running vertically down from the fastener to the seat – the negative g strap – designed to stop me floating upwards when we turned upside down and pushed negative g.

Next, I found and connected my main and emergency oxygen hoses and mic-tel lead, and clipped the main oxygen hose to my life preserver to stop it flailing about and getting in the way.

By this time, I was so trussed up I found it difficult to move. This was far from a joke, as reduced mobility had been a factor in some delayed ejections, adding time to the action of reaching for the face screen handle. Investigators thought it may even have been a factor in some fatalities. So my final action was to reach up for the face screen handle with both hands. I could reach it - just.

So there I sat, sweating profusely and breathing heavily. I'm not sure how long I'd taken. Not long enough for Dingdong to think he had to chivvy me along, but long enough for me to wonder if I'd ever come to grips with the procedure, or feel comfortable at the end of it.

No time to relax, though. We had to arm our seats.

One at a time, the airman standing on the wing handed Dingdong five pins, smooth sided bolts about one and a half inches long with a red tab on one end. Dingdong pushed each pin into the appropriate hole in a stowage on the right cockpit wall below the canopy rail, before reaching for the next. When he'd finished, both ejection seat main guns and face screen handles, and the canopy jettison gun were armed. Then, he turned to me and raised a hand.

The pin for the seat manual separation handle was down by my left hip close to the cockpit wall. It had to be removed by feel, something I'd practised many times in groundschool. On occasion, I'd dropped it. Not a problem there. But in the aircraft, it could fall into the bowels of the cockpit, from where it could migrate in flight to jam the engine or flying controls with potentially catastrophic consequences.

So, if I dropped this, or any other pin, unless we were lucky enough to spot it straight away, we'd have to disarm the seats and unstrap for a search to be carried out, leading, inevitably, to a slip in the flying programme. And if the pin remained hidden, the aircraft would have to be taken to the hangar for the seat to be removed for more thorough checks. In either case, I'd be about as popular as a fart in a spacesuit.

As a result, there was a fair bit of adrenalin flowing as, all fingers and thumbs in my flying gloves, I reached down, located the pin, removed it and handed it to Dingdong. He stowed it and I removed the pin from my seat pan firing handle and handed that to him.

Dingdong then removed and stowed his pins.

We'd follow a reversal of the process after flight, fitting seat pan and manual separation pins as soon as we turned off the runway, Dingdong handing the others to the groundcrew to refit when we stopped on the flight line.

Until then, we were sitting on live seats.

I was especially wary of the seat pan handle, fearing that I might snag it, at which point, like a hair trigger, it would blast me from the aircraft. Thankfully, this wariness soon waned, which was just as well. You couldn't be a military pilot if you were in constant fear of your equipment.

The cockpit was now my factory floor, my office, and as with any job, you just had to be aware of the dangers and do your best to minimise them.

That said, on the infrequent occasions I strapped into an ejection seat later in my career, I always felt some of that initial frisson. Never more so than during my flight with the Red Arrows, when such was the proximity of the ground and other aircraft that having to eject seemed a very real possibility!

But that was 25 years in the future, so back to Linton.

With the strapping-in procedure complete, the airman stepped off the wing root and walked round to the front of the aircraft. Dingdong and I put on our oxygen masks, spoke to one another on intercom and operated our oxygen regulators to check that the gas flowed at normal, high and emergency settings.

Such was the vice-like grip of my helmet that I already had a headache. The addition of the oxygen mask failed to make it any more comfortable. After suffering for several flights, I, like many of my fellow course members, eventually convinced the safety equipment fitters to change the helmet fitted at North Luffenham, at which point, the headaches stopped.

Unfortunately, they never identified an oxygen mask that fitted my long face and prominent nose, the bridge of which was bruised and sore for the rest of the course.

As I've already said, I have little memory of the content of this first flight, but my guess is that it was a quick whizz round the local flying area and maybe a climb for a taste of aerobatics before returning to Linton and landing.

Given the deafening roar you heard when JPs took off and climbed away from the airfield, I remember being impressed at the relative quiet in the cockpit. Cocooned within it, flying helmet clamped tightly round my head, the engine noise was reduced to a whine that never disrupted thought or radio communication, even at full throttle.

And although pilots of faster machines took the mick out of the JP - calling it *variable noise, constant speed*, because of its relatively sluggish acceleration and low top speed – I also have no doubt that I'd have been impressed by the rate at which we covered the ground.

Back on the flight line after landing, Dingdong shut down the engine and gave the face screen, canopy and main seat gun pins to the groundcrew. When these had been fitted, we unstrapped.

Traps for the unwary at this point included failing to release the oxygen and intercom connections, leg restraints or the fastener connecting your life preserver to the dinghy pack in the base of the seat. If you stood up with that connected, you began to pull out its 15 feet of cord - and became very unpopular with the safety equipment fitters!

We climbed down from the wing and as the groundcrew prepared to complete their checks and replenish at least the fuel and oxygen, we walked back to engineering ops and Mac's team of tradesmen. Here, Dingdong annotated the F700 with information he'd noted on his kneepad, such as our take-off and landing times and how many hundred pounds of fuel remained in the tanks.

He also recorded a string of numbers taken from the fatigue meter, a device on the rear wall of the cockpit that measured the number of times we'd pulled or pushed certain levels of g-force. These readings were used to calculate the working life of the airframe and some of its major components, such as the wing spars.

Dingdong would also have discussed any technical problems we'd discovered, the same process that had happened in the crew hut when I was an airframe and engine fitter on Vulcans. If necessary, he'd then have written a brief description of each snag on a separate Job Card, initiating repair work by the appropriate tradesmen: airframe, engines, electrics, avionics or safety equipment, or a combination of these.

Complex and time-consuming jobs would mean the aircraft being towed into one of the four hangars for repair. Otherwise, the work would be completed on the flight line. Either way, the duty flying instructor in squadron ops would be trying to negotiate another aircraft for the next crew to fly, or be forced to watch the tiles that made up his flying programme *slipping to the right* until sorties started to *fall off the board*, the term used when delays meant a flight or flights had to be cancelled for lack of time in the working day.

Luckily for the duty instructor on this day, I don't remember any problems with our aircraft. So, as we wrapped up and left engineering ops, the next crew would be somewhere in the pre-flight process, aiming to arrive with the engineers as Mac was signing the paperwork.

We returned to safety equipment and handed over our life preservers, helmets and oxygen masks to be checked, or to have any problems fixed. Then it was back to squadron ops where, as the duty student put a cross through our tile on the flying programme, Dingdong leaned over the authorisation sheets on the ops desk again.

This time, he annotated the remaining boxes along the line on which he'd signed out with information such as take off and landing times and numbers of landings, before initialling the sheets and writing DCO next to his initials to signify that our duty had been carried out. Had we been unable to complete the sortie for some reason, he'd have written DNCO, duty not carried out.

At the end of the day, the DCO annotation would lead to a tick being put on another large board in ops, the progress board. Down the left hand side ran the names of me and my fellow course members, while along the top were the numbers of all the exercises in the flying syllabus, from 1, Familiarization, to 92, the Final Handling Test.

To us humble students, it often seemed that the only thing that mattered were the ticks on this board. To attain them, we sometimes felt we were pushed too hard, flying in unsuitable weather, or with insufficient time to prepare. It fed our perception of our squadron commander as the demon headmaster of *Another Brick in the Wall*. With its theme of callow youth being forced through the sausage machine of education or, in our case, flying training, it became the course song, with the words changed to *Another Tick on the Board*.

Back to December 1st. Having signed in, Dingdong and I made our way from the ops room to the cubicle in which he'd briefed me for the flight. Here we de-briefed, which involved him re-iterating some of the major points we'd covered, and then giving a critique of my performance.

On this flight, I'm not sure there'd have been much to say, but as the syllabus continued, I was to discover that de-briefs could be as long as the initial brief, and more painful, as they tended to focus on things you'd done wrong rather than those you'd done well. In my case, this often meant there was a lot of ground to cover.

After each dual flight, the instructor would also complete a report. The first part was a tick sheet, a grid with a list of up to 70 different disciplines followed by a choice of 6 squares in which to place a tick, 6 for an excellent performance, 1 for unacceptable. On these early sorties, the ticks appeared alongside such disciplines as checks, taxy, take-off, climb, etc. Later, they'd give an indication of my performance when flying aerobatics, navigation and other advanced skills.

The numbers would be backed up by a short narrative covering major points worthy of praise or, more likely, criticism, and any supervisory points for the system to bear in mind, such as airsickness or persistent weakness in key areas. The report would end with an overall grade, from below average – unacceptable; through low average – must do better; average – could do better; high average – doing well; to a grading I'm pretty sure I never gained, above average - excellent.

From the start of the brief to the end of the debrief for that first 30-minute flight would probably have been about two hours, maybe more. Things would progress more smoothly as I became more familiar with the process, but nevertheless, most one-hour flights would eat up at least two and a half hours of the day. Of course, preparing for each flight and digesting the points made in the debrief took much more time, and completing two flights in a day stretched me to the limit.

It wasn't until I trained to be an instructor myself that I spared a thought for the men who'd been teaching me back then. On a good-weather day, they might be expected to complete three or four flights, leaving little or no time for their own preparation, let alone breaks or meals. And then they had to write a report for each trip and find time for any other admin.

No wonder we all sometimes prayed for bad weather!

Perhaps I've taken more time than I ought covering the process surrounding this first flight, but I thought it important. With minor exceptions, I followed the very same procedure for every flight I completed at Linton; in fact, for every flight I completed during my entire RAF career – meticulous briefing and checking of information, rules, procedures and equipment, then flying the sortie and de-briefing.

It's the same for every flight the RAF undertakes.

There must have been some problem with the weather in December 1979, because I completed only four further flights, two on the 6th and two on the 21st. And the problem needn't necessarily have been thick cloud, rain or snow, but just poor visibility.

Many people think pilots fly with their eyes glued to the instruments. In the RAF at least, this is far from the case. It was drummed into us that we had to focus on the world outside the cockpit. Only by doing this could we see what was happening around us, ensuring, not only that we avoided bad weather and collisions with other aircraft, but also in the military context that we spotted the enemy before they spotted us.

So we were taught to fly by reference to the external horizon, sometimes the sharp line between ground and sky, but more often once above a few thousand feet, the line between the top of a haze or cloud layer and the sky. During the early part of the syllabus especially, if this horizon line was obscured, we were unable to fly.

My morning flight on 6th December was the first of many building blocks on the way to becoming a military pilot: Effects of Controls 1. The instructor, who I'm going to call Simon, was a flight lieutenant in his early 30s with the same slim physique and intense manner as Dingdong, but also a flashing smile.

He and I followed the same pre-flight ritual as on my first flight, and once airborne he taught me to use the controls; firstly to roll by easing the control column from side to side to operate the ailerons - small control surfaces on the outboard trailing edge of each wing; then to pitch up and down through the horizon by easing the control column back and forward to operate the elevators on the rear of the tailplanes; and then to yaw – swing – the nose around the horizon by squeezing the rudder pedals to operate the rudder on the back of the tailfin.

Once I'd practised this, Simon taught me how to achieve wings level by rolling to set the top of the instrument panel – the coaming - parallel to the horizon to the front, then pitch up or down to position it a set distance below the horizon, while making sure the wingtip tanks were an equal distance below the horizon to each side; and finally to use the appropriate rudder pedal to stop any yaw and head straight for a landmark in the distance.

The resultant view from the cockpit, a snapshot of the position of the coaming relative to the horizon, is known as an *attitude*.

But to hold any attitude, I usually had to exert a force on the control column. This quickly became tiring, while if I was distracted and relaxed my grip, the aircraft would slide away to a new, unwanted attitude. Simon provided the answer, teaching me to turn a little wheel on the side of the throttle quadrant to move a tab on the elevator and counter the control force.

After this, I could set an attitude, assess the control force needed to hold it and turn the wheel until that force disappeared. Now if I released the control column, the attitude didn't change.

The process is known as trimming.

Although it was rarely necessary, I could also trim out the force on the ailerons, but because the force of the JP's single engine operated along the centreline of the aircraft, there was rarely any residual force on the rudder, so no need for a rudder trim tab.

I was to learn that every time I changed a parameter, such as speed or power, it was necessary to re-trim. In fact, like lookout, trimming is an almost continuous activity for any pilot flying without the aid of an autopilot.

The essence of this first exercise could be stated in three words, Select, Hold, Trim, that is, select the attitude, hold it and trim out the control forces. The three words formed an activity cycle, one of many I was taught at this stage. They were the bedrock of flying training, things that had to become as natural as walking or breathing if I was to become a successful pilot.

Simon was also the instructor for my second flight on December 6th, Effects of Controls 2, during which he taught me how to maintain a visual attitude while lowering or raising the landing gear, changing power settings or operating the control surfaces on the inboard trailing edge of both wings called flaps. Again, the essence was the activity cycle, Select, Hold, Trim.

For Exercises 4 and 5 on December 21st 1979, I had a

different instructor.

Fair-haired and standing about five feet eight inches tall, Roger was an affable squadron leader in his early thirties. He either was then or shortly after became a Specialist Aircrew officer, eschewing further promotion for a status that virtually guaranteed he'd spend the rest of his career in the cockpit. It seemed to work, because he was still a squadron leader instructor at Linton 11 years later, when I was the Station's squadron leader desk officer at Headquarters Support Command.

Roger taught me how to achieve straight and level flight at different speeds. The essence was another activity cycle: Lookout, Attitude, Instruments.

Starting with the lookout element, I was taught more formally a method of scanning the sky I'd been introduced to on the Chipmunk a few months earlier. It meant moving my head in a systematic pattern, darting my eyes over large areas above and below the horizon, relying on peripheral vision to pick up objects or movement which I could then focus on more directly to see if they were a hazard.

Except when flying in cloud, I had to repeat this lookout scan incessantly, just as the best pilots in the Battle of Britain had done. And as an aside, they wore silk scarves, not as an affectation, but to stop the starched shirt collars they wore at that time from chafing their necks as they swivelled their heads in a constant search for the enemy.

While looking out, Roger taught me to assess the attitude, checking the position of the wingtips as I scanned to the sides, and that of the cockpit coaming relative to the horizon when sweeping my eyes across our front.

After each complete lookout scan, I was allowed a brief glance at the instruments, say the altimeter to see whether I was climbing or descending, and the air speed indicator to check the speed. Adjusting one variable usually meant adjusting another; for instance, if I was climbing and the speed was low, I might regain speed merely by lowering the nose, but I might also have to increase power. But whenever

I made adjustments, I had to be looking outside at the attitude, not inside at the instruments, and I had to re-trim.

As the syllabus progressed, we were also taught the attitudes for turning at different angles of bank, and for climbing and descending. Although vastly different from the attitudes for straight and level, they were still snapshots of the position of the instrument coaming relative to the horizon, and if you could remember them, you could fly accurately with only the odd glance inside to check the instruments.

I spent hours on the ground trying to commit the various attitudes to memory. But like many of my peers, my attempts met with limited success. And in the air, having invariably set the wrong attitude, I'd attempt to adjust it while looking at the instruments rather than out of the cockpit, a habit known as *chasing the instruments*. Pilots doing it tend always to be trying to catch up with events, rather than controlling them.

Again, it was only when I became an instructor myself that things like visual attitudes fell into place. And when I had my own students, although I always did my best to help them, I did so in the realisation that many would fail to grasp the concept at that early stage of their training.

I hope I haven't banged on too long about activity cycles, but just as with the pre- and post-flight procedures, they were the bedrock of every flight at Linton and beyond, even if by then they were second nature and I barely realised I was doing them.

With each exercise, I was completing more of the checks and learning other skills, such as taxying, taking off and the rudiments of landing. And of course, although there'd been little flying in December, there were still plenty of groundschool exams, and those early morning station exercises. There'd also been plenty of sport and two social functions, the Squadron Christmas Party and the Station Christmas Draw.

As the name implies, the Christmas Draw was a lottery, for which tickets were sold in the weeks leading up to the event. The more tickets sold, the more and bigger the prizes. On large stations, there could be many tens of prizes up to and including cars and holidays, making tickets very popular. There was also plenty of opportunity for eating, drinking and dancing into the small hours.

Unlike most formal Mess functions, the dress for Christmas Draws was civilian dinner jacket, or more usually, dinner suit. Neither as the son of a dustman, nor as an airman had I found it necessary to own such attire. The other ex-Apprentice on my course, Steve Longley, was in the same boat.

We had two options, hire a dinner suit, or buy one. Even if we only wore the suits once a year, buying seemed the most sensible option, so Steve and I visited a tailor in the narrow mediaeval streets of central York. An hour or so later, we left, having paid the eye-watering sum of £120 for our suits. In my case though, this has turned out to be a bargain. As I write this piece 38 years later, it still fits. And the flares adorning the bottoms of the trouser legs have been in and out of fashion several times!

Sadly, Steve had less wear out of his. Relaxed and devil-may-care while at Linton, a decade or so later, he committed suicide. A story for another volume perhaps.

After my two flights on Friday 21st December, I drove to Ludlow for Christmas. Since arriving at Linton at the start of November, I'd returned home only twice, on short weekend visits lasting from late Friday night until early Sunday afternoon.

Although I'd proposed to Geraldine in October, at the time we hadn't set a date for the wedding. This was partly because the RAF discouraged marriage during flying training. It wasn't that many years since it had been forbidden altogether. The flying training establishment - as again witnessed in *Fighter Pilot* - thought the chances of reaching a front line cockpit were enhanced by total immersion in flying and living in the Officers' Mess with your fellow course members, not in a married quarter with the distraction of a wife or, even worse, children.

Who knows, perhaps the principle had merit, but even at the time it seemed hopelessly outdated.

Geraldine and I realised that if we allowed the RAF to dictate matters, we were unlikely to see much of one another for the best part of three years, maybe more, because flying training was deemed to last until you were combat-ready on the front line. As a result, we decided to marry sooner rather than later, whatever the RAF thought.

And anyway, three of my course were already married, and they seemed to struggle no more than the rest of us, while another two had weddings planned in the early months of 1980.

The upshot was that somewhere between October and Christmas, Geraldine and I cemented our plans. On December 28th, we visited the vicar of Bromfield, the village a couple of miles to the north of Ludlow in which Geraldine lived. At the end of the meeting, we'd agreed a date of 24th May 1980.

After a Christmas break of eight full days, which my diary summarises as, *Smashing*, I returned to Linton on Sunday 30th December. On New Year's Eve we had groundschool, including a Navigation test.

Chapter 6 – More Building Blocks

I suppose, technically, my first solo flight had been in an Air Training Corps glider at RAF Cosford in 1971. A couple of other members of 43 Course had achieved the same milestone, while others had flown solo in light aircraft. But none of these experiences seemed to compare with the event that loomed large as we returned to flying in January 1980: our first solo in a military jet, Exercise 14 in the Linton syllabus.

On the 2nd, I completed Exercises 6 and 7. In the first, Roger taught me to climb, level off and descend, while in the second, Simon covered the art of turning. Again, both exercises were based around the activity cycles, Select, Hold, Trim and Lookout, Attitude, Instruments, and by the end, I had many more visual attitudes to remember.

At the end of the day, I could do, or at least make a fair attempt at most of the checks before and after flight, and many of the airborne checks. I could also start the engine, taxy, take off and climb, weaving every 1,000 feet to clear the area ahead of the nose and check that no-one was sneaking up on me from behind. Once at the desired height, I could level, fly medium turns and enter and fly a descent.

The environment still seemed strange, almost surreal. Despite the light streaming in through the domed perspex canopy, the cockpit felt cramped and claustrophobic, its sides rising to shoulder level, the dark instrument panel sitting a few feet ahead up to chin height, and the instructor and me sitting shoulder to shoulder on our ejection seats, like green Michelin men, swathed in layer upon layer of uncomfortable flying kit. I still struggled to pick out the words on the intercom and radio, and my nose had a tendency to drip, which was becoming annoying. But at this stage, I was coping, and enjoying my flying.

Two days later, I had the first of two flights with Roger, during which he taught me how to take off, fly a circuit and an approach to a runway. To stop us getting in the way of others flying in the circuit at Linton, we aimed to complete most of the exercise in the upper air, utilising an imaginary runway among the clouds.

Using all the skills I'd learned so far, I climbed us to a sensible height. Following a short period of revision, Roger taught me how to climb from our imaginary runway, turn onto a downwind heading, fly straight and level downwind while doing the landing checks, fly a finals turn and then a final approach. After several practices, we returned to Linton.

Lining up with the airfield from several miles out, he now taught me to recognise the view of the runway needed to fly a good approach. Initially, from our distant position, I could see the concrete strip was too foreshortened, too dumpy. It was the sign of a low approach. But as we flew on, the aspect of the runway changed, becoming longer and less tapered from the landing point to the far end. When the aspect was ideal, Roger lowered the nose to fly an approach, drumming home the visual cues I should remember if all was going well. Finally, he raised the nose and showed me how the runway looked when we were too high, a plan view with hardly any taper from one end to the other.

In the run up to first solo, I'd fly approach after approach until I recognised the ideal picture of the runway. But I also had to know what to do when the picture wasn't ideal, so reiterating a skill taught at height, on a second circuit, Roger showed me how to raise or lower the nose to regain the correct flight path, while using power to maintain the correct speed.

After touching down, he gave me control to roll a short distance along the runway and take off again – in RAF terms, a *roller*. This was my opportunity to fly a complete circuit.

All I can remember is that everything happened so fast – too fast. Take off, after take-off checks, turn onto downwind, landing checks, radio call, finals turn, another radio call, line up with the runway, fly the final approach and land.

Throughout, Roger prompted and cajoled, encouraging me to maintain the correct heights and speeds all the way to a landing – or barely controlled crash. By the time we'd taxied in and shut down, I felt like a complete dish rag.

I fear my words fail to bring home the pace of our training. But in just seven flights comprising six hours 30 minutes in the air, I was expected to have come to terms with a bewildering range of equipment and procedures, and to have learned the basic checks and skills necessary to fly a JP in the circuit of an airfield.

Although the syllabus at a civilian flying club would be similar, the environment and atmosphere would generally be much more relaxed. After all, the student is paying for his or her own instruction, so if they have the money, they can revise and repeat exercises as necessary, effectively progressing at their own pace.

The training of airline pilots would probably be more constrained, but they too pay for themselves. In our case, it was the taxpayer that was footing the bill, which, at a conservative estimate, amounted to £4,000 for each hour in the air. As a result, we were granted little time for revision. Most of the time in the air was spent learning new skills. It was all-too-easy to drop behind.

I was still coping, but also beginning to feel the pressure.

Before I could be allowed to go solo in the circuit, I had to be familiarized with a hazard of flight known as a stall.

It may sound like the embarrassing moment when your car engine cuts as you try to pull away from traffic lights, but stalling an aircraft can have much more serious consequences. Failure to recognise the condition and take the correct recovery action has caused the loss of many aircraft over the years, among the most high profile in recent times being Air France Flight 447, an Airbus 330 that crashed into the Atlantic on 1st June 2009, with the loss of all 228 people on board.

So my second trip on 4th January, Stalling 1, was an important part of my education as a pilot.

In the pre-flight brief, Roger set the scene. He was holding an aluminium model of a JP that looked like a child's glider, one shaped metal sheet for the fuselage, and sheets representing the wings and tailplanes riveted to either side in roughly the right places. There was a similar model in every briefing cubicle. Not exactly state of the art training aids by today's standards, but they seemed to fit the bill.

In summary of the aerodynamics lessons we'd had in groundschool, Roger began, waving his free hand over the model.

'The curved top surfaces of an aircraft's wings cause air to speed up and flow over them in a smooth layer, like the water flowing over rocks just beneath the surface of a stream. This fast, smooth, flow creates a lower pressure above the wing than beneath it, and the wing is sucked upward, producing lift.

'If we increase the angle of attack of the wing by pulling back on the control column,' he continued, tilting the nose of the model upward, 'the air rushes faster over the top surfaces, producing lower pressure and more lift. But, at the same time, the air toward the back of the wings starts to break off, like the ripples behind our rocks in the stream.'

He continued to raise the nose of the model.

'At some point,' he said, 'if you had your wits about you, you'd probably notice that the nose of your aircraft was a bit high and the speed was getting a bit low. But, if you missed these signs and kept pulling the nose up,' – he angled the nose up even more – 'the air would break off the wings earlier and earlier, until the lift began to reduce and the ripples of turbulence began to buffet the tailplane and elevators.'

He tapped a finger on the tailplane of the model.

'Now, luckily for us, you can feel that buffeting through the control column. It's the cast iron indication that you're approaching a stall, and on this flight I'll make sure you recognise it.

'But,' he continued, 'let's say you ignore this buffet and carry on raising the nose. The air will break off the wing even earlier, destroying lift and flowing back like the bubbling chaos in white water rapids, until it's really smashing against the back end. At this point, the whole airframe will begin to shudder and you'll be able to feel it through the seat of your pants.'

Roger shook the model, setting the wings and tailplanes rattling.

'Eventually, because of the loss of lift, the nose and maybe a wing will drop, and you'll begin to sink in a full stall.'

He fluttered the aluminium JP downward, like a falling leaf. 'Not a great situation at any time, but potentially lethal if you don't recover.'

The model fell to the floor with a loud clatter.

After a short pause, he continued, 'So, the aim of today's exercise is to recognise and recover from a stall with minimum height loss.'

An hour later, up among the cloud tops, Roger spent several minutes making sure I could recognise the buffet. Then he taught me how to fly the aircraft into a full stall. I followed through on the controls as he closed the throttle and raised the nose to maintain level flight. When I could feel the buffet through my fingertips, he continued to raise the nose until the whole airframe began to shake. Then the nose dropped, followed by the left wing and we began to descend rapidly.

Roger told me to relax while he recovered and climbed away. I flew the next stall entry. When the buffeting increased and we began to descend with the nose and left wing low, he took control to teach the recovery.

'Simultaneously move the control column and the throttle forward until the buffet stops, then level the wings and raise the nose to climb at full power.'

Under his watchful gaze, I practised entering and recovering from two more full stalls. Both times, we lost several hundred feet before we began climbing away. This is hardly surprising, since not only were we losing height because of the stall itself, but also because I was pushing the nose forward and adding power to fly clear of the buffet.

And herein lies the reason that many aviation pioneers, but also many other pilots over the years, have killed themselves and their passengers.

If you don't understand the nature of stalling, the natural response to a situation where your aircraft is descending is to raise the nose, not lower it. But in a stall, if you raise the nose before the buffet has disappeared, you increase the rate of descent not decrease it. Counter-intuitively, you have to lower the nose and descend before you can climb.

Only when Roger was sure I'd learnt that fundamental lesson, did he move on.

'But isn't it stupid to go into a full stall and lose hundreds of feet when each time you had a cast iron warning it was about to happen?'

His inflection begged an answer. 'The buffet, sir,' I responded.

'Correct, Ron. So now let's see what the height loss is if you recover as soon as you sense the buffet.'

The technique was the same - add power and lower the nose until the buffet disappeared and climb away. But doing it before we entered the full stall, I found I could recover in around 100 feet, sometimes less, and well before any significant nose or wing drop.

Of course, even the loss of 100 feet could be catastrophic if you were close to the ground. So, when I next flew, four days later, on the morning of Tuesday 8th January, Simon taught me how to recognise and recover from a stall on the approach to a runway.

The complication here is that many of the things you do when preparing to land, such as lowering the undercarriage and adding power, tend to mask the signs of the stall, including the buffet, which becomes harder to detect and more fleeting. Any inattention can quickly lead to a full stall, the last thing you want close to the ground.

So, up at several thousand feet again, I learnt to recognise the buffet at various stages of the approach to a runway, and to recover as soon as I did so, well before we entered a full stall. After each of our practices, Simon had made a point of stating the speed at which the buffet had made itself felt, usually around 75 knots. Once he was happy with my recoveries, he moved the lesson on.

'Okay, I'm happy you'd recover if you felt the buffet on the approach. But we shouldn't be letting things get that far. What could we monitor during the approach that would tell us things were going wrong long before we felt the buffet?'

'The airspeed, sir,' I answered, thinking back to the pre-flight brief 90 minutes previously.

'Correct,' he responded. 'And given that the speed in the finals turn should be 115 knots, and over the runway threshold it should be 95 knots with fuel in the tip tanks, 90 knots without, we shouldn't let it get anywhere near 75 knots, should we?'

'No, sir.'

'Right, you *must* carry out the standard stall recovery if you feel the buffet *anywhere* in the circuit. But even if there's no buffet, you should still do the standard stall recovery if you let the speed drop to 105 knots in the finals turn or, depending on the fuel state, 85 or 80 knots on the final approach. Any questions?'

'No, sir.'

Armed with the ability to recognise and recover from a stall close to the ground, I was ready to begin training in the circuit in earnest.

Chapter 7 – Into The Circuit

There was now a change of routine. We still spent mornings or afternoons in groundschool, but our flying moved to RAF Elvington, an airfield a few miles to the south-east of York. It had been a bomber base in the Second World War and Cold War, but was now a relief landing ground for Linton and Church Fenton, the local flying training units.

The move was necessary because 43 Course were about to begin *pounding the circuit*. At any hour of the working day, four or five of us were to be seen circling the airfield and descending to attack the runway in a series of more or less controlled crashes. If we'd all done this at Linton, none of the other courses would have had time to take off and land, let alone fly circuits themselves.

So, for a month or so, after morning met brief, those flying the first sortie of the day took off from Linton and landed at the relief landing ground. The remainder, staff and students, boarded a coach for a journey of between 40 minutes and an hour, depending on the weight of traffic in and around York. At the end of the day, those flying the last sortie landed at Linton, while the rest boarded the bus for the return journey.

Life after flying had also developed a routine. In my case, on returning to Linton, I'd usually play some form of sport: squash, five-a-side football or volleyball, leaving just enough time for a shower before dinner, a swift beer after, and a couple of hours' swotting before a fitful night's rest and another early start. Although there were still some groundschool exams outstanding, most of the swotting was linked to the next few sorties on the flying syllabus.

I don't remember much partying, and several of my peers had adopted a similarly studious routine. Others though, perhaps more gifted, and certainly more relaxed, found time to become regulars at pubs in and around York, while at least a couple seemed to have taken up residence in the local nurses' home. They'd return to Linton just in time for morning met brief with tales of dodging matron on the way in or out of the home, or diving out of windows when a room inspection seemed likely.

I remember matron gaining the upper hand on only one occasion.

Having spotted him driving away in the early morning, the beleaguered guardian passed the car registration of one of our course members to the Station. The Lothario was given a fairly tongue in cheek interview and told to lay low for a few weeks.

But of course he wasn't the only young man matron had to worry about. A proportion of all the trainee pilots at Linton and our sister station at Church Fenton seemed to spend at least some nights in the nurses' home. I couldn't help thinking that if she really wanted to stop the shenanigans, matron needed help with security, starting with a barbed wire fence and a minefield.

The first of my two Pilot Flying Log Books shows that my second flight on 8th January was Exercise 11, and that I completed nine landings. This was my introduction to pounding the circuit. The big unknown was just how many times I'd have to pound it before I was deemed safe to go off on my own, if ever.

On this, my first dedicated circuit sortie, Simon was prepared to give me a fair amount of leeway, and instruction. But by the end of it, I was expected to fly our JP from take-off to landing without too many interventions on his part. After all, first solo, Exercise 14, was only three trips away.

Within the limitations of my memory after 38 years, what follows is an explanation of how I'd hope to fly a normal circuit in the JP with a 10 knot breeze blowing straight down the runway.

Apply full power, release the brakes and keep straight, pull the nosewheel off at 75 knots and ease into the air at 80. Raise the landing gear before the aircraft has accelerated to 140 knots, the speed above which the wheels should never be dangling into the airflow.

Before take off, I'd lowered the trailing edge flaps by 15 degrees to the take-off position to improve lift. Now, select them up before reaching their limiting speed of 150 knots. With the aircraft *cleaned up*, complete the after take-off checks and climb straight ahead.

Approaching 500 feet, a good look out for other aircraft and enter a climbing turn to the left through 180 degrees at about 25 degrees of bank. About a third of the way round this upwind turn, level at 1,000 feet. After the remaining two thirds of the turn, roll out and fly downwind, parallel with the runway, which is tracking beneath the left wing, just inboard of the tip tank.

While on the downwind leg, make a radio call to the visual control room atop the air traffic control building. A call of, say, 'Delta Two Three, downwind to roll,' – informs the circuit controller that I'm on the downwind leg and intending to touch down and roll along the runway for a further take off. If I called 'downwind to land,' it would mean I intended to remain on the ground.

With the call acknowledged, complete the landing checks, which include ensuring that the speed is below 140 knots and selecting the landing gear down, checking that three green lights appear on small circular indicators on the instrument panel in front of each pilot. These confirm that the nose and both main undercarriage legs have locked down.

Check that the speed is below 150 knots, lower the flaps to the take-off position, simultaneously easing the nose forward to counter the increase in lift. Confirm the flap position on another indicator in the cockpit. The lower nose attitude gives a slightly better view to my front.

Now, in my mind's eye, I extend the runway centreline about a mile and a half out into the countryside to a feature on the ground – something like a barn, a small wood or a solitary tree. I want to be over this landmark at 500 feet pointing back at the runway. But for now, continue downwind, pegging the speed at 115 knots.

Abeam my chosen feature, and after a good lookout to make sure I'm not going to impede other aircraft on approach, throttle back a little and lower the nose to enter the finals turn, rolling left to about 25 degrees of bank, adjusting power to maintain 115 knots.

Once established in this turn, make another radio call: 'Delta Two Three finals, three greens.'

This tells the controller where I am, and that I believe my landing gear to be down and locked. But hard won experience of aircraft landing with their wheels up when pilots said they'd lowered them had led to a belt and braces system of extra checks on RAF airfields.

If the gear is locked down, the controller will have heard three short beeps at the end of my radio call. In addition, a red and white vehicle – always known as a caravan – is parked next to the runway. From this, an airman will look out for a flashing white light on the nose of my JP, visual confirmation that the gear is not only down, but locked down. If the airman doesn't see the light, he'll fire a red flare to warn me not to land.

Having heard the beeps and checked for conflicting traffic, either in the air or on the runway, the controller should clear me to do what I requested downwind – roll. But if a vehicle is crossing the runway, or an aircraft is landing or taking off ahead of me, and the controller expects them to be clear by the time I reach 200 feet on the approach, they may clear me to continue. If they suspect the runway won't be clear, or there's any other confliction, they could tell me to overshoot.

An overshoot is a climb away from anywhere on final approach before landing. I could do one at my own request, but I may have to do it if the controller tells me to, if the caravan fires a red flare or because I recognise that I'm flying a dangerous approach.

Let's pretend I'm cleared to roll.

Once lined up with the runway 500 feet above my feature, ensure the speed is below 115 knots and lower the flaps to Full, a position in which they droop 40 degrees into the airflow. This increases, not only lift, allowing me to lower the nose and gain a better view of the runway, but also drag, so that extra power is needed to maintain speed, putting the Viper engine in a more responsive rpm range.

Now, assess the picture of the runway, looking for the finely tapered aspect I should have learnt to recognise. If too high or too low, use the flying controls and power to adjust to the correct approach path, then maintain it, whilst also trickling the speed to arrive over the runway threshold at 95 or 90 knots, depending on whether the tip tanks contain fuel or not.

At this delicate stage, the idea is not to fixate on the runway – and risk driving the nose straight into it – but to look to its far end and. As the horizon in my peripheral vision comes *up round my ears,* close the throttle and gently raise the nose to the landing attitude.

After touchdown on the runway centreline, hold the nosewheel up until 60 knots, then lower it gently to the ground. Keep straight while opening the throttle for a further take-off.

From take off to touchdown usually takes about 5 minutes.

Of course, for simplification, in explaining this standard model of a circuit, I've missed out many of the nuances of positioning and control, the detail of the checks and the incessant trimming. Additionally, all manner of complications are likely to interfere with my efforts, not least other aircraft, either pounding the circuit themselves, or returning to the airfield to land.

But the major variable that makes every flight different is the wind speed and direction.

Take the instance of a wind blowing from the left as I line up for take off. Once airborne, if I don't want to be blown to the right of the runway centre line, I have to swing the nose to the left, into wind. And in the climbing left turn, if I used the standard 25 degrees of bank, I'd roll out downwind far too close to the runway, because the wind had blown me towards it all the time I'd been turning. So I have to reduce the angle of bank, the amount dependent on the strength and direction of the wind.

When I've rolled out of the turn to fly downwind, the breeze will be from the right, blowing me toward the runway, so I need to swing the nose right, again into wind, ensuring that I track parallel with the runway. And as I make my radio call and do my landing checks, I need to check that I'm not drifting towards or away from the runway, and adjust my flight path accordingly.

On the finals turn, the wind will be trying to blow me through the runway centreline, so I need more than 25 degrees of bank to line up over my chosen barn, wood or tree. And on the final approach, with the wind from the left again, I'll have to swing the nose to the left in order to fly straight towards the runway.

When it comes to the landing, I don't want to touch down with the nose – and the tyres - pointing left, so, just before touchdown, I need to squeeze on right rudder to straighten the nose. If I do this too late, I'll land with a potentially de-stabilising, lurch, too soon, and the wind will blow me toward the right hand side of the runway, perhaps so far that I'll have to overshoot to prevent a landing on the runway lights or the grass.

Finally, on the runway, I may need to ease the control column left to stop the wind lifting the left wing.

And of course, the wind on any given day could be coming from any direction, right or left, and be blowing at any speed. It can even change markedly in the course of hour in the circuit.

There is a saying that pilots use incessantly in all sorts of situations: *flexibility is the key to air power*. Nowhere is flexibility more necessary than when coping with the vagaries of the wind.

I have no idea what the wind was doing on the 8th January, but I doubt it was blowing straight down the runway. It rarely does. So the instructor would have had plenty of opportunity to introduce me to the nuances of *allowing for wind*. No doubt there were other aircraft in the circuit as well, so he'd also have been able to emphasise the need to look out for conflicts and adjust our flight path to avoid them.

I also know that he'd have spent the whole hour encouraging – nagging – me to fly accurate heights, speeds and headings.

A bit like foot drill for raw military recruits, circuit flying is a great vehicle for instilling discipline in baby pilots. My instructors always emphasized that I must strive for accuracy, even if it meant adjustments of 20 feet in height, one knot in airspeed or one degree of heading. And just like the foot drill at Swinderby and Halton, my best was never good enough. But, after many hours of this quest for perfection, I found myself striving for accuracy in every area of my flying, whether or not anyone else was watching or nagging me.

I also learnt that if I ever thought things were going well and no adjustments were necessary, I should be at my most nervous and vigilant. I'd probably missed something, and probably something very important. That said, throughout the entirety of my flying on the JP, I never reached a stage where I thought things were going well. Adjustments were always necessary.

During my next two flights, Exercise 12 on Wednesday 16th January and 13 on Tuesday 22nd, I completed at least another 17 circuits. I know this because the number of landings appears in my log book in brackets against each flight, not only these two, but every flight throughout the rest of my career.

Just out of interest, the number of landings I completed during the Linton course was 433. You'll have to forgive me for not totting up those I completed during the rest of my flying career. I might have attempted to count the Jetstream and Hercules totals, but the approximately 2,500 flights I completed in ten years of Bulldog flying made the task too daunting.

During the first flight on the 16th, I also completed another series of stalls, ensuring that I'd practised the exercise a minimum of three times before I flew solo. However after my second flight on the 22nd, going solo began to seem less likely.

My diary describes both flights as, *Lousy.*

Of course, only the instructors really knew how well people were performing, but I sensed that 43 Course had already divided into three groups: those doing well, those doing okay, and those who seemed to be struggling.

Among those I thought were doing well were John McBoyle, a Scottish graduate with a ready smile who exuded an air of quiet confidence and competence; Dave L, a tall, dark-haired, school leaver with a laid-back manner who seemed able to do anything he turned his hand to, in the air and on the ground, where he was a gifted pianist who can now be found in the orchestra pit of West End musicals. Then there was Neal, a tall, moustachioed Canadian and another relaxed character who went on to organise our five-yearly reunions; and Mike Burrows, a quiet, slightly earnest, but extremely affable, graduate.

Both Mike and John McBoyle seemed to have benefited from flying on a University Air Squadron during their undergraduate years.

The RAF had 15 University Air Squadrons, small units located at airfields around the UK. Undergraduates at all the UK's universities could apply to join one and be taught to fly, free of charge and without commitment to the RAF. The units also provided flying training to undergraduates who were being sponsored through university by the Service.

Before I started officer training, I don't think I'd even heard of University Air Squadrons, but later in my career, I went on to serve as an instructor on one and command two. My final job included command of all of them, and it probably won't surprise you to learn that I became a big fan, not least because their graduates had a marvellous record of success in RAF flying training.

It was disgust at the conduct of a study that reduced their flying that led me to retire after 32 years in the RAF. Again, a story for another time.

Back at Linton, those doing okay included Bob, known as Bawb, a school-leaver from the Isle of Man with some civilian flying experience; Glyn, one of the married students and a survivor of the guinea-pig flying selection course at Swinderby; Dave B, another tall, moustachioed, Canadian; Rich Hobbs, a slight, fair-haired, man-about-town with something of the air of Toad of Toad Hall - he'd already crashed his bright red MGB GT sports car; Dave Benson, with whom I'd been at Swinderby on the Chipmunk; Ian, a diffident school-leaver with a relaxed air; Keith Whittaker, the ex-policeman and one, if not the leader of the group that frequented the local pubs; and the two other ex-airmen, Steve Longley and Dave H, both of whom seemed more relaxed about their flying than me.

Which leaves those who already seemed to be falling behind: Mike Daly, the New Zealander, who'd also been at Swinderby; Pete, a dark-haired Welshman of whom I can recall little beyond a quick temper; and Dick Winterton, a graduate with the cultivated air and moustache of a Second World War pilot. Dick had also been a student on the Chipmunk at Swinderby.

I think you can probably guess that I, another graduate of Swinderby, now counted myself among those finding the going tough.

One thing that stands out is that three of the four who were struggling were graduates of flying selection at Swinderby. It may have been all four, because I think Pete, the mercurial Welshman, had also been on a Swinderby course. And a fifth Swinderby graduate would join our ranks a few weeks later.

Now those who'd followed the Swinderby route had been warned that we were likely to make a slower start on the JP than those with more flying experience, and especially the University Air Squadron graduates. But we'd also been assured that it wouldn't take us long to catch up.

I had my doubts. These were borne out many years later when I discovered just how successful University Air Squadron graduates were in comparison with other categories entering flying training.

Anyway, lack of experience wasn't the only reason I was struggling.

With my feet on the ground, my speed of thought and action were generally good, sometimes excellent, as in the sporting arena. I was also top of the course in groundschool at this stage, and I worked hard to prepare for each and every flight. But once in the air, I began to struggle.

It was if a switch was flicked as the JP's wheels left the ground. My thought processes became slower, as did my actions. It was as if my brain cells and limbs were wading through treacle. I could feel it happening. It was a sort of sensory overload leading to paralysis.

The ability to receive inputs from multiple sources, absorb and analyse them, come up with an appropriate response and act in a timely fashion is the key to success in military flying. And identifying the people with this ability is the holy grail of aircrew selection. It's what the Officers and Aircrew Selection Centre attempts to do.

You might think that in the case of aircrew, aptitude testing would be the primary selection tool. And even some selectors are seduced by high aptitude scores. But even the highest scores in such tests are no guarantee of success beyond the earliest stages of flying training.

The further someone progresses beyond the selection point, the more factors such as motivation, standard of instruction, continuity of flying due to poor weather, ill health or personal problems can dilute the benefits of good aptitude, if not totally negate them. This is why other parts of the selection process aim to assess character traits such as motivation and reaction to pressure and add these to the mix. Even then, it's difficult to identify how someone is likely to react to the reality of flying training, when a multiplicity of factors impossible to replicate during selection come into play.

From the moment I became a flying instructor, I developed a growing interest in selection, and the management of people passing through the pilot training pipeline. Many of my jobs were in this field, culminating in command of the Officers and Aircrew Selection Centre itself. I find the subject endlessly fascinating, but I'd better save further discussion for a later volume.

At the Linton stage, all I knew was that my inability to live up to the potential I'd demonstrated during selection was endlessly frustrating, for me and my instructors.

Take flying the final approach to the runway. I could tell when I was, say, low and slow. I also knew what I needed to do to recover the situation: push on a handful of throttle and raise the nose to recover to the correct approach path, then remove some power and lower the nose.

But knowing what to do and doing it proved to be two very different things. Even when my mind finally launched my body into action, I tended to over-correct, doing the wrong thing at the wrong time, making things worse rather than better, leaving my JP weaving eccentrically toward the runway.

My landings were similarly inconsistent. I'd either round out too early and float along above the concrete with the prospect of dropping onto it from a less than ideal height, or fail to round out at all, attempting to drive the nose into the ground - until the instructor intervened.

One of the problems, and one aptitude testing couldn't predict, was that I seemed to be overwhelmed by the whole experience. For a start, I couldn't believe it was me, Ron Powell, dressing up in this ostentatious flying gear, strapping into this little red and white jet and launching into the sky. It was as if I was standing to one side, looking at myself and saying, *what on earth do you think you're doing?*

The ex-England and British Lions rugby player, Brian Moore, explains a similar feeling when appearing in the spotlight and gaining accolades. He didn't think he deserved or merited any of it. At a much lower level of achievement, that was me. I suppose it's basically under-confidence, a sense of being somehow unworthy. It would raise its head at other stages of my career, but never more so than at Linton.

Another exacerbating factor that selection was unable to predict was my inability to switch off.

I believe it's no coincidence that many of those doing well were those who found time to visit the pub and take part in high jinks, while those of us who were struggling were more intense, less able to relax. In my case, I already seemed to have entered a downward spiral. The harder I tried, the worse I performed.

I wasn't the only one in the same boat, but that hardly seemed to matter.

You may think that the selection process should have picked up my under-confidence and reaction to pressure, but OASC provides only a snapshot of candidates passing through it, and again, the reality of training can produce unexpected results and problems.

And finally, there was a factor that the selection process could certainly not take into account. It was shared by many of us, and not only those that were struggling. We'd ceased to enjoy our training. It wasn't just the anxiety created by striving for a level of performance that seemed unattainable, but the whole atmosphere of RAF flying training at the time. The major topics of conversation in any gathering at Linton tended to be difficulty, stress and failure.

For some of us, entering RAF pilot training had been our life's ambition. Now we'd reached our goal, we were wondering whether we'd have been happier doing something else.

A case of be careful what you wish for, perhaps.

The series Fighter Pilot offers several telling insights into why some students became unhappy in the run-up to first solo and beyond. Perhaps the best example is a scene in Episode 4 which features an increasingly exasperated instructor talking his student through the circuit and final approach to the runway.

Well, don't just sod about like that, get the height right! What're you putting power on for? You're not even looking at the right things! Christ, the air speed indicator tells you how fast you're going. Come on! What do you think you're doing? It's a throttle not an armrest? Now come on, where do you think you're going? You're just not listening! This will not do. It will not do!'

The whole scene contains not a single example of calm, considered, flying instruction.

And then, just as the student is about to land after minutes of being harangued, the instructor has the gall to say, *Don't get so tense! Relax!!!*

Now, I realise that editing is a powerful tool in the hands of a director who's trying to make a point. But there are other instances in the series where the instructors appear to be doing little beyond berating their students for their inability to perform to the required standard. It goes some way to explain why some student pilots during that period struggled, not only to learn, but also to enjoy their flying.

Such scenes led to a fundamental review of RAF flying instructional methods in the aftermath of the series.

Five years later, when I trained to become an instructor, one legacy was an emphasis on giving the students, even those who were struggling and would ultimately fail, a more positive experience. I wouldn't claim the strategy was entirely successful, after all there were years of cultural baggage to overturn. Some saw the changes as the system *going soft*. They still believed that students – and would-be instructors - had to suffer to succeed.

But institutional and human frailty apart, my experience was that most instructors, at least on the Bulldog, attempted to instruct rather than berate.

Now having said all the foregoing, although some at Linton had to put up with this form of instruction, I did not. My problems were solely down to my own inadequacy.

But at least I hadn't yet been chopped, the fate that befell Welsh Pete at about this stage. He departed to become a navigator. The only other time I heard mention of him was a decade or so later, when he was a flight commander on a Tornado F3 squadron.

He was the first casualty on 43 Course, but we knew he wouldn't be the last.

Chapter 8 – First Solo

Ideally, Exercise 14 would be two flights: the first, pounding the circuit for up to an hour with an instructor; the second, if all went well, a single circuit and landing on my own, my first solo. But if, within the hour, I was unable to convince the instructor I could land without damaging myself or my aircraft, I'd have to fly at least one more dual sortie.

If this happened, I wouldn't be the first student with a log book showing several attempts at Exercise 14, each entry bearing the name of an instructor in the column headed, Captain. Hopefully though, at some stage, I'd get to write the word *SELF* in the Captain column, proof that I'd been flying alone.

But of course I was only too aware that some students never get the chance to go solo, or to record any flights beyond their last, unsuccessful, attempt to impress their instructor.

My log book shows three Exercise 14s, all flown on Thursday 24th January, the first two with my flight commander, John Dignan.

The first was very short, only 25 minutes. In my memory, Dingdong threw the sortie away early because my performance was so dire he judged it better to land and try again later rather than soldier on for a full hour. But in a recent exchange of emails, he informs me that the short sortie was merely a chance for him to look at me anew, as we hadn't flown together since Exercise 1. It was flown at Linton, after which he flew the 15-minute transit to Elvington, where we landed.

Sending someone solo is one of the biggest, if not *the* biggest, responsibility an instructor will ever have. Only he can decide whether the student he's sitting alongside can fly a successful circuit and landing on their own.

No-one wants to ring the parents of a young trainee and

say, *I thought Johnny was good enough to fly solo, but he wasn't - and he won't be coming home anymore!*

So, no matter how nonchalant instructors try to look as they watch their charges take off without them, there's always a frisson of doubt in the air, fear even. That's why only experienced instructors are authorised to do it, ones who've had time to see several students approach the milestone, and to adopt strategies and measures to minimise risk.

Perhaps the most obvious and oft-quoted measure of whether a student is ready to be sent solo is the ability to fly three circuits and landings without the instructor feeling the need to intervene.

It's not a bad starting point, but if adopted dogmatically, it means that from the moment the student takes off on Exercise 14, the instructor is trying not to say anything, assessing rather than instructing. Under this regime, some students will never make progress, partly because the instructor isn't helping them to improve on progressive circuits, and partly because they wilt under the intense scrutiny, knowing that every time the instructor intervenes, any chance of flying solo is at least another three circuits away.

The best instructors make it plain to their students that although the exercise they're embarking on appears on the syllabus as first solo, it's just another instructional sortie, one that may for all sorts of reasons end up without them going solo, leading to another attempt at a later date.

In practice, this was the strategy I adopted when I became an instructor. I continued to teach a student right up to the point when I sent them solo. But I was also assessing, assuring myself that they'd be able to fly a safe circuit despite my need to intervene on occasion.

There are all sorts of other nuances.

Some students who've been struggling will suddenly have a Eureka moment, when everything clicks into place. With experience, you can sense it. And if it happens toward the end of a sortie, you may back your judgement and give them their chance on less evidence than a dogmatic approach would dictate.

You may also decide to strike when the iron's hot with a student who has struggled, but slowly becomes more consistent and by the end of the sortie is just about there. Ideally, you'd give them another dual, but experience tells you that if you don't send them off on their own this time, it will be such a dent to their confidence that they'll never recover, and never go solo.

This can be a very difficult call, but I suspect it may have been the one Dingdong made when he sent me solo. In the recent email exchange, he denied it, but I suspect the insight into his reasoning given at our last reunion may be closer to the truth.

He stated in his speech, 'Ron was so dangerous, and scared me so much, that I just had to unstrap and leave him to his own devices.'

Whatever the reason, after 40 minutes of my second dual attempt at Exercise 14 on 24th January, we landed and taxied to the Elvington Air Traffic Control tower rather than our dispersal.

That was a hefty clue as to what was about to happen, but I still couldn't quite believe it when Dingdong started to unstrap.

I've spoken to many pilots who express similar surprise about the same point in their careers. I think it's because, by this stage, we've all become hyper-critical of our performance. So, even though our instructor seems to think we can do it, we think they're delusional.

That said, I didn't think Dingdong was delusional. I knew it.

Had he not been sitting next to me for the last 40 minutes? Did he not sense how thin the margin between success and disaster had been on every one of my approaches, and my seven landings?

Well, it'd be his funeral!

Only it wouldn't be, would it?

Now, as Dingdong made the ejection seat safe and unstrapped, I'm sure I didn't think I was going to die. If I'd had that mindset, I'd have definitely chosen the wrong profession. But I did harbour the concern that I'd make some form of mistake, hopefully embarrassing rather than dangerous. After all, not only Dingdong would be watching. The rest of the Course would be sitting on the grass by the hangar, waiting to dissect my performance, just as we'd dissected the first solos of those who'd already achieved the milestone - about half of us.

The brief given before Dingdong unplugged his R/T lead was short and succinct.

'You are authorised to fly one circuit to land. But if at any time you're unhappy with your approach, throw it away and overshoot. And don't be afraid to overshoot as many times as you have to. You've got plenty of fuel.'

I sincerely hoped I wouldn't have to make multiple approaches, but I knew he was trying to relieve me of the pressure to land first time, no matter what.

He added that if anything happened to the aircraft that required abandonment, I was not to hesitate, but eject. JPs were ten-a-penny – not strictly true – but baby pilots were not.

After that sobering piece of advice, and after patting me on the helmet and wishing me good luck, his final words were another surprise.

'Enjoy yourself.'

It may seem strange, but if he hadn't said that, I'm not sure I'd have given enjoyment a thought. As it was, after returning the thumbs-up he gave as he walked toward the metal steps zig-zagging up to the visual control room, I sat back and tried to savour the moment.

Here I was, sitting on my own, not in a glider, but an RAF jet. The moment of reflection was fleeting, but nonetheless sweet for that.

Re-focusing, I checked everything was as it should be and called for taxy, avoiding at least one of the mistakes notched up by some of my predecessors by remembering to use my own rather than my instructor's callsign.

Unfortunately, I can't recall what that callsign was now, but let's pretend it was Delta Five Five.

Tower came back with my clearance to taxy just as Dingdong reached the door to the visual control room, 30 feet up. I added power and released the brakes. He gave another reassuring smile, and I was off.

During the long taxy to the runway, there was little to do beyond make sure I stayed on the centreline, so I went over what I was about to do – several times. Holding short of the runway, I completed the take-off checks – twice – then checked there was no-one on short finals, took a deep breath and called for take off.

'Delta Five Five, take off.'

'Delta Five Five, clear take off.'

'Take off, Delta Five Five.'

This was it!

Another deep breath, and I taxied onto the runway, confirming for the third time that I'd set the flaps to take-off. Once lined up, I opened the throttle and, having checked all seemed well with the engine, released the brakes. The acceleration caught me by surprise. Without Dingdong on board, my JP – XN589 – displayed a marked increase in performance.

As the runway lights fairly skipped past, I concentrated on keeping straight, using the brakes until the rudder gained authority. A quick check of the engine instruments and frequent glances at the airspeed, before, at 75 knots, I raised the nose to fly off at 80. At a safe height and before 140 knots, I raised the landing gear and flaps and set the climb attitude, then carried out the after take-off checks. Again, without Dingdong, the climb performance showed a marked improvement.

Just before reaching 500 feet, I had a good lookout, especially to my front left and above and behind, then began a climbing turn to the left. I can't remember the wind on the day, so can't say for certain how I had to adjust my circuit to allow for it. I do remember that almost as soon as I'd rolled on bank, it was time to level at 1,000 feet, continuing to turn through 180 degrees and rolling out on the downwind leg.

With the aircraft trimmed and doing roughly what I wanted – right height, speed, heading and distance from the runway – I took another few moments to relish the experience. Writing about it now, I feel quite emotional, remembering all the people who'd helped me get that far, like my parents and men like Derek Crowther on my old ATC squadron. But I'm pretty sure that back then, as I watched the green fields tracking by, the feeling was more uncomplicated and joyful.

Once again, though, there was little time for reflection. After the downwind radio call, I carried out the landing checks, making sure I wasn't exceeding the limiting speed, before lowering the landing gear – three greens – and then the flaps, dipping the nose slightly to maintain 1,000 feet, trimming to remove the altered control forces and letting the speed trickle back towards 115 knots.

I took a little more time to savour the view, something I rarely did with an instructor sitting next to me. But all too soon, the feature I wanted to be over at 500 feet approached the leading edge of the wing. After another good look round for other traffic, I eased the throttle back, lowered the nose and rolled into a descending left turn. Now, I took a few seconds to make sure the speed, angle of bank and rate of descent looked about right, then made the finals call.

'Delta Five Five, finals, three greens.'

On occasional visits to the towers at Linton and Elvington, I'd experienced the atmosphere when other students flew solo. As a result, I knew the controller would have been watching my progress diligently throughout. But

I wondered whether, until this moment, Dingdong had been showing the studied indifference of the instructors I'd seen on those visits, reading the paper or chatting casually to someone. If so, I was pretty sure he'd be on his feet now, watching me through binoculars.

'Delta Five Five, clear land.'

'Clear land, Delta Five Five.'

I rolled out of the turn and concentrated on the approach to the runway. After a quick check that the speed was below 115 knots, I selected full flap and, as they dipped into the airflow, I lowered the nose to point at the threshold of the runway, adding a smidge of power and trimming.

This part of the approach was where I'd struggled before, so maximum concentration. Drifting left, so pressure on the control column to roll gently right to regain the centreline, then level the wings and angle into wind to maintain it. A bit low, so ease back on the control column and push on the throttle to climb to the ideal descent path, then lower the nose and ease back the power to hold it.

This makes adjustments sound like one-off, sequential, events. But in truth, corrections - to fly left or right, up or down, faster or slower - should be, smooth and continuous, deviations from the ideal being countered almost before they become apparent to an observer.

My skill level was far below this ideal, but I wasn't flying a bad approach – for me – and the speed was trickling back to the 90 knots I wanted over the runway threshold.

Fifty feet to go, so a final check that the gear was down and my feet weren't on the brakes. Then, with the ground rushing up and speeding past, look up and along the runway. Once over the concrete, slowly close the throttle...then raise the nose...to the landing attitude...and hold it...hold it...until the mainwheels touch...

'Shit!'

Not a bad landing until I let the nosewheel slam down. I'd lose points in the assessment of both Dingdong and my peers, but worse things could have happened. And would do, if I didn't keep concentrating. Brake to a sensible speed, clear the runway and stop.

'Wow!'

I'd done it.

Of course, it was only the first of many small steps on the way to becoming an RAF pilot. But at the time, it felt massive. And once again, I couldn't help wondering if it was actually me, sitting there.

This could be a dangerous time. Dingdong and others had warned us to be on our guard, because the trip wasn't over until you'd signed in on the authorisation sheets. Even so, I had to fight an intoxicating mixture of elation and fatigue, the aftermath of an immense adrenalin high. But I managed to taxy back to dispersal and shut down without mishap, again feeling strange that there was no-one sitting beside me to prompt, or at least keep a wary eye on my every action.

It seemed appropriate somehow that the first person to congratulate me was a young corporal of a similar age. I'd never met him before, and the sheer numbers involved in running the lines at Linton and Elvington meant I might never meet him again. But I couldn't help wondering whether he'd believe me if I told him that just nine months earlier I'd been doing a similar job.

Because the thing was, I'm not sure I believed it myself.

Chapter 9 – Grounded By The Weather

If I'd suffered a dip in performance and confidence in the run-up to first solo, my logbook and diary indicate that achieving that milestone led to an improvement – for a while at least. My next dual sortie on 30th January was followed by an immediate solo, one hour, spent consolidating my grasp of flying in the circuit.

To avoid the danger of mistakes brought on by repetition and fatigue, after every third circuit, I had to take a break, engineered by flying wide downwind until I was about three miles from the airfield, then turning in and calling to rejoin for another three circuits.

I'd been taught to fly this wide downwind leg and rejoin at a sensible 180 knots. But of course, left to my own devices, I couldn't resist opening the throttle to see how fast I could go. I remember achieving close to 250 knots, nearly 300 miles an hour, and finding the aircraft quite a handful at this speed. It bounced around and wanted to climb, a tendency I had to counter by pushing the nose down and trimming to an attitude much lower than any I'd yet seen when flying straight and level.

And having accelerated away from the airfield, on my return, in addition to closing the throttle, I found I had to use the airbrakes – small metal slats that popped out on the upper and lower surfaces of each wing – in order to decelerate to a sensible speed by the time I came in sight of the tower.

Chats with fellow course members indicated that most had done the same – and only one person was caught out. When returning to the airfield, his rejoin radio call had concluded with the three tell-tale beeps that told air traffic control his landing gear was down.

This prompted the controller to say, 'Check gear,' at which point my friend looked in at the instrument panel to see three green lights glaring back at him.

'Shit!'

Either he hadn't raised the gear after take off, or he'd inadvertently lowered it as he'd accelerated away downwind. Whatever the reason, here he was haring along at 240 knots, ten knots slower than most of us had achieved because of the drag of all that metal and rubber dangling into the airflow, but an impressive 100 knots in excess of the landing gear limiting speed.

And yet, he could probably have got away with it. There were no other aircraft about, so all he had to do was acknowledge the call and say in answer to any questions that he'd decided to fly his departure and recovery at less than 140 knots with the gear down. Unusual, but if that's what he said he'd done, they were unlikely to investigate further, especially if there were no obvious signs of damage after landing.

But, laying aside the issue of personal integrity, we'd had it drummed into us in briefings and flight safety films that if we ever exceeded a limit for the airframe or the engine, or even suspected we'd done so, we should return to land as soon as possible and come clean to our authorising officer. The engineers could then investigate to see if any damage had been caused.

If we chose to keep quiet, the likelihood was that any damage would lay undiscovered, leading to a failure on a later flight, almost undoubtedly when someone else was flying the aircraft. The consequences could range from the inconvenient to the catastrophic, including loss of life, both in the air and on the ground. There were plenty of instances of the latter in aviation history.

The flip side for anyone admitting their mistake was a few days of unremitting banter, and the possibility of official sanction and punishment; although, in the interest of fostering openness, the authorities tried not to punish flight safety infractions, preferring to use them as examples of what could happen if you weren't vigilant at all times.

My mate admitted his error and landed to take his punishment, which I seem to remember comprised nothing more than a lecture on being more careful in future, followed by a few days of jokes at his expense. For the rest of us, it was a timely reminder of the dangers of inattention.

I'd like to think that any of us would have confessed to a similar mistake. I've certainly had to admit to a few like it over the years.

When not flying, January had been a month of groundschool exams and plenty of sport, badminton, squash, five-a-side football and volleyball. I played volleyball for the Station team throughout my time at Linton, and turned out for the football team when the flying programme allowed. I'd also been home a couple of times.

On one visit, my diary notes a trip to the cinema to see Apocalypse Now, and gives the verdict, *very powerful film*. I'd also been offered and decided to buy a car belonging to the father of one of my childhood friends, a blue Vauxhall Viva with 93,000 miles on the clock. I picked it up on my second weekend at home at the end of January, and described the journey back to Linton as *magic*, which seemed to be my go-to word when I found something enjoyable.

Although my choice of vehicle didn't enhance my standing as an officer or pilot - none of my cars ever did - it turned out to be the most reliable to date, and served Geraldine and me faithfully for several years. One of my course mates bought my MG 1300 on the last day of January. Amazingly, he still speaks to me.

My next dual flight on 1st February must also have gone well, because it led to an immediate solo, another 45 minutes in the circuit. In fact, I know it went well. My diary describes the flight as, you've guessed it, *Magic*.

I flew only once more in February though, a dual sortie on the 7th. The reason for the break in flying was the weather. This would probably have come as a surprise to those interested solely in ground activities. In the Vale of

York, the last three weeks of February 1980, although chilly, were blessed with bright sunshine and blue skies. There was little if any rain.

But at this stage in our training, we were still learning to fly visual attitudes, for which we needed a crisp horizon. And unfortunately, there was persistent haze all the way up to 20,000 feet or more. Those who flew found themselves shrouded within a featureless grey bubble, known as goldfish bowl conditions.

The lack of reference points made visual flying, not only difficult, but, as the disorientation rig at North Luffenham had demonstrated, positively dangerous. Only more experienced pilots who could fly by reference to the cockpit instruments were able to get airborne.

We were grounded.

The met men said a high pressure system over the UK was well established, and there was little chance of an improvement in flying conditions for the foreseeable future, perhaps until the end of the month. For the first few days, we turned in as normal, hoping the meteorologists were wrong. But after a week of poor visibility, our instructors accepted that they were probably right.

By this time, the break seemed to have lifted a weight from our shoulders and we pursued a range of activities with great gusto. I was relieved of even more pressure when I handed the mantle of course leader to someone else.

I like to think I was given the position on arrival because they wanted someone to set 43 Course off on the right footing. And at the end of my two and a half month stint, I also like to think I'd succeeded. I was more than happy to pass the baton on though.

On 11th February, I did my first ever stint as Orderly Officer. I saluted the RAF Ensign as it was lowered by the orderly corporal at dusk, and again when it was raised at dawn.

Perhaps because of my memories of sitting in the

guardroom as Orderly Corporal, feeling lonely and unloved, I dropped into the guardroom a couple of times in the evening to chat to the Orderly Corporal and Sergeant, lastly at 10pm. If there'd been any defaulters, that is, airmen ordered to report in their best uniform as part of their punishment for some crime or misdemeanour, I'd have inspected them. But there were none, so after chatting for a few minutes, I returned to the Mess, where I remained on call overnight, ready to deal with anything the Orderly Sergeant decided to push up the line. I had a quiet night, as I did on the three other occasions at Linton when I was Orderly Officer.

One weekend, I attended the tall and moustachioed Dick Winterton's stag night, and the next, Geraldine and I went to his wedding. During the intervening week, he'd shown me round the officers' married quarter he'd just been allocated. Sitting among an estate of similar houses, it was a large, three-bed, semi-detached, red-brick house, dating back to the 1950s. As we walked from room to room, I became more and more impressed.

If Geraldine and I were allocated something similar in a few month's time, we'd have a house twice the size of my parents' council house, although not her parent's tied cottage attached to the Earl of Plymouth's walled garden, which was palatial by working class standards.

Largely on the basis of accent and education, I assumed Dick had been brought up in something akin to a mansion, but even he seemed impressed with his new home, proud even. The dining room had a particularly interesting feature. Above the large, dark-wood, dining table was a lamp with a metal shade like a Vietnamese peasant's straw hat.

'If you pull it down, it dips over the table,' Dick said.

I reached up, grasped the sides of the lampshade and pulled. It dipped all right, clattering onto the table, closely followed by yards of wire and chunks of plaster. Dust billowed to fill the air and coat the table. Mouths open, Dick and I looked up at a jagged hole in the ceiling.

Luckily, Dick saw the funny side. When we visited the house for a party a few months later, he showed me the new light fitting. He also made a point of telling me it didn't pull down!

Mention of Dick brings to mind another aspect of flying that is rarely talked about. His new bride – they separated several years later - was excessively worried about him flying, to the point that he had to ring her after each flight to assure her he was safe. At the time, I sympathised with them both. After all, she'd had no inkling of his likely career path when they'd first met.

But such excessive nervousness was a phenomenon I witnessed several times in my career. In some instances, the concern was genuine, but in others, you had to wonder whether it was an affectation, an overly-public demonstration of deep love – with a hollow ring to it.

When I led the co-pilot section on my Hercules squadron, one wife in particular used to ring the office regularly to check that her husband was safe. Out of office hours, she'd ring me at home to seek reassurance, and when I was away, Geraldine would be expected to offer solace – based on nothing other than that she'd heard nothing to the contrary. No news was good news!

Whatever the reason for such extreme wifely concern, I always felt it placed an incredible burden on a relationship.

For me, the third week of February seemed to consist mainly of sport, including three sessions of 5-a-side football and two games of volleyball, one for the Station. On the Thursday morning, we went for a 10-mile walk that ended in a pub lunch. And on the Friday night we visited another pub, this time with our instructors, for a party to celebrate all bar Pete achieving their first solo. After a meal, we were presented with our solo certificates.

Printed on a small sheet of brown card, they're emblazoned with a cartoon drawing of a generic black bird kicking its startled offspring out of the nest. The wording below states: *This is to certify that on this 24th day of January, 1980, Ron Powell did alone and unassisted take off from and return safely to Elvington, thereby successfully completing his FIRST SOLO JET FLIGHT.* It is signed by Dingdong.

There was one other ritual we all had to perform. Along with our certificate, we were handed a pint of beer, which we had to down in one.

Now I like beer, and although I prefer to savour it a little, I was very content to drink it in one, encouraged by the braying chants of the assembled host. But I felt genuinely sorry for those few who didn't normally drink beer or, in one instance, shunned alcohol entirely.

Unlike today, when such a thing would be frowned upon as an initiation ceremony, no quarter was given, and even the teetotaller had to play his part. Drinkers were loudly chastised for every pause in their quaffing, and every drop spilled down their chins. As a final deterrent to waste, the glass had to be upturned on the drinker's head when it had been drained, which could lead to a beer shampoo and hoots of derision if any liquid remained.

Laying aside the concern about initiations, it seems harmless enough. But in the cold light of modern scrutiny, alcohol and flying are a poor mix, even when separated by the ten hours that was mandated throughout my career. And finally, isn't it strange that going solo in an RAF jet wasn't enough. You still had to prove your manhood through the ability to drink beer.

And no, I wasn't anywhere near as sniffy during my time in uniform, when I grasped every opportunity to drink beer with enthusiasm.

I went home on the Saturday and had a *magic* weekend.

The final week of February was also without flying. On the Monday, I played badminton, 5-a-side football and volleyball. But on the Tuesday, I enjoyed a new experience: potholing.

One of the instructors was a keen potholer, although nowadays he'd probably be known as a caver. Whatever the title, on the Tuesday, he drove five or six of us to the Ease Gill Caverns in Cumbria, the longest and most complex system of caves in England. That afternoon, we descended below ground and spent several hours exploring County Pot.

Over the course of the adventure, we learned to cope with a great variety of terrain and equipment, including the thin wire ladders favoured by cavers. These were hung over the few precipitous, seemingly bottomless, drops we encountered. As it turned out, they were generally no more than a few metres deep, but who knew in the darkness? Less steep descents were tackled by climbing or scrambling down.

There was also a lot of crawling through muddy confined spaces and walking along streams, or following them as they cascaded down narrow, corkscrew-like, canyons, the water lapping up our rubber boots.

The presence of so much water in such narrow tunnels explained the emphasis our instructor had placed on checking the weather forecast before bringing us underground. The consequences of a heavy rainstorm above our heads hardly bore thinking about.

And when belly-crawling for several yards through narrow, horizontal, cracks, I was also aware of the hundreds of yards – millions of tons - of rock above me. Luckily, I'm not particularly claustrophobic, but I couldn't help wondering what would happen if a couple of tectonic plates chose that moment to brush against one another.

Several other things have stuck in my memory.

For a start, it really is pitch black down there. Even on the darkest night, we're used to having at least some ambient light to which our eyes can adjust. And unless you have a house with a cellar that you like to sit in with the lights out, most rooms have windows that allow in some light on the darkest of nights.

But underground, there is no natural light, and you literally cannot see your hand in front of your face. It can be very unsettling, knowing that you're relying totally on the light from your headlamp. Which brings me to the first of several surprises.

I'm pretty sure that by the early 1980s even coal miners would have had electric lamps attached to the fronts of their helmets. But although superficially our lamps looked the same, they relied on water mixing with crystals within the casing to produce a gas which jetted from where the bulb would be on an electric lamp. This jet was lit to form a living bulb of flame, the strength of which was adjusted by a small, knurled, knob on the side. There was no lens of glass or any other material covering the flame.

The system had a couple of drawbacks for the novice caver.

The first manifested itself when descending the little wire ladders. It was difficult to locate and step into the thin aluminium rungs below your feet in clumpy boots. But if you looked down to find your footing, the flame from the lamp was liable to set fire to the sleeves of your overalls. And if looked up to make sure you hands grasped the rungs above you, the flame burned them.

The descent of every ladder became quite comical, at least for those observing. As each person stepped down, there'd be a cry of *ouch* or something fruitier as the flame burnt their fingers. This would be followed immediately by another shout when the natural instinct to look at the damage led to a second burn. And the shock could be so great that the climber instinctively let go of the rungs, leading to more swearing as they scrabbled to regain a hold.

Experienced cavers no doubt had all manner of techniques to prevent this farce, but we had to steel ourselves to look to the side, perhaps catching a glimpse of the rungs in our peripheral vision. Even then there were frequent lapses when a quick glance to confirm a handhold led to more cries of shock or pain.

It was even worse when climbing down the bare rock. Any attempt to look where to place your hands risked burning the flesh, while if you tried to look down at your feet, your overalls were again at risk. I felt in constant danger of setting myself alight.

Another problem with the naked flame was that if it touched rock or mud as you crawled through confined spaces, it blew out with a resounding pop. This left your face covered in little specks of black, like a cartoon character in the aftermath of an explosion.

And then, of course, you had to relight the bloody thing. This had its own nuances. For a start, before you struck a match, you probably had to extricate yourself from the position you were in – hanging on a ladder, descending a slope, or wedged into a confined space where it would have been impossible to even reach your matches, let alone light the lamp. And often, the crystals had dried out so there was no stream of vapour to re-light.

The approved method for moistening the crystals was, our instructor assured us, to pee on them. To this day, I'm not sure whether it was a joke on his part. But anyway, the undignified and messy system of getting the lamps fizzing again seemed to work.

Caving was not for the squeamish, in all sorts of ways.

Several times, there were a series of pops as one light after another went out. It became progressively darker with each pop. But only once did our guide encourage us all to extinguish our lamps at the same time. When the final lamp went out, the gloom quickly became oppressive. In company, I found it easy to contain the primeval fear of the monster in the darkness, so powerful in childhood. But I was aware of it, and on my own, I'm not sure how I'd have fared.

After a few seconds, during which I for one had pondered how we'd find our way out if none of the lamps would light again, our instructor said, 'Apologies, everyone.

I usually bring a torch, but I seem to have forgotten to pack one today.'

Great, I thought. But after only a few seconds wondering if at least one of us could light their lamp by feel, a flashlight beam banished the darkness to reveal his mischievous smile.

On only one other occasion did he cause a moment of trepidation. We'd been descending for several hours before we entered a small cavern with several exits. He paused, standing in uncharacteristic silence, face etched with uncertainty.

'I can never remember which way to go from here,' he said.

We looked at one another, unsure whether to believe him. He let the doubt bubble for a while, before he relented, flashing another mischievous smile.

'Oh yes, there it is. Come on then, follow me.'

When we emerged from the complex, it was dark, but not pitch black, as it had been for the last several hours. I have no idea how far we'd travelled down to our exit point, possibly several miles. I was muddy, tired and covered in scrapes, bruises and burns, but it had been a marvellous experience. Not marvellous enough for me to become a potholer though. I prefer walking or running around in the light.

I did go potholing once more, in a very different cave system in Wales. Again, a story for a later volume.

Chapter 10 – Onward And…Well, Onward

I went home for the first weekend in March. On the Sunday, Geraldine and I attended the morning service in St Mary's Church, Bromfield, the village two miles to the north of Ludlow in which she lived. We were there to hear the reading of our Banns.

Banns are an announcement of a couple's intention to marry. Although an ancient tradition, they're still a legal requirement for a Church of England wedding, and they have to be read on three consecutive Sundays in the parish churches of the bride, the groom and the church they're to be married in if that happens to be different. They give parishioners the opportunity to make an objection to the marriage for reasons such as one of the couple already being married.

I can't remember whether I attended the reading of the Banns in my parish church, St John's in Ludlow, but I do know that no-one raised any objections there, or in Bromfield.

Truth be told, Geraldine and I were only marrying in church because it was expected of us. At the time, the alternative, a civil marriage in a registry office, was seen by many people, including our parents, as inferior, something done by people with something to hide, like a previous marriage, or an unplanned pregnancy.

Geraldine had never been religious and, by this time, neither was I. If we had our time again, we'd certainly have had a civil wedding, although our parents would have been very disappointed, if not outraged. After all, weddings then – if not now - were as much for the parents as the couple. We certainly ended up inviting more of their friends and relatives than we would have if left to our own devices.

But if nothing else, the Banns focused the mind, widening the circle of people who knew our intentions. A few weeks later, this circle was widened again when the engagement appeared in the Ludlow Advertiser. Somehow, seeing it in print made the wedding seem more official, more serious – and, well, imminent.

Over the weekend, the weather cleared and I returned to Linton ready to pick up the flying syllabus where I'd left off. But after our three week break, we all needed a flight to get us back in the swing, and to complete any pre-solo legal requirements, such as stalling. So, on Monday 3rd March, I flew what was known as a flex sortie, one hour of revision with an instructor who appears in my log book just this once.

The trip must have gone well, because I flew solo that afternoon, my last hour of dedicated circuits. The next day, I flew a pre-set route round the local flying area, known as a sector recce. The instructor was a tall, dark-haired, ex-Vulcan pilot, named Clive Crouch, universally known as Croucho.

A quietly spoken bear of a man, he was to be my primary instructor for the next couple of months. He was the one who wondered why I couldn't transfer the mental agility and physical prowess I displayed on the football pitch to the cockpit. Alas, I couldn't. But bless him, no matter how much I tried his patience, I don't remember him ever getting ratty. Exasperated yes, but ratty no. I still apologise to him every time we meet at our five-yearly reunions.

I suspect his exasperation began on that first trip together. Following the dual sector recce and a few circuits, I should have flown the same profile solo later in the day. But, although the weather may not have been suitable, I suspect that either my navigation of the route or the circuits at the end weren't up to scratch. Whatever the reason, we flew the dual sortie again two days later. Only then did I fly my solo sector recce.

It was the flight with which this volume of memoir opens, the one blighted by my nervousness at approaching bad weather, and which resulted in me descending with the wrong pressure setting on my altimeter, and flying around York at 650 feet when I should have been at 2,000.

A flight that should have been one of the high points of the course had been a near disaster. Even my diary's stark verdict of, *Awful,* underplays the blow this episode dealt to my confidence. It made me question whether I was cut out for what lay ahead.

As you know, I decided to carry on, partly because we were about to begin a consolidated period of general handling. During it, I expected to have to polish old skills such as stalling and circuits, but I was really looking forward to learning new ones, such as steep turns, aerobatics and spinning. I'd also have to come to grips with an increasingly complex range of airborne emergencies.

But once again, poor weather intervened. This time, we didn't fly for two weeks. Continuity - the period between flights - was becoming a problem for 43 Course.

In later months, we'd sometimes feel our sorties were too close together, leaving us little time to assimilate information. But that was far from the problem now. In our first 14 weeks of flying, poor weather had grounded us for several consecutive days in December and January, three weeks in February and now two weeks of March. Those of us with little or no previous experience were in danger of seeing our newly-acquired motor skills fade, or disappear altogether.

So why didn't the RAF start all its flying training courses in May, allowing the critical early lessons to be completed in good weather?

Unfortunately, for reasons I was to learn much more about later in my career, including the high throughput of students and the cost-effective provision of aircraft and instructors, courses had to start at roughly monthly intervals throughout the year. This condemned some – like us - to start their flying training during the winter months, when continuity was almost bound to be poor.

148

Having just complained about bad weather though, I feel I have to mention that unbroken good weather can also be a problem.

Through much of my career, a small number of students bound for the fast jet stream were sent to Texas for their advanced training. There, hurricanes and tornadoes notwithstanding, the weather was generally excellent. On return to the UK, those who'd been successful in the US were given a short course to re-introduce them to our procedures and weather before they progressed to the fast jet front line.

I was given an insight into the extra layer weather can add to decision-making by an ex-Jaguar pilot instructing such students on the Hawk at RAF Valley.

'You're leading a widely-spaced formation of four jets on a mission to bomb a target beyond a range of hills,' he began. 'To avoid enemy radar, you're flying at 250 feet and 420 knots – covering eight statute miles a minute. In good weather, the high terrain would be no problem. Each aircraft would weave through the valleys, meet up on the other side and continue to the target, which has to be hit by all four of you.

'But ten miles before the hills it begins to rain, the visibility reduces and the cloudbase lowers to sit a few hundred feet above you. You know the higher ground will be in cloud, but the valleys?

'What should you do?

'Remember, while you're thinking, the hills are getting one mile closer every seven and a half seconds.

'You could stay as you are and hope to weave through the valleys as planned. But there's a risk that some of you will run into cloud and have to climb, trusting to luck that there's a gap on the other side of the hills in which to descend and carry on to the target. And of course, in the worst case, someone could leave their climb too late and crash into a hillside.

'So, should you call your wingmen in and try to weave the whole formation along the same valley? You'd be together, but now you'd run the risk of all four of you running into high ground.

'Right, so perhaps it'd be better to close up and climb early? That way, you'd be certain to avoid the high ground. But what if you couldn't find a gap on the other side to descend through? You might never find the target, which is unthinkable.

'Okay, so what about telling your wingmen to scatter, leaving each pilot to cope with the weather and attempt to reach the target on their own?

'Of course,' my friend concluded, 'all the solutions have advantages and disadvantages, but you need to make a decision. And you need to make it now.'

Well I'm sorry, but give me an hour or so lying in a darkened room and I might - just might - come up with a decision. But truss me up in a jet bouncing along in bad weather at eight miles a minute and my brain would explode, or at least freeze in panic.

The pilots returning from Texas were much better than me, but sadly, a significant number always failed their familiarization course, and the UK weather was often the deciding factor. The blue skies of Texas had not prepared them to cope with it.

The bottom line is that students need to be exposed to bad weather at some stage in their training, just not at the very beginning.

On the penultimate day of our two week lay-off, I met His Royal Highness, Prince Philip, The Duke of Edinburgh. It was a very brief meeting. I was first in a line-up of flying suited students detailed to meet the Prince in our crewroom.

I was to meet him once more, much later in my career, and I have to say that on both occasions he was just as curmudgeonly as he comes across in some interviews. His barbs on this first occasion were directed at one of the senior officers accompanying him, so we students warmed to him immediately.

With a twinkle in his eye and mischief in his voice, he opened with a rhetorical question. I can't remember the exact wording, but it was something like, 'I suppose you'd all much rather be flying than standing here waiting to see me?'

None of us felt moved to attempt an answer, but our squadron commander did.

'Oh, of course not your Royal...'

Whether the squadron leader was about to make an attempt at flattery or flannel, we never found out. The Prince fixed him with a hostile stare and addressed him sternly.

The sub-plot was *I wasn't talking to you*, although the actual words were something like, 'Don't give me that baloney!'

All bar the squadron commander struggled to stifle their mirth, and the Prince moved on, having lightened our day immeasurably.

Even when the weather improved, it often wasn't good enough for us to concentrate on general handling. The individual elements of this discipline all required a better horizon than was available for much of late March.

But the pressure to put ticks on the progress board was so great that we had to fly if at all possible. So, on days when the weather wasn't good enough for general handling, we jumped ahead to a discipline that could be flown in slightly poorer weather: instrument flying. And it was while learning to fly on instruments that I suffered a dip in performance and confidence that I seemed unable to arrest.

So, what was the problem, and what is instrument flying about?

Any pilot with a job to do – fly passengers, deliver freight, hit a target – has to be able to fly when there's no visual horizon. Usually this involves flying in cloud, and often for the vast majority of a flight, from soon after take off until just before landing.

Flying in cloud is like walking or driving in an all-enveloping bubble of thick fog, uniform greyness in every direction, no white lines, hedge or tree to draw the eye and give a clue as to which way is up.

Now, you might think your body would provide clues. And it does. But they're invariably false. The disorientation rig at North Luffenham had given us an insight, but on a brief introduction to instrument flying, Croucho had driven the message home.

First, he told me to look down and close my eyes. Then, after thirty seconds or so, during which I'd sensed no movement, he told me to look up. We were turning left. He'd rolled to 20 degrees of bank, but at a rate below the threshold that disturbed the fluid in my inner ear, fooling my vestibular system.

After another short period with my eyes closed, I was convinced we *were* turning and maybe descending. But of course, when I looked up, we were flying straight and level. The demonstration ended with Croucho manoeuvring while I, eyes closed, tried to give a running commentary. It wasn't long before I had to admit that I had no idea what the aircraft was doing.

The punch line was the same as that at North Luffenham. Without visual cues, the only things a pilot can trust are his instruments.

So far so good. But there are more instruments dotting the instrument panel of even a relatively simple jet like the JP than any car. The sheer number and variety can seem overwhelming. Thankfully, when flying in cloud, you don't need to look at all of them all of the time, any more than you do when flying in good weather.

But where do you start?

The most important requirement is for an instrument that

provides a picture of the world outside the cockpit, and its horizon. Unsurprisingly, the instrument that emerged to fulfil this requirement was called an *artificial* horizon. Because of its importance, it tended to occupy the top middle spot on any instrument panel, as it did in the JP.

Over the years, artificial horizons have evolved greatly, to the point where modern aircraft have various ways of displaying aircraft attitude, usually on computer screens. But the main artificial horizon in the JP3A was very basic.

About three inches square, beneath its glass cover was a curved black surface with a gyro-stabilised white bar representing the horizon. Over this sat a representation of an aircraft. Known as a gull-wing, its kinked white wings reaching halfway across the face of the instrument to either side of a central dot, representing the aircraft nose. The gull-wing was fixed to the instrument, remaining static and horizontal relative to the pilots whatever the aircraft was doing, whilst beneath it, the horizon bar behaved like the real horizon outside the aircraft.

For example, if I pulled my JP into a climb, the gull-wing would rise above the horizon bar, just as outside the aircraft the nose had risen above the visual horizon. If I pushed into a descent, the gull-wing would dive below the horizon bar, just as the aircraft nose would be below the visual horizon to our front. The distance between the gull-wing and the horizon bar indicated the angle of climb or descent.

If I rolled, the horizon bar would tilt relative to the gull-wing, an arrow at the base of the instrument sweeping its circumference to indicate the direction and angle of bank. So in a right turn at 30 degrees bank, the arrow at the base would be to the right, under the 30 degree mark.

The instrument would continue to give accurate information even if I rolled through 360 degrees, but its gyro would topple if I exceeded 85 degrees of pitch, at which point I'd have to regain straight and level flight to allow the gyro to re-erect, an operation I could expedite with a fast-erect button.

So as long as I didn't climb at an angle greater than 85 degrees, I could set any attitude on the artificial horizon I could set on the real horizon outside the cockpit. I just had to get used to a small black and white representation of the world, rather than the large technicolour one I was used to.

Groundschool had various mock-ups in which we could practise instrument flying, including a cockpit trainer in which we'd complete 25 formal sessions alongside the flying syllabus.

In a classic example of Sod's Law, my first dedicated instrument flying sortie was not only my first flight after our 14-day lay-off, but also the first since my confidence-sapping solo sector recce.

The instructor, who I flew with on just this one sortie, set about teaching me how to set attitudes on the artificial horizon. This involved placing the central dot of the gull-wing various small distances above or below the horizon bar to achieve straight and level flight at different speeds, or to climb, descend or turn at different angles of bank, or any combination of the above.

We'd discussed the approximate performance - speed, height, heading, rate of turn, rate of climb or descent – I could expect for a given attitude and engine power setting. Now, the instructor taught me which instruments to check to confirm performance – the altimeter, air speed indicator, gyro compass, vertical speed indicator and altimeter. These were clustered round the artificial horizon, making them easy to find with a quick glance.

The frequency with which I needed to scan any particular performance instrument depended on the mode of flight, but I learnt never to check more than one before returning to the artificial horizon to check the attitude. Of course, I still had to scan more distant gauges, such as those displaying engine performance or fuel contents, but much less often.

The pattern a pilot's eyes should follow, looking from the artificial horizon to a performance instrument, back to the horizon and then out to another performance instrument is called a selective radial scan, and it is the fundamental building block of instrument flying.

My diary gives no indication how this flight went, so I don't think it can have been disastrous. There was then a break in the weather that allowed a couple of general handling flights, before a return to instrument flying with Croucho a week later.

This flight probably started with him teaching me an instrument take off – that is, looking out of the cockpit until safely airborne, then peering in to concentrate on the instruments until the final few seconds before landing. The sortie would have included a mixture of teaching and practice, covering climbing to a prescribed height, levelling, flying medium and steep turns, at 30 and 45 degrees of bank respectively and descending for an approach to the runway, before looking up from the instruments to land visually.

It merited the diary comment, *Awful*.

So what was the problem? After all, in theory, instrument flying should be no more difficult than visual flying. However, the reality is that many would-be pilots struggle with the skill. All I can do is try and explain why I was one of them.

When looking out of the cockpit in good weather, I found it easy to see what the aircraft was doing. But when instrument flying, it could take me quite a while to interpret what the artificial horizon and performance instruments were telling me. It could then take even longer to work out what I needed to do - turn, climb, descend or whatever - and even longer to operate the controls and do it.

When flying on instruments, I also tended to become tense, leading me to make jerkier movements and spend more time making adjustments. This led to a cycle of constant corrections, meaning the aircraft was never flying a truly settled flight path, exacerbating another problem.

As demonstrated by Croucho and the disorientation rig, manoeuvring in poor visibility can upset the balance mechanism in the inner ear. This often leads to a feeling of giddiness, or worse, the feeling that you are flying at a permanent lean, anything from a few degrees off kilter to 90 degrees left or right. The sensation is given the generic name of *the leans*, and it can be very disconcerting, to the point where it takes real determination to ignore what you're feeling and trust the instruments.

I experienced the leans regularly. It made instrument flying immeasurably harder. I've already mentioned an unnerving instance later in my career when flying a Bulldog across the Channel. By that stage I was able to cope. At Linton, the leans were harder to counter, and they were made worse by my tendency to fly jerkily and over-correct.

And finally, to replicate the condition of being in cloud, we wore a special black screening device known as *the hood*. Attached to the top front of the flying helmet above the visors, it protruded maybe six inches forward and down to the sides. When in the correct position, it cut out the view of the outside world, allowing you to see nothing other than the instrument panel, your own legs and those of your instructor. If you needed to look outside, say to take off, or because your instructor wanted to show you something outside the cockpit, you had to flip it up or tilt your head back.

It was universally accepted that *simulated* instrument flying under the hood was harder than *actual* instrument flying in cloud. This was certainly my experience. Whenever I wore it, the cockpit seemed infinitely darker and more claustrophobic than when flying in even the darkest cloud. And like many of my peers I came to view it as a torture device. Putting it on made my heart sink and my thought processes curdle to the point of near paralysis.

So, I struggled to cope with instrument flying from the

outset. Now, I accept that this was largely down to deficiencies in my own physical skill, mental acumen and confidence. But I also think the trough that I - and others - seemed to fall into at about this time was at least in part due to the way we'd begun leaping about the syllabus.

My logbook shows me completing Exercise 22, general handling, one day, Exercise 28, instrument flying, the next, with jumps in subsequent days from Exercise 25 to 29, then 36 to 24. Then followed two weeks of general handling, before a return to instrument flying.

I can't help wondering whether those who'd already displayed signs of weakness might have coped better if we'd been allowed to follow the syllabus, improving our skills through the medium of general handling *before* moving on to instrument flying.

The counter-argument is that it would have led to further delays in our training. And anyway, flexibility is the key to air power. We just needed to man up and cope.

Sadly some of us couldn't. Eventually, my problems with instrument flying began to threaten not only my future as a pilot, but also my mental well-being. That may sound over-dramatic, but it's true. And the effects lasted well beyond Linton.

While still in downbeat mood, around this period I was suffering an added complication.

From the moment I donned my oxygen mask at the start of each flight, my nose seemed to produce abnormally large amounts of mucus. By the time we were airborne, it was often beginning to drip. As the flight progressed, the drip could become a stream, especially when I was hot and bothered, which could be quite often.

On the early trips, I'd ask the instructor to take control, rummage for a handkerchief, lower my oxygen mask and blow my nose. But as the syllabus moved on, it became too embarrassing and time consuming, so I'm afraid I took to just sniffing and having a good clean up when I landed.

Another manifestation of the same problem was that towards the end of a flight, my nose could become blocked, which seemed to make my ears *sticky* and difficult to clear. Sometimes, when I descended, they became painful and only a prolonged period of squeezing my nose and blowing actually made them *pop*, allowing the pressure to equalise. The stickiness also seemed to affect my hearing, making it more difficult to hear radio calls.

Generally, I just kept quiet and put up with it. But days when I couldn't fly because I couldn't clear my ears seemed to become more frequent.

I often wondered whether at least some of it was psychosomatic, brought on by the pressure. I think some of my peers and instructors had similar suspicions. Only when confronted with the evidence in my medical records years later did I accept that the problems were very much physical rather than mental. And even now, decades later, there are long periods when I wouldn't dare fly, even though I don't have a cold.

Back then though, all I knew was that I was beginning to fall behind, a situation that would eventually lead to a series of medical tests.

Chapter 11 – Spinning and Other Delights

Although worries about my flying were beginning to monopolise my thoughts, to the point that I may have seemed distant and distracted at times, I still enjoyed the time I managed to spend with Geraldine and was really looking forward to our marriage.

One weekend in March, we went to the Royal Shakespeare Theatre in Stratford to see As You Like It. The next we chose a photographer for the wedding. I say chose when what I think I mean is that we booked the photographer whose portraits of families and newborn babies appeared on the sideboards of everyone we knew.

And as it turned out, family portraits were his forte. He proved hopeless at shepherding wedding guests. Neither the number nor quality of the photographs in our wedding album seem to justify the length of time we spent standing around in the cemetery of Bromfield Church as he gathered the people for the next photo on his list.

I don't think he'd have lasted long in today's wedding industry. On the other hand, I doubt we paid today's inflated prices.

I also continued to enjoy many of the extra-curricular activities on offer at Linton. One weekend in April, a large group of students and a few instructors completed a 40-mile walk across the North York Moors.

Known as the Lyke Wake Walk - because meetings of the organisers are known as wakes - it runs across the highest points of the Moors, from Osmotherly in the west to Ravenscar in the east. The aim is to complete the 40 miles in less than 24 hours. We set out at six in the morning and did it in 14.

We'd have been quicker, but in a fine example of military planning, a support party fed and watered us every time we crossed a road, which was fairly often. By the finish, I'd eaten breakfast, brunch, lunch, tea and dinner, and probably a couple of snacks in between. Not that this stopped us celebrating our achievement with another meal and a couple of pints at the Ravenscar Hotel.

I'm not sure how many teams put on weight during the Lyke Wake Walk, but we did.

Whilst instrument flying was already casting its cloud, I still enjoyed general handling, including one of its major elements: spinning.

Many people I've spoken to over the years are horrified at the thought of plummeting earthward in a rapidly spinning aircraft. But for reasons that I hope will become clear, despite a tinge of butterflies before every spin, I always found them tremendously exhilarating. And never more so than my first spin sortie on 25th March, which my diary indicates was *Magic fun*.

Starting at about 20,000 feet, Croucho set our JP up as if preparing to enter a stall. But this time, as the speed reduced, he moved the controls in such a way that the aircraft rolled swiftly onto its back and kept rolling until the nose settled about 45 degrees below the horizon. At this angle, we spun downward, completing one turn every few seconds and losing up to 800 feet with every revolution.

It may be a cliché, but the ground really did seem to rush up to meet us. And as the fields and clouds whirled like the spin cycle of a washing machine, my eyes struggled to make sense of what they were seeing.

After several turns, Croucho set about recovering. His actions included pushing the nose forward, at which point the rate of rotation increased until we were looking straight down and spinning like a top. I began to wonder whether the aircraft was ever going to recover. When it did, it was with a jolt that left my head and stomach still spinning, a sensation compounded by g, my vision dimming as Croucho pulled us from the headlong dive.

It was a while before I really knew what was happening, by which time we were in a gentle climb.

The physical sensations in a spin are exciting enough,

but there's a cerebral element that gives the experience an added frisson. As you drop like a stone, you're all too aware that only one set of actions will make the aircraft recover. Get these wrong, or enter a spin with insufficient height to carry them out, and your aircraft is going to spin into the ground, with you in it if you don't have enough height to get out and float down on your parachute.

As with stalling, many pioneers found this out the hard way, and aviation history is littered with spinning accidents, many of them fatal. This knowledge can add to the apprehension some people feel before spinning, while extra checks and precautions can also ramp up the tension.

For instance, when preparing to spin, we had to calculate several heights, starting with an entry height that allowed sufficient margin for the planned number of turns and the recovery; then a minimum height to commence the recovery; and finally – something which always focused the mind – a minimum height at which to eject if the aircraft had not recovered.

To minimise the chances of disorientation, there had to be a good horizon at the height we entered the spin and the height, perhaps several thousand feet lower, at which we intended to recover. For the same reason, we weren't meant to spin over a monochrome surface, such as complete cloud cover or a smooth sea, and we needed at least one readily identifiable feature – the sun, a distinctive cloud or something on the ground – that we could use to keep track of the number of turns.

Just a bit about the aerodynamics of spinning.

An aircraft in a spin is rotating, nose down, as if around a fireman's pole. In its headlong rush, it's actually pitching, rolling and yawing toward the pole, the inner wing stalled, or more deeply stalled than the outer wing.

Many things, including the method of entry and subsequent handling of the controls can affect the rates of rotation and descent, as can the type of spin, with variations including high rotational and inverted, the latter a type I feel delighted never to have experienced.

To recover, it's important to know the direction of spin, which may not be apparent to the naked eye, especially if the spin is entered from a mishandled manoeuvre. The cast iron indicator once again is an instrument, in this case the turn needle - in the JP, a small gauge to the left of the central artificial horizon.

Once the direction of turn is known, and ignoring the subtle differences between aircraft types, the generic spin recovery is to apply opposite rudder to oppose the yaw; then - counter-intuitively when you're already descending rapidly – push the nose forward to un-stall the wings; and, when the spin stops, centralise the controls and ease out of the dive.

Simple. And that, with the necessary variations for the JP is what Croucho set out to teach me on my first dedicated spin sortie.

Of course, the lesson was broken down into digestible chunks, but I'll skip to the end and describe my first practice of a four turn spin.

After working out the various heights, I fly a 360 degree steep turn to check the airspace below us is clear, then roll out pointing at the sun. I close the throttle and maintain straight and level flight as the speed reduces. At 90 knots, I simultaneously push on full left rudder and pull the control column centrally back into my stomach with both hands.

Our JP rolls swiftly left onto its back. The nose drops and tucks under until we're pointing down at a rapidly spinning kaleidoscope of colours, from the greens of fields and woods to the brilliant white of clouds.

The airflow buffets the rudder and elevators, but I hold on, checking that the control column is fully back and central – any aileron could make the spin unstable. As the world rotates below me, I count aloud each time the sun appears.

'One, two, three...'

After the fourth turn, I chant, 'Recovering now, sir,' words that are meant to reassure Croucho that I'm on top of things.

I glance inside at the altimeter. We're above our minimum height to commence recovery, so I take one hand from the control column and close the throttle – or in this case, check it's closed. As I was to find out on a later sortie, if you enter a spin with the throttle open and don't close it, the rate of descent winds up alarmingly.

Another glance inside, this time to find the turn needle and confirm the direction of spin. Unsurprisingly, with me holding on a bootful of left rudder, the needle is to the left, so I push on full right rudder.

I now have to pause for three seconds, which, I can tell you, seems a very long time when you're spinning earthwards at many thousands of feet a minute. Then, slowly and steadily, I push the control column forward. As I do so, the rate of rotation increases alarmingly, but I steel myself to keep pushing.

We're pointing straight down by the time the spin suddenly stops. I centralise the rudders and, bracing against the onset of g, ease out of the dive into a climb attitude. Once there, I open the throttle slowly and check the engine temperatures and pressures.

The whole event has probably lasted little more than ten seconds, during which we've lost thousands of feet – many of them in the recovery. At every stage, I've sung out what I'm doing, again to reassure Croucho. So, after the fourth turn, my spin recovery would have sounded like this:

'Recovering now, sir.

'Height sufficient.

'Throttle closed.

'Needle left.

'Full right rudder.

'One, and two, and three.'

'Control column centrally forward, until...spin stops.

'Centralise the rudder and eeeaaasse out of the dive… to the climb attitude.

'Smoothly open the throttle.

'T's and P's,' shorthand for engine temperatures and pressures.

It was a speech which had to – and did – become second nature – whichever aircraft you flew. Out of interest, the Bulldog recovery is very similar, but the control column has to be pushed forward as soon as opposite rudder has been applied.

There was one final step.

Just as I'd been taught to minimise height loss in a stall by recovering as soon as I spotted the earliest sign – often the buffet – why on earth should I wait until I was in a fully developed spin before initiating recovery? So Croucho taught me to spot the wing drop - known as autorotation - that is the precursor to a spin, and to centralise the controls immediately, preventing the spin developing and minimising height loss. It is known as an incipient recovery.

From this point on, there was no reason to end up in a spin because I could recognise the signs and recover before it happened. But of course I still had to demonstrate that I could recover if I failed to catch the incipient stage, so there were still plenty of full spins.

The fact that I enjoyed spinning didn't mean my execution was always flawless. In a recent email, Croucho reminded me of a spin I've obviously chosen to forget. He says I moved the control column forward *before* I'd applied full opposite rudder. This put us high-rotational, the rates of both spin and descent increasing markedly.

Croucho had taken control and sorted things out, but by the time we recovered we were much lower than we should have been. Unsurprisingly, he says we were both pretty shaken, and our post-spin conversation was brief.

He says that I croaked, 'I think I'm going to be sick!' to

which his reply was, 'I think I need a change of flying suit!'

On another occasion, I remember pushing the control column forward a little too fast and too far, so that we found ourselves hanging upside down in our straps waiting for the spin to stop. It was a very uncomfortable experience, one that Croucho made all too plain he didn't want to repeat.

To show that not all the near-death experiences were my fault though, I seem to remember Croucho demonstrating a spin from manoeuvre and forgetting to close the throttle. This also led to a very high rate of descent, and another recovery much lower than planned. I did the same in a Bulldog ten years later, by which time I realised how much composure instructors required.

To be able to talk calmly about the characteristics of a spin, then teach how to maintain and recover from it, all the while descending as if in a runaway lift, requires a certain sang-froid, if not downright courage. Even some experienced and gifted front-line pilots struggle to teach spinning, as I learnt at first hand when I began teaching them to become instructors.

And as Croucho had discovered, even if you pass the instructor course, nothing really prepares you for the reality of sitting next to a student seemingly intent on killing you. Over the course of my several thousand spins, I certainly had some frighteners, including students letting go of the controls in a panic, or, more alarmingly, holding them in such a vice-like grip that I had to wrestle them free before I could recover.

An added complication for pilots who fly several types of aircraft is that each type has a subtly different spin recovery. The dangers of this were outlined in an anonymous article in the RAF's flight safety magazine, Air Clues. Although I know the name of the author, who regularly flew in the Hawk, the JP or the Bulldog, I'll maintain his anonymity.

Flying solo one day, he entered a spin, maintained it for four turns and prepared to recover. To his horror, and despite the obvious differences in their cockpits, he couldn't for the life of him remember which type he was in. And the harder he looked for clues, the further his befuddled brain seemed from solving the puzzle. Eventually, knowing he had to do something, he flew the recovery for the type in which the correct drill was most critical – the Bulldog.

He had an agonising wait to see whether he'd made the right choice, but his logic was sound.

Some believed the Bulldog so capricious that it would occasionally fail to recover from a spin even when you did fly the correct recovery. Several were lost to spinning accidents over the years, one a few months before I arrived on the staff of the University of London Air Squadron at RAF Abingdon in 1985. Sadly, in that instance, the instructor died, having parted company with his parachute when abandoning the aircraft.

Whether he was ultimately the victim of a rogue spin, I don't know. Personally, I always believed my Bulldog would recover if I carried out the drill correctly. On the other hand, I also knew it wouldn't if I didn't.

Luckily, on the day of his dilemma, the author of the Air Clues article *was* flying a Bulldog, and it recovered. If he'd flown the JP or Hawk recoveries, the aircraft would have crashed, although hopefully he'd have taken to his parachute before that happened.

The lesson to be taken from his article was that if you fly multiple types, make sure you remind yourself which you're flying *before* you enter a spin.

Given the potential for catastrophe, why on earth does the RAF teach its pilots to spin in the first place?

Well, the first reason is practical. Because military pilots tend to operate towards the edge of the flight envelope, there's always a chance they'll end up in a spin, especially if they make a hash of something. In training, the most likely scenario is a mishandled aerobatic manoeuvre, but fast jets especially can end up spinning from a range of seemingly innocuous manoeuvres. And if it happens, the pilot needs to be able to deal with the situation.

This is why I had to prove I could recognise and recover from a range of incipient and full spins before I could fly aerobatics solo.

The second reason is to do with character. A military pilot has to be prepared to fly his or her aircraft into situations which others might consider dangerous, foolhardy even. And one of the best ways to see if a student has what it takes to do this is to ask them to fly a manoeuvre that will lead to the loss of their aircraft – if not themselves – if they don't complete a precise set of actions promptly.

If the student can do it, it's not only a great boost to their confidence, but also a sign that they may have what it takes to become a military pilot. If they can't, military aviation is not for them.

As I said, I always enjoyed spinning. It takes all sorts.

It was at about this time that we lost another member of the course.

Dave Benson had left school to work in a Job Centre before achieving his ambition of entering RAF pilot training. We'd completed the selection course at Swinderby together. He laid out the reasons for his failure in a recent telephone conversation. Chief among them was continuity, not of weather, but of instruction. And again, there was a wrinkle.

Despite the RAF placing a heavy emphasis on standardisation of flying instruction, each flying instructor develops their own style; indeed, they're encouraged to do so. But even the best instructors also tend to develop habits that are non-standard, if not downright wrong.

Everyone who's been through flying training will have flown with an instructor who suddenly says, *who taught you that*?

The questioning of things you've been taught by others can be wearing, even if it only happens occasionally. But imagine sitting next to a succession of different instructors, each of whom insists that you unlearn what's gone before and adopt his way of doing things. So the ideal is to fly with only one good instructor. But there lies the rub. Pity the student who has good continuity, but with a bad instructor.

Surely the RAF didn't have any of those? Well, unfortunately, as illustrated in *Fighter Pilot*, I have to tell you that it did – and probably still does.

Luckily, as I was to discover later, there weren't too many, and where their inadequacies were known, the system did its best to eradicate them, and to protect their students. Sometimes though, the instructor's problem wasn't just a deficiency of skill, but also of manner. And a poor instructional manner was more difficult for flying supervisors to uncover and correct. Often, unless a student complained, usually citing a personality clash, the problem could go un-noticed until they began to fall behind.

This is what happened to Dave. He began to struggle with a poor instructor and, in a case of misplaced loyalty, when offered a change, decided to stay with the devil he knew. And by the time a change was enforced, it was too late.

The added complication was the death of a close friend in the critical week of check sorties that would decide his future. Returning from the funeral, he felt numb and lacking in motivation. But the system at that time was unsympathetic to such personal problems. He was expected to put his feelings aside and get on with things. Unable to do so in the time available, he was chopped, having completed about 30 hours on the JP.

Dave went on to navigator training but decided he didn't want to fly if he wasn't in control of the aircraft and left the RAF. He completed an HND in Mechanical Engineering, specializing in Aerospace, while also studying for the licences to become an airline pilot. Unfortunately, the airlines weren't recruiting when he graduated, so he went to work as a project manager in the power industry.

By the time the airlines opened their doors, his engineering career had taken off and he decided to stick with it. Latterly, he's become a project manager for the decommissioning of nuclear power stations, but he still flies light aircraft in his spare time.

I continued to enjoy the individual elements of general handling, even more so when I passed my Spin/Aeros Check on 3rd April and was allowed to attempt aerobatics solo.

I use the word attempt advisedly, because although I enjoyed aerobatics, I was never very good at them on the JP. It wasn't until I became an instructor on the Bulldog that I gained a degree of proficiency. For the whole of my time at Linton, I had a limited repertoire of barely recognisable manoeuvres. Lacking in polish would be a polite way of putting it. There were several reasons.

Once the aircraft left straight and level flight, the sensations of movement and g tended to overwhelm me. In my excitement, I'd lose spatial awareness and begin pushing and pulling the controls without proper reference to the visual cues I was meant to be using. It was one of the things that already marked me out as a poor prospect for the fast jet stream.

I was keen though, as the following description of my early aerobatic flying should demonstrate. Starting with a loop.

I check the airspace around me, then open the throttle, push the control column forward and dive through 200 knots - 230 miles per hour. A quick glance up. All clear, so, doing my best to keep the wings level, I pull back on the control column, by which time the speed is approaching 220 knots.

The g force increases rapidly, forcing me into my seat. I fight to keep my head up and strain as if I'm on the toilet, trying to prevent or at least delay the draining of blood from my brain. The eyes are the organs most sensitive to lack of blood oxygen and, at 4g, when every part of me weighs four times normal, my vision dims as if a grey mist has descended.

I hold the back pressure and the JP's nose sweeps upward. To my front, the view of grey-green fields gives way to white pillars of cloud, then their crisp, bubbling, tops and the deep blue above. As the speed reduces, so does the g force. My vision clears. But the reduction in speed also reduces the effectiveness of the elevators, so I have to pull the control column back further to maintain the same rate of pitch.

Upside down at the top of the loop, the whine of the engine vies with the whoosh of the blood pumping in my ears. There, I float, hanging in my straps, light-headed, stars sparkling before my eyes. Almost overwhelmed by the sensations, I look *up,* marvelling at the sight of the ground and the clouds below me.

A voice nags me to snatch a quick glance to either side and check if the wings are level. Luckily they are. Just as well. When they're not, I'm never sure which way to move the control column to sort it out.

Now for the second half of the loop.

I ease the control column back, gently, so as not to pull into a stall or, much worse, a spin. The nose arcs down the blue to the tops of the clouds, then over their flanks. The speed passes 200 knots. I strain and pull until my weight quadruples and the green fields turn misty grey again.

Eventually, the nose sweeps through the horizontal into a gentle climb and I unload the back pressure and the g. Oxygen-rich blood returns to my head, making my cheeks flush and my eyes speckle with stars.

If my schoolmates could see me now! I think most would be impressed, but only until they looked behind the dark visor and Top Gun flying kit.

Some of my fellow course members are already linking their manoeuvres into an aerobatic sequence, whereas I'm happy to have completed a solitary, recognisable, loop. And while they'd be moving straight into the next manoeuvre, I take a few moments to settle down by flying a wing over – pulling the nose up to about 45 degrees, dropping the left or right wing and pulling round – buying time to regain my composure, lookout for other aircraft, and find a feature on the ground I recognise.

Once I'm content that I know where I am, I move on to attempt a barrel roll.

A barrel roll is a combination of a loop and a roll. It should be big and graceful, flown at a maximum of 3½g, the aircraft flying a corkscrew motion as if it's bottom skin is sliding around the inside of a barrel.

Despite the emphasis on grace, the cocktail of looping and rolling can be disorientating and the barrel roll has been something of a widow-maker over the years. Tens of display pilots have died mishandling the manoeuvre, often in front of large crowds.

Luckily, my attempts are flown at height. Let's pretend I can fly a proper barrel roll.

Pointing at a distinctive feature, such as a fluffy cloud, I pitch down and roll until I'm at about 45 degrees nose down and 45 degrees left bank. At 200 knots, I ease the stick back and right, pulling the nose above the horizon and rolling around the fluffy cloud, until I top out above it at 90 degrees of right bank. At this point, I continue to roll and pitch, passing through the inverted abeam my cloud and on until I'm left wing low directly beneath it. To finish, I coordinate roll and pull until I'm straight and level, pointing at my feature again.

Occasionally, I fly something akin to this ideal. But some of my attempts go awry when I lose situational awareness as I'm upside down. Now, if I pull too hard and roll too little, I end up diving at the ground and losing hundreds of feet before I recover to straight and level. For a display pilot flying close to the ground, this can be lethal, and too often is. For me, it's a little discombobulating, but

I'm still thousands of feet up.

Ideally, at the first hint of disorientation, I roll rapidly to avoid this excessive loss of height. The problem with this of course is that I fly more of a semi-circle than a barrel.

But at least it's safe.

After another wingover, it's time for a stall turn. Again, let's pretend I know what I'm doing.

At 180 knots, having had a good scan of the airspace above, I pull up into the vertical, looking out to the sides and checking the back pressure when the wing tanks are perpendicular to the horizon, which should mean my JP is pointing straight up. As the speed washes off, I apply a little forward pressure on the control column to maintain the vertical.

Now, I want to go from pointing up to pointing down, rotating like a Catherine Wheel nailed to a post, the nail passing through the cockpit floor between the ejection seats. So, as the speed reduces, I pick a distinctive feature on the horizon by the left wingtip – probably another cloud – close the throttle and smoothly push on full left rudder.

As the noise of the engine fades the nose slices left. To counter the secondary effect of yaw – roll - I ease the control column right. Then, using a combination of all the controls, I fly the nose through the cloud on the horizon and look to the right wingtip, flying that onto the same feature. Once the tip tank sits over my feature, I centralise the rudders to leave me and my JP pointing straight down.

After a brief pause that always intrigues and excites me, the aircraft begins to slide earthwards, building up speed until I raise the nose, straining against the onset of g, and smoothly open the throttle.

In reality, I very often lose track of things as soon I pitch upwards to start the manoeuvre, which means I tend to end up either slightly short of or just beyond the vertical. In some cases this is okay and I can continue the manoeuvre, producing a stall turn of sorts. But on other occasions, I'm

172

so messed up that if I try and continue, something nasty could happen, like a potentially damaging tail-slide, or a spin.

To prevent this, I fly a vertical recovery, closing the throttle, gripping the control column, bracing my feet on the rudder pedals and waiting for the aircraft to fall forward or onto its back. In either case, after a brief period of excitement as the aircraft sorts itself out, the end result is the same as if I'd competed a flawless stall turn, me and my JP pointing down at the ground.

On occasion though, the aircraft hesitates in the vertical, the nose wavering as if deciding which way to fall. In these instances, I know the recovery will be more dramatic, the nose whipping forward or backwards, the control forces buffeting the rudder and control column, attempting to wrench it from my hands. I hang on for dear life until I end up looking straight down, swaying back and forth like pendulum. Eventually, the aircraft settles into a headlong descent from which I can recover as normal, albeit with a raised pulse rate.

Being able to fly such a variety of vertical recoveries safely was another essential element of the Spin/Aeros Check.

After either a successful stall turn or a vertical recovery, I take a few moments to settle down and find out where I am, before flying a wingover and attempting either another stall turn or the next manoeuvre, a slow roll.

I'm still not sure why the slow roll is considered one of the basic five aerobatic manoeuvres. It's actually quite complex and difficult to fly without losing height. For this reason, it's another manoeuvre that has led to the death of many a low-level aerobatic pilot over the years. Again, the ideal and my own attempts are likely to be somewhat different, but let's pretend otherwise.

Flying at 180 knots, I pick a point on the horizon and ease the control column to the right to start the roll. As the roll progresses, I slowly feed on left rudder to keep the JP's nose up until, at 90 degrees of right bank, I'm holding on full left rudder to prevent a descent.

Beyond 90 degrees, as I roll towards the inverted, I ease the control column further right to maintain the roll rate, whilst simultaneously moving the rudder pedals toward neutral and pushing the control column forward to hold the nose above the horizon and stop us descending when we're upside down after 180 degrees of roll.

There is now a brief excursion into negative g, an uncomfortable condition that forces the blood into my head. It feels as if my brain and eyes are bulging. The feeling in my eyes is no illusion. At high values of negative g, pilots can experience a condition known as red-out, where the vision dims in a red mist. In extremis, blood vessels in the eyes can burst.

None of that here though, the slow roll is just a taster, little more – or should that be less - than zero g.

Beyond the inverted in the third quarter of the slow roll, I progressively reduce right aileron deflection to maintain the roll rate, whilst also reducing the back pressure and feeding on right rudder to hold the nose up and stop a descent as we reach 270 degrees of bank.

For the final quarter, I progressively reduce the right aileron input, maybe even move the control column a little to the left to counter a tendency for the roll rate to increase. Simultaneously, I progressively reduce the rudder input to neutral and increase the back pressure to stop a descent, leaving the nose pointing at the original feature on the horizon as we reach wings level.

The reality of my early attempts was that I didn't fare too badly until we were upside down, but after that, the nuances of control movement tended to escape me. If I concentrated on maintaining the roll rate, the nose was likely to drop and I'd lose a fair amount of height, so I generally kept the rate of roll high, which meant a quickish slow roll.

It wasn't going to win me any prizes in aerobatic competitions, but again, it was the safe option.

The last of the five basic aerobatic manoeuvres is the roll off the top, which is supposed to be a combination of the first half of a loop and the second half of a slow roll.

This time, after my wingover, I dive to 250 knots – 287 miles per hour – before grunting and pulling into a loop at about 4½g. Hanging upside down in my straps, I pull over the top until the nose is pointing slightly down, then roll left, feeding on left rudder to keep the nose up and progressively adjusting the rate of roll and back pressure to complete the second half of a slow roll.

You can probably guess that, in practice, I was able to fly the looping portion of the manoeuvre fairly well, but the second half, the slow roll, less well. This was partly because I didn't want to end up rolling at slow speed with lots of rudder and back pressure, a control combination that seemed to screamed spin. So I tended to roll far too quickly, making my rendition of a roll off the top far from classic, but safe.

Chapter 12 – The Problems Mount

From the notes in my diary, my mood over the majority of April seemed to follow a predictable pattern. Instrument flying days were *bad*, or *awful*, while those when the weather was suitable for general handling were much better – *good*, or even, as when spinning with Croucho, *Magic fun*.

But then, towards the end of the month, Croucho's debriefs of my instrument flying began to mirror my own diary assessments. My performance was usually bad, and sometimes awful. In the end, I was placed on Review, a formal process that included an interview with my flight commander.

Dingdong explained that Review was a way of acknowledging my problems officially, and gaining help in the form of extra hours, should I need them. But we both knew that it could also be the first formal step on the way to me being chopped, and that things could come to a head in a matter of days.

He went on to explain that I was now assessed as low average.

My face must have dropped, because he jumped in with a more upbeat tone and said, 'But you're solidly low average.'

I appreciated his attempt at sweetening the pill, but I can't say it worked.

My flying to date had provided many challenges, but also much enjoyment. From now on though, I couldn't afford a dip in performance in any area, and the threat of the chop hung over me every time I strapped in. The result was that from the last week of April 1980, there are very few positive comments about flying in my diary, and when instrument flying was on the cards, the prospect of getting airborne filled me with a kind of dread.

I was still determined to succeed, but the constant battle to improve had wrung most of the fun out of flying. And I wasn't the only one in the same boat. Several of us openly admitted to praying for bad weather so we wouldn't have to fly. It was weird. We were doing the very thing we'd always wanted, but the reality was proving so much less enjoyable than we could ever have imagined.

One of the other strugglers was New Zealander, Mike Daly. The catalyst for his dip in mood was also instrument flying. We tried to support one another, endlessly dissecting our problems, although we both realised the only solution was to start producing the goods in the air, something neither of us seemed able to do.

I felt especially sorry for Mike. He'd travelled so far to pursue his dream. And the distance left him more isolated than most of us, who could visit friends and family pretty much whenever we wanted. At least once, I took him home with me to Shropshire. I'm not sure how much this helped, but at that stage we were both determined to soldier on.

The incessant pressure to succeed is another theme covered in *Fighter Pilot*, where several of the aspiring pilots describe changes in personality brought on by the stress of flying training, which they too had ceased to enjoy.

Like them, the prospect of my dream coming to a sudden end affected every aspect of my life, making me a much more insecure and serious individual, one who found it increasingly difficult to switch off. I suspect it was the start of me becoming the *task-oriented workaholic* described by a senior officer in a report toward the end of my career.

Geraldine had met a fairly happy-go-lucky young corporal. I feared she was about to marry a neurotic officer. If she had the same fear, she never mentioned it.

On the positive side, I suppose you could say that the battle to survive gave me the drive to work hard on every aspect of Service life, not only in the air, but also on the ground. In that way, I suppose it became the basis for my eventual success, such as it was.

But I jump ahead again. At Linton, the pressure was

never greater than when I pulled on the hood for an instrument flying lesson or test. And of course, while I still struggled to master the basics, new skills and procedures had to be learnt, such as instrument approaches.

Modern aircraft and airfields have sophisticated approach aids that allow a pilot - or the aircraft itself - to fly all the way down to a runway enveloped in thick fog. Back in 1980, the equipment on RAF airfields and aircraft was more basic. So the rules dictated that a pilot flying an approach to a runway could fly no lower than 200 feet before deciding if they could see enough – usually the runway threshold and its lights – to land. If not, they had to overshoot and try another approach, or divert to an airfield with better weather.

Even with the most sophisticated aids, not every pilot can descend to the minimum height possible. Most have to add a safety margin that reduces with experience and the ability to pass airborne tests, known as Instrument Ratings. So, the more experienced and skilled a pilot is, the lower they can descend in cloud when attempting to land.

One day, I'd be taking Ratings, but at my stage of training I was working toward lesser qualifications known as Gradings. At the end of each instrument flying sortie with Croucho, I'd practise approaches to either an airfield or a specific runway. These were usually directed by a controller sitting in the air traffic control tower, tracking us either with radar or by taking frequent radio bearings.

The controller would tell me headings to fly and heights to which I should descend as they positioned me to commence the final descent. Sitting blinkered under *the hood*, I'd strive to fly as directed, scanning the artificial horizon and performance instruments, and adjusting attitude and/or power to correct height, rate of descent, speed and heading as necessary.

For an airfield approach, the controller's aim would be to put me at my minimum descent height - generally in the region of 1,000 feet - a few miles from and pointing at the airfield. Approaching this height, I'd look up and hope to see the ground or, better still, the airfield, and join to land from a visual circuit.

If I looked up and was still in cloud or poor visibility – or Croucho told me to pretend I was - I had to lock back onto the instruments and overshoot, transitioning from a descent to a climb without dipping below my minimum descent height. *Busting* this height was one of the easiest ways to fail an instrument flying test.

There were a range of runway approaches, but most involved me striving to fly down an ideal glide path on headings passed by the controller. At decision height, I had to look up and decide whether I could see enough to continue my descent and land, or climb into a missed approach procedure for another attempt.

Runway approaches are more pressured because they're like descending down a cone, the point of which is on the runway. The closer to the runway you get, the narrower the cone and the easier it is to fly out of it, either by drifting off heading, or straying above or below the ideal flight path. To stay within the cone nearing decision height, no more than a few hundred yards short of the runway, requires corrections of as little as one degree in heading and less than 50 feet a minute in rate of descent.

There was so much information to absorb from the instruments and the controller, and so many things to do that I found it all extremely difficult. I could also become so overwhelmed approaching decision height that I'd omit to look up, another sure-fire way to fail a test – or to fly into the ground if you failed to spot your mistake when flying solo in bad weather.

However, despite all these problems, I did improve, and things began to look up; that is, until the introduction of another new skill: limited panel instrument flying.

I had to be able to fly in cloud and get on the ground safely even if my primary flight instruments - the artificial horizons and gyro compass – failed. Croucho would simulate this by shielding them from me with purpose made covers that allowed him to see them. I'd then have to fly by reference to the alternatives, in the JP, a turn and slip indicator and a magnetic compass.

The turn and slip was a small circular gauge to the left of the main instruments. Beneath its glass cover, a white needle little more than an inch in length sat above a ball in a tube of viscous fluid, like a spirit level. In the piston and multi-engined aircraft I flew later in my career, the ball would become something of great import, but in the JP it was generally of peripheral interest.

So my main focus during limited panel flying was the needle. Fixed at the bottom, when vertical it indicated that the aircraft wasn't turning. But when I rolled into a turn, it tilted in the direction of turn, and marks around the top of the instrument indicated the rate of turn.

Almost all turns in the JP were made by rolling until the tip of the needle settled over the first mark, at which point, I'd be flying a *rate 1 turn*. This meant the aircraft was turning at three degrees per second, allowing me to work out how long a turn would take: for instance, 120 seconds for a turn through 360 degrees, or 43⅓ seconds for a turn of 130 degrees.

The turn needle had several annoying foibles, the worst being a property known as lag. When I rolled into a turn, it would take a second or so to react, and it would continue to lag, only stopping a second or so after I'd centralised the ailerons. Then, if the tip of the needle had settled short of or beyond the rate 1 mark, I had to make an adjustment, again allowing for the lag. It would be the same when I rolled to wings level, the needle lagging my control movements and taking time to settle, hopefully in the vertical.

The other substitute instrument, the magnetic compass, also had its foibles. Attached to the central windscreen pillar above the instrument coaming, it bobbed about in a viscous fluid and provided trustworthy heading information only in straight and level flight. In a turn, and for several seconds afterwards, there was no point in looking at it as it would just be swinging about randomly.

So, on limited panel, to go from a heading of north, 360 degrees, onto east, 090 degrees, I first had to work out the change in heading - 90 degrees right - then divide this by three to give the time for which I should turn, in this case, 30 seconds. Then, having noted the position of the second hand of the clock on the instrument panel, I had to roll into and maintain a rate 1 turn, scanning between the turn needle and the performance instruments to maintain height and speed, with the odd glance at the clock to keep an eye on the time. After 30 seconds, I'd roll left toward wings level, again anticipating the lag of the needle.

If I'd judged right and the needle stopped in the vertical, I still had to wait a few seconds before checking the compass. And then, if I'd overshot the desired heading, rolling out on a heading of, say, 100 degrees instead of 090, I had to fly a three second rate 1 turn to the left to adjust.

I found the whole process extremely taxing.

Most of my mental capacity was taken up by the simple act of flying, so working out the heading change and time of turn could take what seemed an age, especially when the heading change was something like 135 or 250 degrees. And even if I was able to achieve and maintain a consistent rate of turn at the right height and speed, I still had to remember to look at the second hand of the clock before rolling in and in time to roll out.

And just a reminder that while all this was happening, no matter how nice the weather outside the cockpit, I was under the hood; that is, unable to see anything beyond two pairs of legs and the instrument panel.

And there was more.

Flying on instruments, I found it all too easy to get

distracted, or to fixate on one instrument to the detriment of the others. Both these things could, and often did, lead to a breakdown in my selective radial scan. When this happened, the aircraft would drift off the attitude I'd set, so that when I glanced back at the artificial horizon, I was confronted with a picture I hadn't expected. Generally, I could regain control by making a fairly minor adjustment of attitude and power.

But if I looked at the artificial horizon and saw something vastly different from the attitude I'd set, I was in what was termed an *unusual position*, or UP. In this instance, there was a set recovery drill. Toward the end of every instrument flying lesson, Croucho would give me several opportunities to practise UP recoveries.

To set these up, he'd tell me to lower my head and look down from the instruments while he flew a series of increasingly extreme manoeuvres. It was like riding a rollercoaster in a blindfold, complete with unexpected changes in g, either pulling my head down and dimming my vision, or leaving me floating with stars before my eyes.

When he eventually gave me control, I'd almost undoubtedly be suffering from the leans and maybe a hint of nausea. No time for tea and sympathy though. I had to look up, locate the artificial horizon and interpret what it was telling me; that is, where the angle of bank marker was around the circumference, and the position of the gull wing relative to horizon bar. This could take me a while, but let's say I work out that our JP is almost upside down – say 160 degrees of right bank – and in a steep descent.

I then had to locate the altimeter. If it indicated that we were below a safe height based on the terrain and obstructions over which we were flying – or Croucho said we were – he'd expect to hear me say that I'd eject. Even if there was sufficient height to attempt recovery, I'd still have to keep the possibility of ejection in mind as things progressed.

Of course, for practises, there was invariably enough

height to attempt a recovery, so next I'd look to the airspeed indicator. If the speed was high and increasing – as was likely to be the case in my high bank/low nose example - I had to close the throttle. If the speed was low or reducing, I had to open it.

Only then could I return my gaze to the artificial horizon and try to work out the shortest way to roll to regain wings level - in this case left - and roll as swiftly as possible using full aileron. Once within 60 degrees of wings level, I could also pull, aiming to set the straight and level attitude, then trim out the elevator forces.

Croucho had a seemingly unending repertoire of UPs with which to test me, anything from arrowing upwards near the vertical to screaming dives, and any angle of bank you can imagine. After each recovery, I had to tell him what height and heading I needed for a recovery to base, then go through the possible reasons for ending up in the UP in the first place – options such as distraction, simple inattention, or something more sinister, such as an oxygen problem dulling my senses.

But things could become even more devious.

When flying aerobatics, the gyros in the artificial horizon and main compass would *topple*, rendering them useless until reset, which could be done only when flying straight and level for a protracted period.

Of course, as long as I was flying visually, the loss of the artificial horizon didn't matter. But if I accidentally speared into cloud, I had to be able to regain straight and level without either a visual or an artificial horizon, that is, on limited panel.

So, after practising UP recoveries with a full suite of instruments, Croucho would shield the artificial horizon and gyro compass from me and tell me to lower my head while he manoeuvred some more.

After the last several minutes of violent pitching and rolling with no sight of the outside world, my leans and nausea would not have improved. My head would be spinning, my skin cold and clammy, my nose dripping and my ears *gummed up*. But when Croucho eventually gave me control, I'd have to ignore these sensations and set about trying to recover on limited panel.

The first couple of actions were the same as for full panel recoveries, that is, check there was sufficient height to attempt a recovery, before noting the speed and either opening the throttle to accelerate, or closing it to slow down. But then, the limited panel recovery diverged, and largely because of another foible of the turn needle.

It was extremely sensitive to g.

High positive g not only pulled the needle down so that it over-read the rate of turn, but also held it down, so that it didn't move when you rolled. And under negative g, the needle under-read. So before rolling toward wings level, I had to establish and maintain 1g.

This meant locating the accelerometer, a small circular gauge positioned just above the centre of the instrument coaming. When flying straight and level, its white needle pointed horizontally left to register 1g, but when manoeuvring, it could sweep clockwise to indicate that I was pulling up to 10g, or anticlockwise to indicate pushing to minus 4g; although I'd have been in a world of trouble, as the aircraft g limits were plus 6 to minus 2½, and my own physical limits without feeling discomfort were even less, about plus 5 to minus 1.

Now, let's say Croucho has put me in a tight descending right hand spiral in which we're pulling 3g; that is, everything in the aircraft, including me and the turn needle, weigh three times normal.

I had to push on the control column until the accelerometer needle registered 1g. This would have steepened our dive, perhaps precipitously, but before I could slow our descent, I had to level the wings. So, looking at the turn needle and attempting to maintain 1g, I had to force the control column fully left. Because of its inherent lag, as soon as the needle twitched, I had to assume the wings were somewhere near level and pull on the control column.

As I pulled, I had to locate the altimeter. Its hundreds needle would be sweeping anticlockwise, but at a reducing rate as the nose of our JP rose. As soon as the needle stopped, I had to check forward to re-establish 1g and stop us ballooning into a climb.

Ideally, as we screamed earthwards, I'd be able to complete the actions almost as quickly as I could say them, the chant being, 'Height, speed, g, roll, pull, trim.'

Also ideally, after this frantic period, I'd be somewhere near straight and level, and could reset the power for a sensible speed and make minor adjustments in slower time, easing the turn needle into the vertical and making tweaks in pitch to keep the altimeter steady – aided by glances at the altimeter and vertical speed indicator – both plagued by lag - to pick up trends in climb or descent.

If I'd achieved something like straight and level, Croucho would probably take control and put me into another UP, perhaps handing the aircraft back at the top of a parabolic curve under negative g, with the speed and one wing low.

Again, there was an endless variety of situations from which he could ask me to recover.

When he'd seen enough or we'd run out of time, he'd say, 'This is the last UP,' before manoeuvring and giving me control, probably in the most extreme attitude to date.

If I managed to recover to straight and level, I'd let things settle and check my heading on the magnetic compass. Knowing roughly where I and Linton were, I could use my kneepad map to work out the approximate change in heading required to point us at base, and the time required to complete a rate 1 turn onto it, turning the long way round.

We always had to turn the longest way. This was to ensure we had plenty of practice at mental arithmetic, and at maintaining a rate 1 turn on limited panel.

For instance, if I was flying on a heading of 270 and a return to base required a turn onto 240 degrees, rather than just turn left for 10 seconds, I had to work out the difference in heading if I turned right - 330 degrees – and how long I should turn for - 110 seconds. Then, I had to note the time on the clock, roll into a rate 1 turn, scan steadily to maintain it and remember to roll out after I minute 50 seconds.

Once I was flying toward base, I was allowed to re-erect the primary instruments and call air traffic control for a full panel recovery; although later in the syllabus, the period of flying on limited panel was extended to include approaches to the airfield or runway, on the assumption that the artificial horizon and gyro compass had failed altogether.

Recoveries from UPs on limited panel were my nemesis. Even when I made progress in other areas of instrument flying, as soon as Croucho put the patches over the artificial horizon and compass in preparation for the exercise, my brain seemed to freeze.

It wasn't fear of the manoeuvres. I wasn't overly concerned that during the recovery we might be hurtling earthwards at nearly 300 miles an hour, or soaring upwards close to stalling speed. It was apprehension based on experience of my senses becoming overloaded by the sensations and the multiplicity of things to look at and do, to the point that I found it difficult to do any of them.

More often than not, rather than recover from the UP into which I'd been put, I merely lurched into another, then another, porpoising around the sky as if on a roller coaster. Sometimes I managed to dampen the sinusoidal deviations and, if Croucho waited long enough, I'd recover. But on other occasions, my self-induced climbs and descents would become more and more extreme until he was forced to take control before we ran out of height or I overstressed the airframe.

Perhaps nothing emphasises my having reached the

limits of my mental capacity better than the farce of the radio calls for recovery I made after the final UP.

Thinking I was talking to air traffic control, I'd transmit, 'Delta Two Three for radar recovery.'

In my headset, I'd hear, 'Delta Two Three turn left onto 370.'

'Left 370,' I'd reply, before Croucho could stop me making a fool of his callsign.

In my fevered state, I'd failed to tune the radio to an air traffic frequency, instead making my recovery call on the *quiet* frequency training aircraft all over Yorkshire and Lincolnshire used for instruction. The reply had been some wag in another aircraft telling me to turn onto an imaginary heading.

I knew a heading of 370 degrees didn't exist for goodness sake. I was a trainee pilot. But so discombobulated was I after performing limited panel UP recoveries that I'd have replied to almost any outlandish radio call. And I did – more than once!

Croucho cringed at the abuse of his callsign and I became evermore depressed and convinced that I was doomed to failure.

General handling sorties were also becoming increasingly challenging, with more complex simulated emergencies and combinations of emergencies, including engine failures, necessitating an attempt to glide to the nearest airfield for a practice forced landing, a procedure that really tested airmanship and judgement.

But, with the odd slip-up, I seemed to be coping with this.

I also seemed to have an unassailable lead in our ground studies, so I'd be awarded the Groundschool Trophy at our graduation – if I made it that far. Surely this was proof that I could compete, at least academically, with those from more affluent backgrounds who'd climbed higher up the ladder of education.

But most of my peers seemed so self-assured, so confident in their abilities – even when there was evidence to suggest otherwise. Their upbringing and education seemed to have given them a bearing, a manner of speaking and a confidence in their own self-worth that I didn't share. It was as if they had access to some life code that I lacked the means to decipher.

I tried to hide my inner doubts and brazen it out, both at Linton and throughout my entire career, but I always felt, if not inferior, different, sure that my Shropshire burr marked me out as every inch the ex-corporal son of a dustman, defined by the term, *five O Levels and a Burton suit*.

Don't get me wrong, I didn't – don't – mind being considered an ex-corporal son of a dustman. Like all inverted snobs, I'm immensely proud of my heritage. And I've always been very grateful that the RAF often seemed to have more confidence in me than I did myself; although I also know that, just occasionally, my lack of poise and inability to speak in the neutral or posh tones of the archetypal officer made some doubt my ability to compete alongside more stereotypical officers.

For instance, as a squadron leader in the early stages of the RAF Advanced Staff College course, I was told that I was obviously not an intellectual. Now this is undoubtedly true, but it seems a strange thing to tell someone, and I think the comment was based as much on my manner and accent as my intellect, because I went on to finish in the top ten per cent of the course.

If only I could have been among the top ten per cent in the air at Linton. But I couldn't. So perhaps all that work on the ground was a waste of time. I know some – usually gifted aviators – who'd say exactly that. Their view is that effort beyond the minimum required to pass ground exams is wasted.

I'd be tempted to agree, but with one caveat. While my work ethic seemed to make little difference in the air, the reputation for effort seemed to garner me multiple extra flights and re-tests, while some deemed less diligent were cast aside, often at the first hint of trouble or failure.

It was just as well. I needed all the help I could get. During April, I had to repeat several instrument flying exercises because my first attempts weren't up to snuff.

Then, on the 30th, I failed my first instrument flying test, the Basic Instrument Flying Grading.

A few weeks earlier, I'd applied for an officers' married quarter. But now, with the wedding barely three weeks away, it began to look as if I'd no longer be at Linton, or a trainee pilot, maybe not even an officer.

Geraldine knew I was struggling, but not, I think, how badly. We'd discussed the likelihood that we wouldn't get much of a honeymoon, but framed against the general difficulty of securing leave at Linton, rather than my impending suspension.

Before the latest crisis, I'd told her there was a chance I'd get two weeks off. But she also knew I might get no more than a few days. So, setting our sights somewhere between these two extremes, we booked six nights in a small hotel in Bath - £12.50 per night, bed and breakfast.

My latest difficulties seemed to put even this modest break in jeopardy. But I still kept the depth of my problems to myself, and during the first weekend in May, we had a meeting with the vicar and gave him the £40 fee for a church wedding.

The next week, after a remedial instrument flying sortie, I passed my Basic Instrument Flying Grading. In the words of my diary, the pass was *marginal,* but I was now cleared to fly solo in cloud, specifically to climb through a layer several thousand feet thick to try and find clear air above, perform general handling and descend through it again to find the airfield.

In the following days, I had a dual and a solo general handling flight, the latter being described as *good fun.*

It's the last positive comment about flying to appear in my diaries. I'm not entirely sure why this is. I know I continued to enjoy some aspects of my flying, or at least individual flights, but perhaps the pressure of being on review and the genuine gloom caused by my problems with instrument flying made these seem irrelevant. Luckily, in areas other than flying, I had much to be cheerful about.

That Saturday was my stag night. As far as I remember, it was a pub crawl round Ludlow with my brother and best man, Brian, and childhood friends, Andy, Nick and Simon – for all of whom I'd been best man – and Ian, by then a corporal RAF driver. It started at The Charlton – the pub for which I'd played darts – and ended at The Unicorn, another favourite watering hole on the other side of town.

I wish I remembered more about it, but I don't, which perhaps emphasises how low key stag nights were at the time – or how drunk I was.

Ten days before the wedding, I took possession of the married quarter we'd been allocated in a row of houses just outside the main gates of the station. The process was known as a *march-in*.

It sounds very formal and military, and it was. I followed the Unit Families Officer and Barrack Warden around the exterior of the house, and then from room to room as they noted any pre-existing damage, pointed out the amenities and went through an inventory.

Since leaving home and joining the RAF, I'd lived in a series of fully furnished barrack blocks or mess rooms and eaten in communal dining rooms, so I'd had no reason to acquire possessions beyond a stereo system and a small black and white television. And Geraldine was leaving home similarly devoid of possessions, beyond a few things, such as table cloths, bed linen and a set of cutlery she'd kept in her *bottom drawer*, a catch-all term for a cache of things that might prove useful to young women if they married.

Most newly-weds of that period were in a similar

position, certainly those from working class backgrounds. In recognition of this, we were able to request a fully furnished married quarter.

So, 7 Linton Place, a 1960's, three bed semi with garage, contained not only MOD furniture – three-piece suite, dining table and chairs, and fully furnished bedrooms, including standard-issue blankets - but also a kitchen stocked with crockery, cutlery and glassware. The only things we had to buy in short order were a washing machine and a fridge.

I'm sure we paid additional rent in recognition of the fact that the house was furnished, but I can't remember how much. The money for the washing machine and most other small items we needed came from Geraldine, who had a nest-egg of £600. I had little or nothing, having spent most of my disposable income up to that point on cars and beer, although I had a small savings insurance policy.

From the moment we married, I became a more committed saver.

At the end of the march-in, with every last spoon counted, I signed to accept the house and its contents, hoping that Geraldine would like it. I thought she would. Compared to her parents' tied cottage, it was modern and airy, while compared to my parents' council house, it was palatial.

Over the next 25 years, we were to live in 14 married quarters. Some were much larger than 7 Linton Place, but it was the best bar one.

The weekend after that first march-in, Geraldine, Brian and I had a run-through of the wedding in Bromfield Church. Everything at the Ludlow end was good to go.

Back at Linton, through a combination of having to repeat exercises and days lost because I couldn't clear my ears, I'd dropped behind most of the course. So, in an effort to regain lost ground, during the week of the march-in, I flew nine times. The trips included a dual navigation sortie with our new squadron commander.

His arrival had led to a tremendous lightening of mood on 2 Squadron. But, by this stage, my own underlying mood was so downbeat that I was unable to enjoy the new atmosphere, something I've always regretted.

The week before the wedding, I should have been on a survival course. I'd been looking forward to it, but I was one of a small number who were kept back, flying seen as a greater priority than running around the hills. In my case, I also had to make some headway so that I wasn't too far behind when I returned from honeymoon.

It was hoped I'd reach Exercise 59, my Basic Handling Test. This was the mid-course test of progress. Mostly, it would be general handling, but it could also include assessments of my instrument flying and navigation. Historically, it was one of the major stumbling blocks on the course.

On the Monday, I flew three general handling sorties, one solo and two dual, which earned the diary comment, *Pretty Bad*. This was worrying, because general handling had been my main source of hope and enjoyment. Now, I had only one dual and one solo flight in which to improve before the test, which was likely to be on Wednesday.

But on the Tuesday, I didn't fly because of poor weather, and on the Wednesday, it wasn't clear enough for general handling, so I jumped ahead in the syllabus again to complete an instrument flying sortie. This meant my test had slipped to Friday at the earliest, the day before the wedding.

If I passed, we'd get our honeymoon. If I didn't, I'd either be chopped on the spot, or have to return early the next week to fly the remedial sorties that would seal my fate. To say that I felt under pressure would be an understatement.

Fate had contrived to bring together two of the biggest days of my life. Although I was still excited about the wedding, the upcoming test was casting a very dark shadow. And if it went badly, I wasn't sure I'd be able to hide my disappointment, even on my wedding day.

On the Thursday, I flew a solo general handling sortie followed by a final, pre-test, dual with Croucho. There's an old chestnut in flying that you shouldn't peak too early, meaning you should save your most polished performance for the test rather than the pre-ride. Using this measure, I'd left the field open for an outstanding test performance, because I really screwed up the pre-ride. It was so dire that I had to fly the trip again on the Friday morning.

Whether this extra hour went well, I can't recall, but whether it had or not, I could be granted no further leeway. My next flight, the Basic Handling Test, was to be flown with Dingdong.

I was so overcome with nerves that the following couple of hours are hazy to say the least. But, from years of conducting such tests myself – albeit many years later and in a different aircraft type - I'm pretty sure Dingdong would have briefed me to perform steep turns; an incipient and a fully developed clean stall, and a stall in the approach configuration; aerobatics, preferably with the manoeuvres linked into a sequence; an incipient and a four-turn full spin; and a full suite of circuits – normal, glide, flapless and low level. He was also likely to have asked me to fly, either a short navigation leg, or a practice diversion to another airfield.

To test my sortie management, he'd have told me to choose the order in which I did things, and the heights and areas in which I did them, based on factors such as the weather, avoiding airspace busy with other aircraft and time constraints.

As far as possible, he'd have wanted to observe and not intervene beyond engineering at least one major emergency for me to deal with, and probably a few minor ones as well.

One thing my log book does reveal is that both the pre-ride with Croucho and the test included a climb and descent through a layer of cloud, leading to ten minutes of *actual* instrument flying, and an approach called a flame-out controlled descent through cloud (FOCDTC).

This is a means of gliding to an airfield and descending through cloud to carry out a visual forced landing pattern below. Its appearance in my log book indicates that the major emergency Dingdong gave me was a catastrophic engine problem, probably a mechanical failure or fire. The drill for either of these necessitated a simulated engine shut down, after which, having contacted air traffic control, I'd have trimmed my JP into a gliding descent and headed toward the overhead of Linton.

Assuming I was some distance from the airfield when given the emergency, I'd aim to approach the airfield using a one-in-one descent profile. That is, if I was at 15,000 feet, 15 miles from the airfield, I'd push the nose down and attempt to lose 1,000 feet for every mile counted down by the controller. If I was too high at the next mile point, I'd push the nose forward to increase the rate of descent, if too low, raise the nose for a mile.

The aim was to pop out of cloud three miles from the airfield at 3,000 feet – the minimum cloudbase for this type of approach – giving me time to orient myself and bleed off excess speed while heading for a point 2,500 feet above the in-use runway, from where I could fly a forced landing pattern and a glide landing.

Of course, you were unlikely to have an emergency at exactly the right height and distance. So, if it happened when you were below the one-in-one profile, you made your glide as efficient as possible until height and distance coincided. If you were above the ideal profile, you could either spiral down to intercept it, or glide to the overhead and then spiral down through the cloud. I'm pretty sure this is what I did on my trip with Dingdong, but whatever the profile of my descent, it would have been a severe test of my instrument flying skills.

Overall, my Basic Handling Test lasted one and a

quarter hours and included four landings. As we taxied clear of the runway after all that, I knew my performance had been far from flawless, but I had no idea what Dingdong had made of it.

Some testing officers would let you know whether you'd passed straight away, while others kept you waiting until you'd unstrapped and were walking across the pan, and the odd one would keep their own counsel until you were sat in a briefing cubicle ten or 15 minutes after landing. The latter was torture, not least because everyone you met as you walked in raised an eyebrow as if to enquire, *well how did it go then?* when all you could do was shrug, *I don't know*.

I'm familiar with these different scenarios because, over the years, I've been on the receiving end of all of them. I also know that a testing officer may not tell you at the earliest opportunity because he's still trying to decide whether you merit a pass. He may even disappear to consult someone before giving his verdict. Invariably, you pick up on all the indecision, another exquisite form of torture.

I can't remember how long Dingdong kept me waiting, and I didn't hug him when he told me I'd passed. I could have done though.

I was very aware that the success was probably only a reprieve. But, for the moment, I could drive to Ludlow, looking forward to my wedding, my honeymoon and, as it turned out, a total of two weeks' leave.

Chapter 13 – A Joyous Interlude

May 24th 1980 dawned bright and sunny. During the morning, I parked my blue Vauxhall Viva outside the Angel Hotel in Broad Street, the broadest thoroughfare in Ludlow. Lined by tall brick, mainly Georgian, townhouses, it sweeps downhill to the River Teme, and has been described as the handsomest street in England.

Toward its top end, the Angel, an impressive black and white building, had been a coaching inn and hotel since Tudor times. It was probably second in fame only to the Feathers Hotel, another landmark of Tudor Ludlow, and it had once accommodated Admiral Lord Nelson, the victor of Trafalgar, when he visited the town. Our reception was to take place in The Nelson Room. The hotel frontage remains, but the interior is now given over to shops and apartments.

As I parked, Geraldine was watching from the hairdresser opposite. I didn't see her, which some would say was a very good thing, as it could have led to years of bad luck.

The next thing I remember was standing in Bromfield Church next to Brian at 2.30pm, waiting for Geraldine to arrive. From the moment I first laid eyes on her on 7th June 1977 – the day of Queen Elizabeth II's silver jubilee celebrations – I was smitten. But when the Wedding March stopped and I turned to see her and her father next to me, her beauty took my breath away.

I couldn't believe my luck then, and I still can't to this day.

Bromfield Church pre-dates the Norman Conquest, and parts of the current structure date from the 12th and 13th centuries. Originally a priory, it had suffered under, first, Henry VIII and then Cromwell's zealous religionists, but it's still quite a large church for a small village, easily swallowing our 70-odd wedding guests.

About two-fifths were friends and work colleagues, perhaps a few more from my side than Geraldine's; two-fifths were relations; and one fifth were friends of our parents, the majority villagers from Bromfield.

Although I elected to wear uniform, I asked my other serving guests to attend in civvies. It meant we missed the opportunity to have my coursemates form a tunnel of ceremonial swords for Geraldine and I to process through on exiting the church. But I hoped it would prevent my two non-commissioned guests, Sandy and Ian, feeling sidelined or uncomfortable, something that was more important to me.

After the ceremony Geraldine says I marched her down the aisle so swiftly she had time for little more than fleeting eye contact with her friends and relations. But as I've already mentioned, there was plenty of time for her to catch up as we stood around in the churchyard waiting for the photographer to take his snaps. Luckily, the sun continued to shine.

The reception is a total blank, but there are pictures of Geraldine and me cutting a traditional, three-tiered, wedding cake, and Brian says his best man speech seemed to go down well. He also read aloud a few messages from those unable to attend. One was a telegram from Croucho I still have in a scrap book.

It reads, *I hope the slow rolls go better on your honeymoon than they did on your test!* a reference that would have been lost on the majority of the guests, but caused much hilarity among those in the know.

We also had a set of glasses and a card from Lord and Lady Plymouth, for which I can claim no credit, as I'd never met them. But I think it's a demonstration of how generous the Earl and his wife could be to their estate workers, and their families. The generosity was on show again when Geraldine's parents retired from the family's service. They were housed in a chocolate box cottage on the edge of the estate, next to an abandoned mill on the River Teme. They lived in it for 25 years, until its remoteness and narrow, vertiginous, wooden stairs forced a retreat to an apartment in Ludlow.

As the reception wound down, we disappeared to change out of our wedding finery and into our going-away rig. At about 6.30pm, we walked out onto Broad Street to say our final goodbyes, get in the car and set off for our honeymoon. As we approached the Viva, I knew that giving my keys to the hotel, *in case they needed to move it,* had been a mistake, or more likely, a ruse.

An assortment of tin cans and old shoes dangled from the rear bumper, and we caught my mother scattering the contents of a box of confetti over the inside. We were finding it for years. Someone had sprayed messages and heart symbols in shaving foam all over the doors and roof, and it was pretty obvious my friends from Linton had been involved, because the bonnet was adorned with the front profile of a Jet Provost. And when we came to get in, we were encased in a spider's web of string wound between the rear-view mirror, steering wheel and door handles.

Playing along with the jolly japes, we drove off down Broad Street, waving to the guests. But as soon as we disappeared from sight, we had to stop, not least because every time I turned the steering wheel, the string set the car's indicators blinking, or the windscreen wipers sweeping.

We unravelled ourselves, removed the tins and old shoes and did our best to wipe off the shaving foam. I don't know how long this had been on, but it had faded the paintwork, leaving shadowy hearts and the outline of a JP that took weeks to remove with T-cut and car polish.

The rest of the journey was uneventful, but it was 9pm by the time we reached the small hotel in Bath. The landlord seemed a bit grumpy at our arrival time, which didn't bode well for the rest of our stay. Slightly worried by this reception, we unpacked and went for a meal.

The next morning, we were having a lie-in, with the intention of going down for a late breakfast when there was a knock on our door. I scrabbled to find something to put on and opened it. There was the landlord with a nervous smile and a trolley bearing two full English breakfasts and a little vase of flowers.

How wrong can you be?

It was a touching gesture, and one that would be unheard of in a large corporate hotel – unless you'd bought the *honeymoon package*. It was also much appreciated, the atmosphere only slightly dented when he backed out, saying in all seriousness that we couldn't expect the same level of service every morning.

When reviewing my diary, scrap books and photographs, it became apparent that our honeymoon was no different from any of our subsequent holidays; that is, full of activity, with little or no sitting about.

After our room-service breakfast on Sunday, we toured the city, visiting attractions such as the Roman Baths, the Abbey and the Royal Crescent. In the evening, we went to the cinema – which we still called the pictures – to see 10, starring Bo Derek and Dudley Moore. On Monday it was Stonehenge and a nearby Bird Gardens. Tuesday was Wells, Wookey Hole and the Cheddar Gorge and Caves.

On Wednesday, we visited Yeovilton Fleet Air Arm Museum, which included a Concorde as one of its exhibits. I then had, *an ideal night, lovely meal, lovely company*. Whether Geraldine felt the same of course, I can never really know, but I've had many more ideal days and nights with her since.

Thursday, we visited the stately home and safari park at Longleat. In the evening, we went to the pictures again, this time to see The Spy Who Loved Me, starring Roger Moore as James Bond. Afterwards, we had a meal and spent the last of our cash on a Drambuie and a Crème de Menthe, not our usual tipple of choice, so I can only guess it was an attempt to appear sophisticated. I doubt we pulled it off.

On the Friday, we left Bath and returned to Shropshire to spend the weekend there, a married couple.

At the time, it felt as if we'd taken a tremendous gamble, marrying after less than three years of seeing one another for little more than a few hours a month. But over the years, seeing couples who'd had much more time together before tying the knot grow apart and divorce, I don't think the length of our courtship had much bearing on the longevity of our marriage.

People change, and somehow, you've got to find a way to navigate those changes together. So far, Geraldine and I have managed to pull it off, but I well remember how strange it felt driving back to Linton on the Sunday and walking into 7 Linton Place, truly alone in one another's company for what felt like the first time.

Until that moment, I don't think I'd realised how radical a change in lifestyle we were both about to experience.

It's something all couples go through at some point, whether marrying or just deciding to move in together, but that doesn't make it any less profound. We were about to live as a couple for the first time, waking up in the same bed and, although spending much of most days apart, sharing the evenings before going to bed again. I remember being excited and nervous at the same time.

And unless I'd missed something, because we were so conventional in upbringing and outlook, I appeared to have by far the easiest task in our new relationship. My only duties seemed to be emptying the bins and mowing the front and back lawn. Geraldine would do everything else. And before this moment, she'd never kept house, or cooked more than the odd, simple, meal.

Although it may sound patronising, I feared for her, not least because she was beginning this new life in a totally unfamiliar place 200 miles from family and friends.

We were both from the same working class background, but I'd had seven years to settle into RAF life, ten months of which had been as an officer. I was used to living among and interacting with people that were, to use an old-fashioned term, above me in station. I'd also got used to the formal customs and atmosphere of the Officers' Mess. And no matter how much I may have been churning inside, and how little I knew about etiquette, I just bulldozed my way through.

Geraldine, less confident and shier than me at the best of times, had to be nervous about meeting, not only my fellow officers, but also their wives and girlfriends. I knew these women were far from dowager duchesses, but most had the same middle class assuredness as their partners. I also knew the vast majority would go out of their way to be friendly. Nonetheless, by dint of background and accent, Geraldine was going to feel terribly out of place.

She coped. Of course she did. But I'm sure she wouldn't mind me saying she was often more comfortable in the company of airmen's wives than the wives of officers, some of whom basked in the reflected glory of their husband's rank and tended to look down on the wives of those lower down the pecking order. That said, Geraldine made friends in both camps.

For the drive to Linton, all our worldly possessions, that is the few items from Geraldine's bottom drawer and our wedding presents, had fitted easily into our car.

This was a never-to-be repeated feat. The on-going acquisition of furniture and possessions meant that future moves would require, initially, mini-vans and then full-blown removal lorries, complete with three removal men: an older one directing operations, a younger one doing most of the lifting and a slightly creepy one that made Geraldine, and later Sarah, feel uncomfortable.

As I'd hoped, Geraldine liked the house, which was a good start. We unloaded the car, stored more sets of wine glasses than any couple could possibly need and the much-more useful kitchenware, and went upstairs to make the bed. Geraldine dug out a set of sheets from among the wedding presents, but when she opened the packet and laid them out, they were for a single bed.

Who buys a married couple one set of single sheets?

We dissolved in fits of laughter, any tension banished as Geraldine went to find the double sheets from among her bottom drawer items. Perhaps it's laughing that's kept us together. There have certainly been plenty of situations meriting a choice between tears or laughter over the years, and often linked to house moves. But invariably, we've chosen to laugh.

We had another week in which to settle in before I had to go back to work. The first three days were spent in and around the house, *tidying up*, inside and out, and visiting York to buy a washing machine - £203.39p – and a fridge - £200.

While in the city, Geraldine went to the Employment Office to *sign on* as looking for work. This entitled her to a small weekly amount of unemployment benefit, a payment still known as the dole.

It was a term with negative connotations for my parents' generation, being seen as an unmerited reward for feckless people unwilling to work. Unfortunately, there was an element of truth to this, as I'd discovered when growing up on the Dodmore Estate. And no matter how hard successive governments have tried to encourage such people into work, they still exist, although in small numbers, costing the exchequer nowhere near as much as greedy bankers and expenses cheats in the commercial and public sectors.

So, although it wasn't long before Geraldine was in regular work, she felt the stigma of the dole as she walked into the building and signed on. Even a later re-branding of Employment Offices as Job Centres has failed to banish their aura of shame and failure, a ridiculous state of affairs for those genuinely seeking work.

On the Thursday, we visited Scarborough, a traditional seaside resort on the east coast of Yorkshire. It merits only a fairly damning entry in my diary: *Cloudy and nothing but bingo!* To be fair to Scarborough, though, the same could be said of most traditional seaside resorts.

On Friday, we returned to Shropshire and the places we still thought of as *home*. In practice, this meant staying with Geraldine's family in Bromfield and visiting mine in Ludlow. Over the next few years, even as we moved from base to base, and married quarter to married quarter, we continued to think of these two locations as our respective homes. This only began to change when our son, Robin, was born five years later, at which point, we reduced the frequency of our visits and stopped returning routinely for holidays, such as Christmas. And when Sarah arrived three years after that, the succession of quarters we danced about all became home.

That said, even to this day, Geraldine and I still say we're *going home* whenever we visit Ludlow. I guess all strangers in a strange land are the same.

Chapter 14 – Back to Work

On my first day back, Monday 9th June, I had three general handling trips: two hours with Croucho and a 30-minute solo in the circuit. Then it was back to instrument flying in preparation for the Advanced Instrument Flying Grading.

It quickly became apparent that my success in the Basic Grading a month earlier hadn't signalled a breakthrough. I could fly reasonably well on instruments until the workload became high, such as during runway approaches, at which point my scan tended to break down. I'd look at the instruments, but not take in what they told me. As a result, I'd fail to spot errors and take corrective action.

And on all but a few occasions, I still struggled to recover from limited panel UPs. There's a saying that when instrument flying under the hood, *one peek is worth a thousand scans*, meaning that having a sneaky look out of the cockpit at the visual horizon and recovering using that is much easier than trying to recover solely on the instruments. In essence, the easiest thing to do is cheat.

Both at Linton and afterwards, several people told me they always cheated if they felt things getting away from them, and that I should do the same. After all, the likelihood of having to recover from a UP on limited panel for real was vanishingly small. I never had to do it during my whole flying career. But I never did cheat.

I'd like to say it was all down to personal integrity, but I suspect that the real reason was that I became so overloaded and flustered during my recovery attempts that I merely forgot to lift my head for a peek.

It would have been much easier if I had, though, saving years of mental anguish.

Over the next three weeks, the odd general handling trip, including two solos, buoyed my spirits a little, but every time I had to don the hood for an instrument flying sortie, it was as if the life force was being sucked out of me. And I wasn't the only one.

It was at about this time that Mike Daly decided to throw in the towel.

He'd become increasingly unhappy, fed up with banging his head against a brick wall with, in his own estimation, no realistic prospect of success. But I think it was the added complication of being thousands of miles from home that led him to withdraw from training. I know from our conversations at the time that once he'd done it, he felt a great sense of relief, as if he'd emerged from a long, dark, tunnel.

I have to admit that his immediate lightening of mood made me consider following a similar path, but I lacked the courage, or maybe I was just too stubborn and stupid.

After the necessary admin, Mike returned to New Zealand, where he spent some time travelling before becoming a software engineer at the nation's only steel plant. Later, he travelled the world, studying and gaining experience of air traffic control systems, installing and being responsible for many of these in his home country. While in Tokyo, he met and married Kayoko and they have two sons.

Mike's travels included a lucky escape. He was in Washington for 9/11 and due to fly out the next day on a scheduled flight with the same number as one of the aircraft that was hijacked.

As he prepared to go home, I was finding it increasingly difficult to cope with the pressure. Geraldine couldn't help but notice.

At that time, to ensure we were well nourished before flying, aircrew were expected to eat a cooked English breakfast. It was what Messes and Aircrew Feeders across the RAF provided. I suspect the dieticians will have changed their recommendations over the years. Now, it's probably granola, or something similar.

But back then, Geraldine prepared me a cooked breakfast every morning, only to see me sit at the kitchen table in my green flying suit, gagging over the first few mouthfuls until forced to admit that I was unable to eat. She knew it wasn't critical comment on her cooking, but a physical manifestation of my mental state.

It didn't happen every morning, but during that period, it was a frequent occurrence, and it continued to be an intermittent problem throughout my flying training. I don't remember having the same symptoms once the flying day was over, so her efforts in the kitchen during the evening weren't wasted in the same way, but I was keenly aware that it was a less-than-ideal introduction to married life.

That she put up with such things is one of many reasons I have to be grateful to her. And she continued to cook my breakfast for many years, even when I flew the four-engined Hercules around the world. This often meant cooking late at night or getting up to do so in the early hours. As our aircraft climbed away from Lyneham a few hours later, the rest of the crew would be amazed when I turned down the Loadmaster's offer of a cooked breakfast because I'd already had one.

Where could they get a wife like that, they asked? I knew they couldn't.

I also had reason to be grateful to the staff of 2 Squadron. During the period of intensive instrument flying leading up to the Advanced Instrument Flying Grading, I was granted four extra hours of practice, more leeway than anyone should be allowed without being chopped. They must have spotted some potential for improvement that I failed to see.

I also had a change of instructor.

I guess Croucho and/or the Squadron hierarchy had decided he'd done all he could for me and it was time for someone else to have a go. Whatever the reason, after 31 flights together, he and I parted company on 17th June. I'd enjoyed a period of remarkable continuity under his tutelage, and I've always been grateful for his patience in striving to sort out my many problems in the air.

He deserved the break.

In his stead, Rod, a slim, dark-haired, flight lieutenant became my primary instructor. While our continuity was nowhere near as good, I ended up flying with him 17 times. In between, I tended to fly with more senior instructors, including the squadron commander, perhaps an indication that my progress, or lack of it, was being closely supervised.

For the Advanced Instrument Flying Grading, I had to fly more accurate heights, headings and speeds, and there were a couple of additions to the standard sortie profile. The first, a practice diversion, meant taking off from Linton, transiting to another airfield to perform an instrument approach, then climbing to complete the upper air work in our usual operating area. The second addition was a pilot-interpreted instrument approach called an Instrument Landing System, or ILS.

ILS ground installations sit next to runways transmitting two radio signals along the approach path. One marks the runway centreline, the other the ideal glide slope. If I tuned the aircraft ILS equipment to the correct frequency for a particular runway – identified by a discrete three-letter Morse tone heard in my headset – I could fly down to my decision height along the intersection of these beams. To do so, I had to interpret a small instrument in the cockpit with two needles, one telling me whether I was left or right of the runway centreline, the other if I was above or below the glide slope.

Ideally, I'd keep these two needles crossed in the centre of the instrument, making small adjustments before either needle shifted too far. But this had to be done by adjusting the attitude on the artificial horizon, not by chasing the ILS needles. And of course, I still had to speak on the radios and monitor the performance instruments, acting on what they were telling me to control such things as the speed. And the closer I came to the runway, the more sensitive the instrument, and the more prompt and measured adjustments had to be.

Inevitably, I struggled with the higher workload generated by ILS approaches.

The final complication was that my nose continued to run freely before gumming up, causing discomfort and adding to my feeling of embattlement. By now, in addition to giving me a succession of nasal sprays, the medics had begun testing me for allergies.

Despite all the extra hours I'd been given, on Friday 27th June, I failed my Advanced Instrument Flying Grading, putting my future in jeopardy once again. It was the day of the Summer Ball, the major event in the Officers' Mess social calendar.

I can't imagine I was much fun to be with, or that Geraldine wasn't wondering whether she'd have to move to another part of the country, and another house, so soon after moving into this one. And by this time, she was working as a receptionist for the Rowntree Trust in York, another thing that would have to go if we moved. But she doesn't remember anything beyond us drowning our sorrows and having a good time.

The next day was her birthday and we drove to Shropshire. In the evening, we went to the centrepiece of Ludlow's annual, two-week arts festival, a performance of Macbeth in the castle. I've always known how to give a girl a good time!

Back at Linton on the Monday, I had two instrument trips, the second another failure of the Advance Grading. I can only think that I made one, critical, mistake, rather than a litany of errors, because for some reason I was allowed a third attempt the next day, which I passed.

Just as well, because I can't believe there was any way I'd have been granted another reprieve.

Chapter 15 – Navigation and Low Flying

Luckily, there were still areas where my performance was better. One of these was navigation. It was flown in small blocks of a few dual and solo hours spread through the syllabus, progressing from medium level navigation around the 40-hour mark, to higher level nav around 60 hours and low level around 70. It also extended groundschool into June, because as each nav phase approached we'd complete a study guide and take an exam.

Medium level navs were flown at around 2,500 feet, or a bit higher if the cloudbase allowed. They tended to follow triangular routes, setting out from Linton to the first turning point, crossing North Yorkshire to the second turning point and then returning to Linton, each leg ideally about 20 minutes (60 miles) long.

Although eventually we'd have to plan navs at short notice, the early sorties were standard, the routes displayed in a nav planning room. This allowed us plenty of time to prepare our own 1:500,000 (half-mil) topographical maps.

The process began with the selection of features that were likely to be easy to spot from the air about every ten minutes apart, things with distinctive shapes and ideally, vertical extent. They'd be my fixes, used to check position and timing. Once smallish ink circles were drawn round these and the turning points, I could ink in the route.

I'd then add more small circles to the side of the route mid-way between fixes. On the day of the flight, these would be annotated with how much fuel I expected to have at that point, and the minimum fuel required to fly the rest of the nav and divert to another airfield if necessary. I'd also identify danger, restricted or prohibited areas close to the route and highlight the most important with fluorescent marker.

The final additions to the map before the day of the flight were little rectangular boxes at the start and each turning point. Each box had room for four pieces of information, but at this point, I'd write in only one: the track, that is, the magnetic bearing to be flown along each leg, measured from the map.

On the day of the flight, dependent on the cloudbase, I'd choose a height to fly each leg and write that in the relevant box. Then, based on the forecast wind at that height, I'd use a circular slide rule called a Dalton Computer to work out the magnetic headings to fly and the time for each leg. These two bits of information were added to the relevant boxes.

When finished, there could be a lot of ink on the map, and the trick was to make sure it didn't obscure topographical and other information. One of the final skills was to trim and fold the map so that all the information was visible and it would fit into a flying suit pocket. This is where it would spend the vast majority of the flight.

We didn't map read as you might imagine by running our thumbs along the track, keeping a constant eye on where we were. We were taught to consult the map only approaching fixes and turning points. The rest of the time was for flying accurate heights and headings and looking out for other aircraft. Even when I took the map out, it had to be held at eye level so that I could still see out of the cockpit.

Most of the early navs started from the overhead of the airfield. So, on the day of the flight, I'd spiral up and complete the pre-HAT checks, reading from map to instruments to make sure I was going to set out on the right Heading, at the right Altitude, and that I started the stop watch to keep an eye on the Time.

And once I'd set out, I'd carry out the post-HAT checks, reading from the instruments to the map to confirm that I was indeed flying the right Heading, at the right Altitude, and that I'd started the stop-watch and knew the Time of the next event, be that fix, turning point or fuel check. Post-HAT checks complete, the map went away and I concentrated on Lookout, Attitude, Instruments.

The HAT checks were repeated approaching and after each turning point.

One minute to a fix, I'd take out the map and, working from large features to small – lake to wood to edge of village - attempt to identify the chosen feature on the ground. The actual wind at the height I was flying was likely to be different from the forecast, so I'd probably be some way left or right of my fix, and maybe a little early or late.

Before GPS and the like, there were several methods of regaining track. If I could see the next fix, say a distinctive hill, I could fly toward it; or if I knew a road, river or railway would funnel me back to track, I could follow that.

Failing these, I could use a method called the standard closing angle. This is based around a mathematical principle called the 1 in 60 rule (to do with the sine of angles...). The practical application for navigation is that if you are x miles off track you can turn through a standard closing angle for x minutes to regain it. And for a JP3A flying at 180 knots – three nautical miles per minute - the standard closing angle is 60 (the starting point for the 1 in 60 rule) divided by three, which is 20 degrees.

So, let's say the wind has blown me two miles left of my fix. To regain track, I could turn right through the standard closing angle of 20 degrees for two minutes, then turn onto a modified heading based on my experience of the actual wind. I could also modify the standard closing angle to turn through a slightly less extreme angle of say 10 degrees for four minutes, which would have less effect on the timing of the leg.

And as to timing, if my fixes were equally spaced a third of the way along the route, and I arrived abeam the first 20 seconds late, I would expect to be 40 seconds late at the next fix, two thirds of the way along the leg, and one minute late at my turning point.

If the fixes weren't so evenly distributed, I'd have to work out how many seconds per mile the wind was slowing me down. So, if I was 20 seconds late after ten miles, I was losing 2 seconds every mile, so I'd be a minute late after 30 miles.

If it sounds quite complicated, I suppose it is, and I can't say that I always made the right calculations, or that things always went smoothly. But I coped, largely because this was visual flying. If I'd had to perform the same mental gymnastics while flying on instruments, it would have been a totally different matter, close to impossible.

Anyway back to our nav. After that first fix, armed with a new heading and timing, I'd put the map away and concentrate on flying accurately until one minute before the new time for the next fix, at which point, I'd pick up the map and go through the fix routine again, probably having completed a fuel check in the interim.

Then, a minute before the end of the first leg, I'd pick up the map and complete the pre-HAT checks for the next leg - Heading, Altitude and Timing - while trying to spot my turning point. If I failed to do so, I had to turn on time, perform the post-HAT checks and put the map away, hoping to identify the next fix.

After several dual and solo navigation sorties at medium level, we moved up to higher levels above 10,000 feet. At this height, it was impractical to plan routes by reference to features on the ground because, as you climbed higher, more and more terrain was obscured by the airframe and/or cloud beneath you. So we navigated by reference to radio beacons on sorties called radio aids navs.

These were plotted on a 1:1,000,000 (one mil) scale Enroute Map, devoid of topographical features but displaying the network of airways over the UK and the numerous radio beacons used to navigate in and around them.

Airways are generally corridors ten miles wide between airfields and major navigation beacons. They offer protection from general air traffic to those flying along them, usually commercial airliners. At this point in my career, these corridors – shaded green on the map – were to be avoided at all costs.

If I'd become a fast jet or a helicopter pilot, I'd have spent most of my career avoiding them, but as a truckie – transport pilot – I was to spend much of my time on the Hercules flying along many of the world's airways, and enjoying the protection they offered.

For now though, although fixes and turning points were based on ranges and bearings from beacons rather than features on the ground, the techniques for radio aids nav were similar to those at medium level.

I really enjoyed navigation. The skill is a military necessity, allowing pilots to find the target, be that to bomb it, drop supplies over it, or rescue casualties from it. But I liked it for more aesthetic reasons to do with watching the sky and the ground rolling by.

And for that reason, I loved the next element on the syllabus even more: low level navigation, the sport of kings.

For many years it was assumed that unless an enemy's air defences had been neutralised, any aircraft flying into enemy airspace at height was certain to be spotted on radar and, in all probability, shot down. And even now when aircraft can cloak themselves in stealth technology, it would seem foolhardy to assume that a sophisticated enemy won't have some means of spotting an intruder flying high above the ground.

The answer has always been to fly as low as possible, using the terrain as a shield to prevent radar systems picking you up unless you blunder too close, or until forced to over-fly a defended target in the last few seconds of an attack. And much to the chagrin of noise complainers everywhere, the only way to operate safely at low level is to practise, practise, practise.

In the UK and overseas, there are a couple of isolated ranges where pilots can practice flying down to as low as 50 feet, but in peacetime over most of the UK, the limit is 250 feet, not just from the ground, but from any object, natural or man made - hillside, house, tower or pylon. During my first low level sorties, 250 feet seemed quite low enough. Flying at 210 knots – 240 miles per hour – if I made a mistake, I was fractions of a second from hitting the ground.

Hence the need to practise.

At low level, my normal activity cycle of Lookout, Attitude, Instruments morphed into Lookout, Picture, Instruments.

Modern aircraft warn pilots that they're dipping below 250 feet. They even have systems to maintain that or any other selected height. But on the JP, we relied on the Mk 1 eyeball. We had to recognise the view of the world – the Picture - at 250 feet, the rate at which the ground rushed past, the way the horizon sat up around eye level when flying over flat terrain, and how the horizon sloped among hills and hollows.

The only concrete rule of thumb was that at 250 feet cows had legs and sheep didn't. All very well if you were flying over sheep and cows and could see that you needed to ease up because the sheep had developed legs, or ease down because the cow's legs had disappeared, but not much use anywhere else.

Lookout becomes even more important at low level, not only to avoid flying into the ground, but also because unlike in the upper air, where aircraft are likely to be flying at a range of different heights, at low level, almost everyone's flying at 250 feet. And whereas at height aircraft might be spotted against the sky, at low level they're hidden amongst the folds and the greens and greys of the landscape. After all, that's what camouflage is for. At the other end of the spectrum, one of the reasons JPs and other training aircraft were painted red and white was to make them more visible at low level.

And as to the instruments, these were consulted to make sure I maintained 210 knots and that I didn't exceed 60 degrees of bank and pull into the ground when turning, something that was all too easy to do while distracted, or when confused by sloping horizons among the hills.

Confronted with rising ground, I learned to add power and raise the nose to climb early, so that I never dipped below 250 feet when passing over a ridge line or summit. Getting this wrong and *clipping the top* was one of the major causes of fatalities at low level, while pilots discovering higher ground beyond what they'd assumed to be a summit – a phenomenon well known to hill walkers – added to the grim statistics.

A variation on this was trying to sneak through a gap between what was assumed to be a hilltop and a low cloudbase. Known as letter-boxing, it was particularly dangerous, as there was often higher ground hidden in the cloud beyond the letterbox. The resulting crashes were invariably fatal.

When the ground fell away, I had to lower the nose and bring back the throttle to maintain 250 feet and 210 knots. Then, approaching the bottom of a slope, I had to add power and raise the nose early so that I didn't dip below the minimum height or, worse still, slap the belly of the aircraft into the ground.

Thankfully, over the last few years, technological advances such as terrain-following radar have virtually eradicated training fatalities due to height misjudgement at low level. But they were still fairly common when I was flying the JP, as were those due to other hazards, such as birdstrikes.

Because most birds fly no higher than a few hundred feet, they tend to meet aircraft soon after the latter take off, or just before they land. In one such instance in 1980, a Nimrod maritime reconnaissance aircraft and two of its crew were lost when it hit a large flock of Canada Geese shortly after take off from RAF Kinloss. How many geese had flown into and disabled the engines will never be known, but 177 dead birds were found on and around the runway. This and similar cases explain why civilian and military airfields put a great deal of effort into scaring birds away from the vicinity of runways.

But collisions with birds also become more likely when flying at low level, especially near coasts, large bodies of water and landfill sites. Such collisions invariably mean a diversion to the nearest airfield just in case there's damage to engines or vital systems such as flying controls or undercarriages. Bird remains splattering canopies and restricting vision can complicate such recoveries, but when large birds smash through the perspex, it becomes much more serious.

I remember a widely-publicised photograph of a pilot with bird remains splattered all over his visor and oxygen mask. The result had he not had a visor down doesn't bear thinking about. As it was, he had to cope with the sheer shock of the event, then clear away enough blood and guts for him to see and fly his stricken jet to an airfield and land, all the while buffeted by hurricane force winds howling in through the shattered canopy.

As the Nimrod example shows, when birds and jet engines meet, it invariably leads to engine failure, and unless the pilot of a fast jet flying at low level is close enough to a clear strip of concrete several thousand yards long, there's only one option: eject.

No such option existed in light aircraft like the Bulldog I flew later in my career. Then, if I'd suffered an engine failure at low level, I'd have been too low to take to my parachute. I might have been able to attempt a forced landing in a large field, but otherwise I was resigned to *crashing straight ahead, wings level, in an airman-like manner*.

An added hazard that I didn't have to contend with is drones. Hitting one of these would be at least as catastrophic as a birdstrike.

Less spectacular but more insidious are the effects of strong winds at low level.

When flying downwind – that is, with the wind behind me – the groundspeed of my JP would be greater than the 210 knots I was used to seeing in little or no wind. And of course, the greater the wind strength, the quicker the ground would rush past. If I ignored the other elements that made up the correct picture for 250 feet, I might be tempted to slow the ground rush by closing the throttle, putting me in danger of so slowing the aircraft that it stalled into the ground. The other way of slowing the rush would be to climb, which, in a hostile environment, would make me more vulnerable to enemy radar and weapons systems.

Strong headwinds on the other hand could so reduce the rate at which the ground rushed past that I'd be tempted to open the throttle and speed up. Nothing dangerous in that, but the alternative, restoring the ground rush by descending, would make me vulnerable to rising ground, especially if masked by other visual illusions.

The wind was one reason we were taught to give tall obstacles, such as radio masts, a wide berth, keeping them in sight at all times. It was particularly important not to turn before a mast when flying downwind, in case you were blown, belly up, into the supporting wires, or the mast itself.

And finally, there were all sorts of visual illusions to trip you up when flying over featureless grasslands, snowfields or, more insidious, forests. Again, there were well documented cases of pilots misjudging their height above the wastelands of northern Europe or Canada. They failed to spot that the tall pines over which they'd been flying for many miles had slowly reduced in height until they were no taller than domestic Christmas trees. Some had woken up to the fact that they were flying no more than a few feet above the ground. Others had died and become case studies on flight safety courses.

Such things are less likely over the UK, but these and other, similar, illusions had to be borne in mind.

Having had briefings on all the hazards outlined above, and a flight to familiarise ourselves with flying at low level, it was time to navigate, this time using 1:250,000 - quarter mil - maps bearing more detail than the half mil maps used at medium level. I found low level nav both more enjoyable and more demanding than navigating at medium or high level.

For a start, we tried not to overfly human settlements or livestock, so there was lots of weaving around villages, farms and concentrations of animals. In fact, we spent so much time deviating from the line on the map that it was in many ways no more than advisory. So I had to keep a mental plot of how many times I'd veered left or right to avoid something, and ease back to track whenever I could.

And of course, at low level, I couldn't see as far ahead, especially in hilly terrain, so things tended to rush up out of nowhere. This increase in pace, allied with more frequent track and timing calculations, stretched me to the limits of my capacity, sometimes beyond.

Route study became more important. Ideally, it would allow me to visualise the flight cinematically before take-off. And then, as I flew the route, I could anticipate and tick off landmarks and features as I passed them without constant recourse to the map. But of course, if I was too far off track, either because of the wind or because of the need to avoid things, I never saw the landmarks and my mental film quickly unwound.

The better members of 43 Course were able to cope with such complications. Sometimes I could, sometimes I couldn't, an inconsistency that made my selection to either the fast jet or helicopter streams unlikely. I proved myself competent enough to be sent off solo at low level though, something which, in recognition of our inexperience, we did at 500 feet rather than 250.

Mostly, I was too busy to take much more than peripheral notice of the view. But just occasionally, slicing along some valley, I found time to glory in the images of sunlight glinting off the dark waters of a lake, or shadows on grey mountain walls, maybe even the shadow of my own JP, swooping among the crags.

At such times, I loved it. These were the inspirational moments that made struggling pilots persevere. In my case, they made me determined not to be chopped, despite the mental toll my stubbornness was exacting.

It's also said that such occasions can make pilots feel vaguely god-like. While I don't remember feeling in any way divine, I have to admit to feeling tremendously privileged, especially when my lofty perch allowed a glimpse into other people's lives, say flying alongside a valley road, the faces of car and lorry drivers turned towards me as I sped past, no doubt wondering what it was like to be up there looking down.

Well, when all was going fine, when you knew where you were, and where you were going, it was just great.

Some of the high points of my life have been when flying at low level: over the raging South Atlantic in a Hercules off the Falklands, monitoring East European trawlers with more aerials than fishing nets; weaving along the desert wadis between Petra and the Dead Sea in a Super Puma helicopter piloted by Prince Feisal of Jordan; flying through the spectacular terrain of Wales and the north of England on various Hawk flights; over the mountains and lochs of Scotland in a Harrier; and finally, numerous Bulldog sorties among some of Britain's most dramatic scenery.

These highlights were all a long way ahead of me, but I'd passed the navigation phases of the basic course at Linton without any great dramas.

Chapter 16 – Night Flying

It was a good job I'd also passed the Advanced Instrument Flying Grading because it was a pre-requisite for the area of the syllabus immediately following it: night flying. Not that this meant we flew at night by sole reference to the instruments.

On all but the darkest nights there's usually enough ambient light to give a clear horizon, meaning the instruments are paramount only in the few seconds after take off, when you have to avoid fixating on the glare of runway and other lights. For the rest of the flight, a pilot can usually fly visually, the instruments being consulted only as part of the normal Lookout, Attitude, Instruments activity cycle.

There's no doubt that darkness can make disorientation more likely, cloaking hazards such as false horizons of sloping cloud, while in sparsely populated areas, stars and the lights of isolated dwellings on the ground can cause confusion as to which way is up. But these problems too can generally be picked up during the normal activity cycle. Then again, just as by day, when flying in poor visibility or cloud, the instruments become vital.

I liked the heightened feeling of isolation when flying at night. It was as if you were floating amid the darkness in a dimly lit cocoon. The sensation was heightened in cloud, when the eerie glow of the cockpit and aircraft lights reflected off swirling water droplets, adding to a sense of other-worldliness.

Over eight nights, I flew a total of five hours dual and three hours 35 minutes solo, starting in the circuit, but moving on to transits to nearby airfields and then navigation farther afield. As it was the beginning of July, much of the flying took place after midnight, keeping many on the station and in the local area awake. This led to an increase in noise complaints, a problem plaguing all RAF stations, and one I'd have to deal with later in my career.

Another result of night flying was that I saw little of Geraldine for a couple of weeks. After a wind-down beer, which seemed to be traditional after each session of night flying, I rarely returned to the house before five in the morning, when the sun was already up. So I was in bed, if not actually asleep, when she went to work, and I left the house again a couple of hours after she returned.

When I'd worked alternate weeks of night and day shifts at Scampton, I'd been single, so night flying gave me an insight into the problems shift work can cause for married couples. On this occasion, it was only a couple of weeks, but when I began flying the Hercules it often seemed as if Geraldine and I were ships passing in the night.

As we sat in the crewroom waiting to fly, we'd do all we could to avoid bright lights, although even the minimum level of lighting in squadron buildings and on the flight line made this easier said than done. And when we arrived at the aircraft, because red light is less disruptive of night vision, we used torches with red filters to illuminate our external checks.

One mistake that people are more prone to make at night is strapping into the wrong aircraft. We were told of a student a few courses ahead of us who'd strapped in and connected his radio link, only to hear his instructor's voice saying, 'Well done, Scroggins. Now if you'd like to look to the left.'

His instructor was sitting in the adjacent JP, waving, as the voice in his headset continued, 'Perhaps you'd like to come and join me!'

The JP cockpit and many of its individual instruments were lit, not in cool green light as they would be today, but in harsh white. Once the engine was started and we'd taxied clear of the pan, we'd progressively turn down the brightness, so that in the air we could concentrate on the world outside.

Of course, flying at night adds another layer of complication to many emergencies, as well as making things that wouldn't be a problem during the day, such as cockpit or runway light failures, into, if not emergencies, at least tricky situations. We learnt to cope with the full range of these.

Many of the more extreme practice emergencies still ended in ejection decisions. Never a heartening prospect at the best of times, ejecting at night seemed particularly daunting. If it came to it, we were taught to try and minimise loss of life on the ground by pointing the aircraft at a dark area before ejecting.

Beyond steep turns, there was little frantic manoeuvring and no turning upside down, which made some view night flying as boring. But I loved it, mostly for the captivating view from the cockpit.

During my Hercules tour, I saw many wondrous things when flying at night: lightning illuminating monstrous thunderclouds, none more spectacular than those reaching up to 55,000 feet over the South Atlantic off the coast of Africa; St Elmo's Fire, jagged lines of electric blue light dancing on the aircraft windscreen and airframe when flying into Gander, Newfoundland; and the well-lit coasts of continents, countries and islands, including the outline of, first Lands End and then the rest of the southern United Kingdom when returning from the South Atlantic.

And it all started on those early flights, looking down on the lights of Linton and its surrounds, from the isolated glow of single dwellings, to villages with tens of house and street lights, to York, awash with so many lights of varying size and colour that they were impossible to count.

Many of the settlements were linked by thin strings of orange, beneath which short white beams and pinpoints of red moved in opposing directions.

What were all those people doing?

It was a question that fascinated me every time I looked down on humankind, but never more so than at night, when, quite literally, they had a light shone onto their lives.

There tends to be less turbulence at night. One of the main reasons is the absence of the up-currents associated with daytime heating, but we concocted a more whimsical explanation.

Bernoulli was a Swiss mathematician and physicist who came up with many of the equations explaining flight, and especially lift. We'd learned these in groundschool, but we took them a step further, postulating a new fundamental particle that thrived in the dark, called the Bernoulli. The air at night was smoother simply because there were more Bernoullis!

Whatever the explanation, the smoothness made it easier to achieve and maintain accurate heights and speeds, something from which I derived great pleasure. This marked me out as multi-engine rather than fighter pilot material. I was content striving for accuracy over long periods, while a fighter pilot would want to be turning upside down and pulling g.

So, apart from the view out of the window, most night flying is very similar to flying by day, but I think it worth mentioning the final approach and landing.

In the run up to my daytime first solo, I'd been taught to recognise the correct aspect of the runway on final approach. Now, I was taught the same at night, when it was based on the view of the lights positioned every hundred yards or so down each side of the runway. If they appeared to merge into one continuous line, I was too low, while if they were widely spaced, I was too high. Only if they stretched out like a *string of pearls* was I on the correct approach path.

And then to land, I had to continue down into the black hole that was the runway until the lights to either side came *up round my eyes*, then take off the power and raise the nose to sink until I kissed – or crunched - onto the tarmac.

In contrast to the hours it had taken for me to go solo by day, Rod sent me off on my own after only 45 minutes of instruction at night.

So I had made progress, at least in some areas.

The weekend midway through night flying, Geraldine's parents visited. I don't remember much, except that they were very impressed with 7 Linton Place.

A short time earlier, Geraldine and I had been introduced to Bibi's, a pizza restaurant close to one of York's impressive mediaeval gates. I'm pretty sure we'd never eaten pizza, but we became regulars. The restaurant and its food seemed the height of sophistication to us, and Geraldine says we took her parents and all subsequent visitors from Shropshire there.

I'm not sure how much they enjoyed their pizzas, but I can't believe they weren't impressed by York. Geraldine and I certainly loved it, and it remained top of our retirement list until we discovered the Cardiff area in the early 1990s. We especially like wandering around the Minster and the City walls, activities that still form an important part of our 5-yearly visits for 43 Course reunions.

By this time, investigations into my nasal problems at station level had indicated that I might be allergic to something in the oxygen system or mask, although exactly what remained a mystery. My fellow course members joked that I was allergic to oxygen, and as I sniffed my way through most flights, it often felt like it.

If the specific allergen remained elusive, the other cause, my hopelessly bent and constricted nasal passages were examined during a visit to a specialist at the RAF Hospital at Nocton Hall, a few miles south of Lincoln. Afterwards, he came up with a plan, but it would be a while before I heard what it was.

From Nocton, we travelled the short distance to Lincoln and spent the Saturday with my friend from Halton and Scampton, Sandy, and his fiancée, Lyn. It was the first time we'd seen them since they'd announced their engagement. The next day, we travelled to Telford and stayed with Simon and Jane, for whom I'd been best man a few years earlier. By then, they were living in a police house in Stirchley, part of Telford.

The following weekend, we went to a friend's after-wedding party in Ludlow and brought my parents back to Linton for the week. They too were impressed with our first home. The following two weekends, we also entertained visitors, first, Geraldine's older sister, her husband and children, then Andy and Ann, the couple for whom I'd been best man the previous September.

When I look at my log book over this period, I was doing plenty of flying, and I know Geraldine was working. So when Squadron and Station events were added to the busy schedule of visits, we were living life at quite a pace.

Things rarely slowed down until I retired 25 years later.

Chapter 17 – Role Selection

My diary entry for 31st July trumpets, *Finished 100 hr course*. Surely reaching this milestone assured my future in flying training?

But of course it didn't.

One hundred hours was merely the amount of flying allowed to complete the syllabus up to Exercise 92, the last night flying sortie. It included an allowance for flights abandoned for reasons such as a failure to find suitable weather once airborne; to regain currency after prolonged breaks due to bad weather or illness; or, as in my case, for the repeat of exercises when the first attempt hadn't been up to scratch.

Because of the poor weather in the early months of 1980, I don't think anyone on 43 Course had completed the 92 exercises in 100 hours. The majority, though, had exceeded the allocation by no more than a small margin, whereas I'd taken 110 hours 35 minutes!

Having reached the milestone though, I and my fellow Course members were about to find out whether we'd done enough to continue in RAF pilot training, and if so, in which role: fast jet, helicopter or multi-engine.

Over the preceding six months, we'd lost three of our original 17 members, but we'd also gained someone. Graham, an enthusiastic young Scot from a course a few months ahead of us had returned to Linton after a spell at Farnborough, where the aviation medicine specialists had attempted to cure his airsickness. It appeared to have worked, although he'd still be known as a *sicky* for the rest of his career. He was desperate to be a fast jet pilot.

Most of the Course were, but following my months on Review, my dreams of becoming a Harrier pilot were long gone. I hadn't even expected to survive as far as night flying. Now that I had, the best I could hope for was a chance to have a crack at the multi-engine role.

But first I had to ensure I met the course standard. If I

achieved that and there were no multi-engine slots - as we'd been told might be the case at our initial briefing in November – so be it. At least I'd have given it my best shot.

So, in the run-up to the role selection point, I was trying to impress. We all were. And we were all feeling the pressure, with every hour in the air more demanding than the last, and more important to our future career paths.

Perversely, it was perhaps the best of us, those still in the hunt to be fast jet pilots that were feeling the most pressure, trying to convince their instructors they had what it took to succeed in a fast jet cockpit.

The Role Selection Board met while we were night flying.

Prior to this, the Squadron collated and reviewed all our paperwork and presented it to officers from the Station and Support Command Headquarters. They decided if any of us had failed to meet the course standard. With these individuals out of the picture, they could discuss the abilities and personality traits of the survivors, before recommending which future role they should follow.

Their recommendations were presented to the Role Selection Board, chaired by a wing commander from the RAF manning directorate. He'd make the final decision.

As I write this, I can hardly believe that for just over two years at the turn of the millennium, I was that wing commander. With a team of six squadron leaders and six civil servants, I was responsible for managing the careers of all the junior officers in the air traffic control, fighter control, intelligence and RAF Regiment branches - and the operations support branch when that was formed – and all the junior officer pilots, including those in training. It was a total of about 2,500 officers.

Throughout the period, I decided not only to which role every pilot in training should go, but also which aircraft they should fly at the end of their advanced flying training. Additionally, I signed off the postings of each and every junior officer for which I was responsible, including exchange tours overseas. I even ratified the selection of pilots for the Red Arrows. And all this while launching and administering two major retention initiatives designed to stop the RAF haemorrhaging pilots to the airlines.

It's just as well I was a task-oriented workaholic!

Although there was no place for sentiment in any of the role selection decisions, I was always acutely aware that I was making or breaking the dreams of some very able and committed young people. I have no way of knowing of course, but perhaps the man deciding my fate was as sympathetic.

The factors to be considered when selecting pilots to roles were many and varied. And like it or not, there was a definite pecking order. Very firmly at the top were those deemed to have the potential to be fast jet pilots. Close behind and usually just short of the fast jet standard were those destined for helicopters. And lagging these were those deemed fit only for the multi-engine role.

Unsurprisingly, those selected to follow the fast jet route needed to have performed well in all areas of the syllabus, but also to have demonstrated high levels of capacity and situational awareness.

Capacity is the ability to take in and process large amounts of information, filter out the unimportant, produce timely decisions and put them into action. Situational awareness is the ability to maintain a mental plot of where you and those around you are in time and space, no matter how hard you're manoeuvring or how fast the situation is changing.

To juggle all the elements of situational awareness, a pilot needs good capacity, but someone with capacity doesn't necessarily have good situational awareness. And both are necessary in those chosen for fast jets. As their flying training progresses they'll have to cope with increasing complexity – higher speeds, larger formations, more complex manoeuvres and tactics, greater distances, worse weather and more difficult emergencies. Lack of capacity and/or situational awareness were the most likely reasons for pilots to be chopped from the fast jet stream.

And last but not least, fast jet pilots need a cast iron determination to achieve the aim, to reach the target, be that something on the ground in the case of bomber pilots, or an enemy aircraft for those destined to become fighter pilots.

Of course, those filling the helicopter and multi-engine streams need the same qualities, but not all have to be developed to the same degree.

Over my career, I was given many explanations of the difference between fast jet and multi-engine pilots. Here are a couple of my favourites.

In the first, a pilot is flying with a mountainous cliff wall close to his right wing. Suddenly he becomes aware of a missile about to hit him from behind. A fast jet pilot would just act on impulse, turning left into the clear air or right into the cliff without thinking. Thus, he'd have a fifty percent chance of surviving and going on to the target.

A multi-engine pilot would note the threat and take time to consider his options: turn right and hit the mountain, or...Too late! He'd be taken out by the missile every time. No chance of survival and no chance to attack the target.

The second example has the same pilots flying a fully laden two engined passenger aircraft that develops a fire in one engine shortly after take off. The swift action of the fast jet pilot, acting on impulse, could be disastrous, shutting down the good engine on 50% of occasions, killing himself and everyone on board. By comparison, the multi-engine pilot's considered response – taking time to identify and shut down the burning engine - would allow a safe return to the airfield every time.

These examples may not stand up to close scrutiny. After all, who's going to turn into a cliff, and many fast jet pilots go on to become successful airline pilots and never shut down the wrong engine. But they highlight differences in mindset between the two groups.

Horses for courses.

But what had our Role Selection Board decided?

Much to my surprise, we'd all been judged, not only to have reached the course standard, but also as suitable to pass on to role-specific training. Not only that, but it seemed there were enough places available in all three roles for all 15 of us to find a niche. In the end, nine were selected to the fast jet stream, one to helicopters and five, including me, to the multi-engine stream.

Because our paths diverged shortly after this, I think I should record how everyone else progressed after Linton.

Of the nine that went into fast jet training, 5 failed to make the fast jet front line. Mike Burrows was re-streamed to helicopters – his first choice anyway, while Graham was forced to withdraw when he suffered a recurrence of his debilitating airsickness. He went on to become a Hercules pilot on the same squadron as me. The remaining three, ex-armourer, Dave H, ex-policeman, Keith, and my ex-apprentice friend, Steve, were sent to fly Canberras in the photographic reconnaissance role. After one tour, Dave H and Keith became multi-engine pilots and Steve Longley a flying instructor.

One of the four to reach the fast jet front line, Glyn, went to Jaguars, but served only a short time before moving via the Canberra to become a flying instructor and then a multi-engine pilot on VC-10 tankers.

So it could be said that only 3 out of the original 17 of us became fast jet pilots. Of these, Dave L went on to fly the Phantom and Hawk, Neal the Phantom, Hawk and Tornado F3 and John McBoyle the Jaguar and Tornado GR1.

All bar Steve Longley went on to become airline pilots.

Canadian, Dave B, went straight to helicopters from Linton and flew Chinooks for six years before becoming an instructor on the Bulldog and Jetstream; while Mike, having re-streamed from fast jet training, flew the Puma and Wessex. Both retired to become airline pilots.

Two of the five streamed multi-engine, Bawb and Dick Winterton, were chopped during their advanced training at RAF Finningly. Bawb went on to become an air traffic controller before leaving the RAF to become a chartered surveyor; and Dick became an education officer before retiring to work in a variety of training and policy jobs in the private and public sectors, both in the UK and overseas.

That left three of us to join the multi-engine front line. Laying the rest of my career aside for later volumes, Rich flew the Hercules on the same squadron as me before moving on to fly baby navigators around the UK in a Dominie, while Ian flew Victor tankers and then Tri-stars. Both went on to fly with the airlines.

Those who are still with me may have noticed that I'm the only pilot on my Course that stayed in the RAF for what could be termed a 'full career'. The remainder all left to join the airlines at one of the intermediate career break points, several, if not all, to ensure they stayed in the cockpit rather than having to sit behind a desk.

I chose not to follow them. Perhaps I lacked the courage, imagination or drive to jump ship and seek out new pastures, but I can honestly say that I never wanted to be an airline pilot. And luckily, most of the time, I found the desk jobs I had fascinating and fulfilling.

Again, horses for courses.

To say that I was relieved to still be in the reckoning after role selection would be an understatement. When the decision was announced, I tried to forget the daunting prospect of another 25 hours at Linton, including much more instrument flying, and focus on the fact that I'd kept alive the hope of achieving my childhood ambition of becoming a pilot in the Royal Air Force.

Chapter 18 – An Unexpected Break and a New Skill

On Friday the 1st August, I flew the first of the 25 sorties designed to prepare me for multi-engine training. A week later, I'd flown another five without any great dramas, even though three were devoted to instrument flying. And then came an unexpected break. The medics had decided to do something about my troublesome nose.

I still had the strong impression that beyond deciding that I shouldn't have passed the initial medical for aircrew, they were a bit stumped. The prime suspect for my problems was an allergen they'd failed to identify. And even if they had, because the side effects of most drugs make flying an aircraft a bad idea, the treatment may have barred me from an aircrew role.

Nevertheless, I think they'd decided they had to do something. So attention transferred to the structure of my nose.

Beneath the nasal linings on each side are three fins of bone called turbinates. Coated with mucous, they increase the surface area of the nasal cavities, making them more efficient at moistening and warming air passing through the nostrils, and at capturing dust and germs. The lower, inferior, turbinates are the largest and if they become inflamed they can block the nasal passages.

Although I was willing to accept that my inferior turbinates were the likely cause of my nose being constricted, I couldn't see how they caused my nose to start dripping in the first place. And I didn't like the sound of the proposed solution: surgery, in the form of a procedure known as a sub mucous diathermy.

Basically, this involved knocking me out with a general anaesthetic before putting hot wires beneath my nasal linings to cauterise – burn out - the troublesome turbinates, in the hope that when the wounds healed, my nasal passages would be wider and less likely to block.

After a week on the ground, I travelled to Princess Mary's RAF Hospital at my old alma mater, Halton. There, on Wednesday 20th August 1980, an Air Commodore King operated on me. I woke to nostrils packed with wadding designed to deal with the major post-operative complication – bleeding.

Immediately after the operation, I had no serious complications, but for the next couple of days I was subjected to one of my least favourite life experiences: nasal toilet. Without going into too much detail, it involved removing the wadding and cleaning out as much gunk as possible from my nose – although it often felt as if the various implements used were rooting around behind my eyes. An exquisite form of torture.

I returned to Linton on the Saturday with warnings not to take aspirin, bend down, lift heavy objects or take excessively warm baths. I also had to keep my nose moist with regular douches of a saline solution that would also help prevent infection.

In the longer term, the procedure has exacerbated some of the things to which we're all prone, such as dryness and crusting of the nose, especially in warmer climes and when subject to prolonged exposure to air conditioning, or in the run up to and aftermath of a cold. My nose also continues to drip more easily than most, which is more of an embarrassment than anything else.

I'd been granted two weeks' sick leave, and during the second Geraldine and I had a few days touring the Lake District.

We spent one night in a hotel in Windermere - £23 for dinner, bed and breakfast; and one in a guest house in Bowness, where we had a restaurant meal. Starters of corn on the cob and melon, main courses of curry and spaghetti Bolognese, two sweets, coffee and wine cost £10.65. We then had two nights in a guest house in Keswick for £25.70, which included a three course dinner for two on the first evening.

Although I returned to work the next Monday, I wasn't able to fly. I didn't know it at the time, but it would be two months before I could. In the interim, most of my time seems to have been spent hosting visits to the Station from organisations as varied as the scouts, a local amateur radio society and several schools.

Geraldine and I also hosted visits from family and friends, and went to York's Theatre Royal to see plays such as A Midsummer Night's Dream and The Importance of Being Earnest.

Once cleared to do so, I returned to the sporting arena, resuming playing volleyball for the Station. In mid September, I took part in a Battle of Britain parade in York, one of the last times I did any foot drill.

At the end of the month, I visited the RAF Central Medical Establishment in London, hoping to be cleared to fly. But they said I needed to go to the aviation medicine specialists at Farnborough for decompression tests. That visit happened a fortnight later and seemed to go well, but it was another two weeks before I regained my medical category, on the very day I should have been starting on the Jetstream at Finningley alongside my friends from 43 Course.

I know the medics have a duty of care, but I wasn't the first pilot to find out that once they get their hooks into you, it can take a long time to escape. For this reason, aircrew are notoriously reluctant to visit the doctor outside their compulsory annual medicals. I became the same.

With even the fast jet candidates on 43 Course nearing graduation, when I returned to flying on 28th October, it was as a member of 44 Course on 3 Squadron. They'd just passed the role selection point. It meant walking into a new crewroom and integrating with a new group of people.

Having been in the RAF for seven years, I'd had to do this several times before, albeit as an airman and tradesman rather than as an officer and pilot. But the process was remarkably similar. It usually involved a fair amount of banter and ribald humour in the crewroom, on the sports field and over a beer at cease work. However you did it though, you very quickly found yourself bonding with the individuals and becoming a part of the group, often in a matter of hours.

Such bonding is an important facet of military life, not always understood by civilians. After all, shortly after you arrive at a new unit, it may have to go to war, or at least some extreme activity in training for war.

One of the major elements of my first novel, Wings Over Summer, was the camaraderie between the pilots of a fictitious squadron fighting over southern England at the height of the Battle of Britain, young men who may have known one another for no more than a few weeks, days in some instances. I emphasised this in a one-page synopsis I read to a group of fellow writers, editors and agents at a literary event in London when I was seeking a route to publication.

One of the editors was disdainful. How on earth could a group of people become such close friends in a matter of weeks, let alone days? Surely friendship was something that grew over a period of months and years, presumably started while one was at university and then cemented over years of literary lunches and dinner parties.

They just didn't understand that you could become so bound to a group – a squadron – and its individuals that you'd be prepared to die for them shortly after having met them. It's a vital but natural process in military units, one that becomes even more pronounced in the white-hot cauldron of war.

I tried briefly to remonstrate, but quickly realised that the editor just didn't understand, and probably never would. Another editor joined in, saying there was far too much action in the book to make it believable. On this occasion, I kept to myself that it was based on the actual activity cycle at RAF Biggin Hill over those two weeks in 1940, and that, if anything, I'd probably underplayed the drama of the period.

It was at this event that I realised my quest for a mainstream publishing contract was probably doomed to failure. This was reinforced when an agent who loved the manuscript of Wings Over Summer said he wouldn't be able to sell it to the gatekeepers of the publishing industry, the editors, because most wouldn't be interested in the subject or have any understanding of it.

Having listened to the editors who'd savaged Wings Over Summer salivate over a book about proto-feminism in a 15th Century school in Manchester, I knew what he meant.

You can take this as a rant based on the bitterness of a self-published author, but the event brought home to me more vividly than anything else since I'd retired that some elements of military life are difficult for outsiders to understand, and that the process that forges unit cohesion and friendship is one of them.

It wasn't too difficult to form friendships with the members of 44 Course. They were a happy bunch, full of character. Unlike 43 Course, many seemed to have known one another long before Linton, having been members of one or other of the Scottish university air squadrons for several years.

Unfortunately, they'd also prove to be a tremendously unlucky course, losing four of their number to flying accidents over the years. I've mentioned them before, but have no hesitation in doing so again.

While still on the Linton course, Paul Bishop died in a Jet Provost Mk5a near Leuchars in Scotland in January 1981. Bill Edward died in a Canberra T17 in Gibraltar in August 1983; Byron Clew in a Harrier Mk3 near Goose Green in the Falklands in November of the same year; and Rob Burge, in a Bulldog near Belfast in October 1992.

Such deaths are a high cost for following the profession

of your dreams, and thankfully, over the ensuing years, the death toll in training has fallen dramatically. Long may that continue.

Like 43 Course, most of 44 Course were also following the fast jet route. Those destined for helicopters had already left for Shawbury, but I joined two other multi-engine students, both at about the same stage of the syllabus. The first was a tall, moustachioed Scot, Rob. Like me, he'd struggled to make it this far, and this helped us strike an immediate rapport. He was also married and Geraldine and I got on well with him and his wife.

The second was Bill Edward, the young man destined to die in a Canberra two years later. Another Scot, he too was joining 44 Course after an enforced break, in his case a period of airsickness de-sensitisation at Farnborough. I think the treatment had been only partially successful, which was why he was following the multi-engine rather than the fast jet route. He certainly didn't seem to struggle with his flying in the way that Rob and I did, and his natural effervescence and laughter were very welcome, helping to raise our spirits during the darker days.

I'm not sure how many hours a student would usually take to get back up to speed before resuming syllabus flying following a two month break, but when I joined 3 Squadron I took ten hours. Five of these were dedicated to instrument flying, which leads me to suspect that my problems in this area had continued.

I flew most of the refresher and syllabus exercises with just two instructors, Chris and Mike. And just like Croucho and all my other instructors, I know I tested their skill and patience on a regular basis. I owe them a great deal.

Once I resumed syllabus flying, a third of the 21 remaining exercises running up to the Final Handling Test, Exercise 117M, focused on instrument flying. The rest included more general handling and navigation, and the final discipline we were to learn at Linton: formation flying.

The arena in which formation flying is most often seen by the public is air shows, where it takes the form of an often very noisy aerial ballet. In my humble opinion, the greatest exponents of display formation flying in fast jets are the Red Arrows.

As a former RAF pilot, you'd have expected me to say nothing else, but I have additional reasons to be a fan. Over the years I was lucky enough, not only to have a hand in training some of their pilots, including the first female Red Arrows pilot, but also to see them working up over three seasons at RAF Scampton, the airfield they shared with the Central Flying School, and on which I'd served as a technician on Vulcans. And finally, in 2003, I was privileged to fly with Red 2 on a full display practice, a magical experience that opens Volume One of this memoir, Preparation For Flight.

Formation flying as practised by the Red Arrows may seem merely decorative, far removed from the hard edge of war. But there are good reasons for military pilots to master the skill.

For a start, large numbers of aircraft can take off from and land on a runway in much shorter time if they do so in formation rather than individually. And being able to land in formation becomes vital if aircraft are recovering to an airfield low on fuel, when there's insufficient time for them to queue up and land one after another. This is especially so in bad weather, when aircraft landing singly would have to be spaced minutes apart to descend through cloud.

Flying in formation is also a proven way of getting large numbers of aircraft to a target in order to hit it with maximum firepower in the shortest possible time. And it's a vital skill for successful air-to-air refuelling, something that extends the range and flexibility of air power immeasurably.

However, alongside low level flying, it's also a sport of kings.

To place your aircraft in close formation, to hold it there

as you manoeuvre surrounded by other aircraft, to see their bright colours superimposed on a shifting background of earth and sky, can be akin to a spiritual experience. Or at least that's how I came to view it later in my career. At Linton, I enjoyed the visuals, but found my two hours dual and one hour solo formation flying incredibly demanding.

The dual formations were of three aircraft, which was convenient as there were three to learn the new skill, me, Rob and Bill. Each of us would lead for about 20 minutes, providing a stable platform for the other two to practise joining up and slotting into one of two basic formation positions: echelon and line astern.

In echelon, I'd try to sit diagonally back from the lead JP, in line with and close to its tailplane. If Rob or Bill sat in a similar position to the other side, we'd form an arrowhead, known as a vic. Alternatively, we could both join in echelon to one side or the other of the leader, feathering back to the right or left. In war films, this is often the prelude to fighters peeling off one by one to dive on the enemy.

To maintain the echelon position, we were taught to use specific reference points. For instance, for the correct fore and aft positioning on the lead aircraft, I had to put myself abeam its tailplane. For the correct up and down position, I had to have an equal view of the upper and lower surface of its wing. We called this splitting the wing. And to ensure I was the right distance to the side, geometry came into play. I had to ease in until a line between my eyes and the lead aircraft's nose passed over its tip tank fuel filler cap - just visible midway along the top of the tank.

If I could hold these three reference points steady, I'd be sitting about 20 feet to the side of the leader's tailplane. Rob or Bill could be holding a similar position to the other side of the leader, or they could be outside me in echelon, making me the meat in the sandwich. Alternatively, I could be the third aircraft of the echelon, attempting to hold position on the other two.

We weren't quite as close to one another as the Red Arrows, but it was close enough when bouncing around at more than 200 miles per hour.

Of course, before we could learn to hold formation, we had to join up, always in echelon to one side or the other of the leader. If I was to join in echelon right, I had to accelerate toward the leader from behind and below and about two wingspans out. As I approached, I had to judge when to close the throttle so that I stabilised abeam his tailplane without racing past. With this achieved, I could ease up to his level, splitting the wing, then apply a little left bank to ease in until his tip tank filler cap was in line with his JP's nose.

Simple. Only of course it wasn't, or I didn't find it so.

Judging the correct distance below and to the side from which to approach the lead aircraft wasn't as easy as it sounds, and neither was achieving the correct overtake speed. Too slow and it could take an age to reach him, too fast and you risked streaking past, even with the throttle closed and the airbrakes out. And if you lost sight of him, you'd have to break away, re-locate him and start from scratch.

I tended to err on the side of safety. So although my join-ups were slower than the ideal, my instructor could be fairly confident I wasn't going to rip the wing off the aircraft in front as I rushed past.

The speed of join-ups and formation changes was one of the things I found most impressive about the Red Arrows. They rush up on the aircraft ahead at a tremendous rate, judging when to close the throttle and use the airbrakes to stop in exactly the right formation position. There is so little margin for error, and the nerve and skill they demonstrate in this and so many other areas is truly amazing.

Anyway, let's assume I managed to join and put myself in the correct echelon position to the side of the leader. To maintain it, I had constantly to scan between the reference points to pick up any movement, then use the throttle and/or control column to correct things.

For example, if I found myself falling behind the leader's tailplane, I had to nudge the throttle forward to accelerate until my JP was nearing the correct position, then ease the power back to sit abeam the tailplane again, ideally at exactly the right speed.

Similarly, if I found I could see more of the bottom of the leader's wing than the top, I had to squeeze back on the control column to ease up to the right position, hold it and trim. And if I found his tip tank filler cap had fallen behind his nose, I had to squeeze the control column to the left to ease closer until the filler cap was in line with the nose again, then gently ease off the bank to hold position.

In reality, it was very unlikely that only one of the parameters needed correcting at any one time. So to hold a stable position, control column and throttle were likely to be in constant motion. The ideal was to make adjustments before an observer had sensed any shift of position. Again, this is what the Red Arrows are able to do.

The same principles apply to the other basic formation position: line astern.

Beginning from vic, if I was No 2, that is, to the right of the leader, I had to slip back, slide across and move forward until I sat about 20 feet behind his jet pipe and slightly low, so that his jet wash tore through the air above my cockpit and tailplane, rather than into them. This was achieved by splitting his wing, so that I could see equal amounts of the top and bottom surfaces.

To ensure I was the correct distance back, geometry came into play again. I had to ease back or forward until the tips of the leader's tailplanes were in line with the colour change two thirds of the way along his wings. And because of the JP's offset seating, to sit directly behind him, I had to be able to see a smidge of the side of his tailplane.

Once I declared I was in a stable position, the aircraft to the left of the leader, No 3, could ease back, slide across and move forward to sit in line astern 20 feet behind me. In fact, he'd probably sit a little further back than that, because I was likely to be moving from side to side and drifting back and forward. And while keeping an eye on my oscillations, rather than following them, he'd be striving to take his fore and aft positioning cues from the leader.

It was very important to develop an awareness of closing speed, and when another JP looked too small or too big - especially too big!

And if things went wrong, you had to break from the formation, pulling up and turning away for three seconds, then reverse the turn, relocate the other two aircraft and rejoin them. There was much practice of this vital skill.

As we made our early attempts, anything less like the precision of the Red Arrows would be hard to imagine. But in our defence, as well as our inexperience, we had to come to grips with the many nuances and complications that make flying in formation challenging. Not least is the fact that the air in which it takes place can be subject to up and down drafts and pockets of turbulence that affect the formating aircraft, making them twitch, if not actually bounce around. And individual pilots may be of differing standards, or subject to their own twitches and lapses in concentration, leading to more unpredictable instability.

As I've already hinted, I found formation flying on the JP extremely difficult. There were several reasons beyond those mentioned above. First and foremost was my inability to relax. To be successful in formation, as in other areas of flying, you need to spot changes or errors early, and make small, measured, control inputs to correct them in a timely fashion. I was invariably too tense to do this.

Second, there was engine response. Piston engines react almost immediately to throttle movement, but the large, multi-stage, compressors and turbines rotating within jet engines have high inertia, meaning there's always a short delay before you decelerate on closing the throttle or accelerate on opening it. This was as true for the relatively small Viper jet engine fitted in the JP as it is for larger, more powerful, jet engines.

So you had to close the throttle a little earlier than you might think to slow down, and open it early to speed up. I'd struggled with this in other areas, notably instrument flying, but it seemed to make formation flying especially problematic. I tended to make larger-than-ideal throttle movements, and then over-correct, constantly hunting for the ideal power setting.

And thirdly, I tended to miss subtle shifts in the position of the reference features. And when I did notice a change, I'd jerk into action, over-correcting with the flying controls as well as the throttle, so that I never established a stable formation position. This made it difficult, not only for me, but for others trying to hang on to my wing or jet pipe.

And sometimes, my control movements would be so out of synch that I'd end up in a pilot-induced oscillation, yo-yoing between much too far from other aircraft in the formation and far too close, well inside the ideal 20-foot spacing. The solution was the same as for other pilot-induced oscillations, hold the controls steady and let things settle down. Not always ideal, or even sensible in a fast moving formation, when breaking away could be the only safe option.

Imagine sitting in a JP as mine arced toward you, not knowing whether I was going to recover in time, break away or crash into you. And then imagine being my instructor, having to decide whether to let me have my head for a while longer, or take control and avert disaster.

Many years later, I had to make such decisions myself when instructing on the Bulldog, but that only gives me more respect for those who bore the brunt of my inept formation flying.

All this was difficult enough when flying straight and level. But of course we also had to be able to hold formation while climbing, descending and turning.

Turning could be particularly interesting, or alarming, depending on your point of view.

If I was sitting to the right of the leader in echelon, when he turned left, I'd be on the outside of the turn, so I had to add power and raise the nose to climb as I also matched his angle of bank. Then, while seemingly hanging in the air above him as he raced over the background of earth and clouds, I had to scan the reference points and keep on top of things as normal.

And if he turned right, putting me on the inside of the turn, I had to take power off and descend a little while matching his angle of bank. Now, he'd be towering above me as I scanned the reference points and struggled to maintain position.

In theory, holding formation in a turn should be no different from doing so when flying straight and level. After all, aerodynamics still hold sway, and just because you're turning, you're not going to fall into the aircraft below, or have the aircraft above slice down into you.

But the mind is a funny thing, and formating in a turn does feel different, especially at high angles of bank. The tendency is to sit wider than the ideal to compensate. This is what I tended to do, not, I think, through fear, but just because I found it more difficult to hold position when turning. Once again though, this put me on the safe side of *not very good*.

And it was probably because I tended to join slowly and sit too far from other aircraft rather than too close that I was judged safe to fly solo after just two hours dual. But I never became truly proficient at formation flying while on the JP, a point that became abundantly clear during my ill-fated return to the type after my time on the Hercules. Another story for another time.

Despite all the foregoing, I always loved formation flying, even on the JP, when the sight of another red and white jet framed against a constantly changing background of blue sky, white cloud and multi-coloured earth never seemed anything other than magical.

And never was this feeling more intense than on my trip with the Red Arrows, when my mind was overwhelmed by the sight of those red Hawks hanging close as we swooped and soared among the clouds. But I also had many exciting and magical moments in the Hercules flying over the South Atlantic from Ascension Island, giving and taking fuel from another Hercules, a Victor or, most nostalgically for me, a Vulcan. To see these giants towering no more than 30 feet above you as you guzzled their fuel could be an awesome experience.

And blowing my own trumpet a bit, I eventually became proficient in formation on the Bulldog, and enjoyed many great moments teaching the skill to students and would-be instructors. And when I commanded the University of Wales Air Squadron, I even led a four-ship of Bulldogs to open the St Athan air show in 1992 and 1993.

Inevitably, our callsign was The Red Dragons!

Chapter 19 – The End of Basic

43 Course graduated from Linton on 21st November 1980, shortly after I'd resumed the multi-engine syllabus with 44 Course. Geraldine and I attended their graduation lunch. It was a bitter-sweet occasion.

I enjoyed the lunch, but they were my Course and I'd hoped to be graduating with them – and receiving the Groundschool Prize. Instead, I was remaining at Linton.

Not that there was anything wrong with 44 Course or 3 Squadron. But I'd been through the majority of the Linton syllabus, including the darker days of my training, with 43 Course. And although I tend not to remember the more upbeat occasions, there'd been many, including various squadron parties and even a treasure hunt. So it was with 43 Course that I identified. I still do. I'd been their first course leader and I've attended all their five-yearly reunions.

Most don't even remember that I didn't graduate with them.

At the end of November, I flew a low-level navigation exercise to the home of the C-130 Hercules force, RAF Lyneham in Wiltshire, with Mike, an ex C-130 pilot. After landing, I remember feeling very small as I taxied our JP past row after row of the camouflaged giants and parked in a far corner of Lyneham's enormous concrete pan.

We spent the night in the Officers' Mess, including several hours in the bar, where Mike introduced me to some of his old friends and comrades. I enjoyed their stories of life *down route* with Fat Albert, their affectionate nickname for the Hercules. But although they were very friendly, their bearing, language and expressions were so different from anything I'd experienced that I felt every inch the third former in the sixth form common room. It emphasised how far I had to go before I could become part of the front line.

The next morning we collected our JP and returned to Linton via a mixed profile navigation sortie. It had been only one night, but the visit seemed a defining moment. I had a new ambition, to become a C-130 pilot. After all, it seemed to offer the best opportunity for seeing the world, something I'd always wanted to do.

Foremost among the many obstacles barring my way were ten syllabus sorties, including an instrument rating and the Final Handling Test, both of which I had to pass before I could progress to my multi-engine training at Finningley, scheduled to start on 21st January 1981.

Inevitably, the winter weather built in delays, as did several repeated instrument flying sorties and the inevitable failure to attain an Amber Instrument Rating at the first attempt. It was the first of many instrument rating tests I'd take at least annually throughout my career. They were more demanding than the gradings I'd taken up until now, with greater accuracy expected.

When I eventually passed on December 21st, the Amber Rating allowed me to descend in cloud to 500 feet above the published minimum height for any instrument approach. Eventually, after gaining the requisite experience over the next several years, I'd hold a White, then a Green and finally a Master Green Rating, the latter two allowing me to descend on instruments to the published minimum height for a runway approach, usually 200 feet.

The delays meant any hope of completing the Linton Course before Christmas had evaporated. And it was just before Christmas that I discovered another unexpected problem.

Like most RAF stations at the time, Linton was short of married quarters. They wanted ours as soon as soon as I finished my course. But when I rang the Families' Office at Finningley to organise a quarter there, although they had one available, they said I couldn't have it.

The problem was that we were entitled to a married quarter only if I was posted to a station for more than six months. My multi-engine course was from 21st January to

10th July, a couple of weeks short of that threshold.

Neither Families' Office seemed willing to compromise. Not for the first or last time, I gained the strong impression that dependants were viewed as a nuisance rather than vital contributors to the morale of an efficient Service, or simply individuals that needed help. Linton wanted us out and Finningley wouldn't have us. That was that!

I'd be alright. I'd just move into the Mess at Finningley for the duration.

But what about Geraldine?

Aside from the fact that we hadn't long been married and didn't want to be separated, where was she meant to go for five and a half months, more if I picked up another short posting? If the separation had been for some important operational reason, fair enough, but this was just some petty bureaucratic wrinkle.

One option was for her to return to her parents. But that wasn't what we'd signed up to. Unfortunately, the only other option was to go to a holding facility in Nottinghamshire, where Geraldine would be expected to live until I was posted somewhere for more than 6 months. If it came to that, I knew she'd make the most of the situation, but I feared she'd feel very isolated; although, of course, Rob Chisholm's wife might also be stranded there. They were in the same boat.

Until this moment, the Station Commander at Linton had seemed a fairly distant figure, someone who stood up at met brief to give little pep talks or bollockings as he saw fit. But he was also a regular presence in the Mess, both at formal and informal events, such as the weekly happy hour on a Friday evening. At one of these in the run-up to Christmas, I mentioned the problem Rob and I faced.

To my surprise and delight, he ignited in anger.

'Ridiculous! Ludicrous!'

Geraldine seems to think his wife was present and that she helped to stoke the flames our few words had lit.

The upshot was an emphatic, 'Leave it with me!'

He was as good as his word. A few days later, Rob and I both received pieces of paper called posting notices. They informed us that we were posted to Finningley on 29th December, early enough to qualify for a married quarter. With the bureaucratic obstacle removed, we were both allocated one.

I like to think that I'd have found a similar champion if I'd still been a corporal. But I doubt it. Not that the Station Commander wouldn't have stuck up for an airman as readily as for an officer, but I'm not sure the airman would have had the chance to fire the old man up. Not for the first time, I was discovering that rank has its privileges – and perhaps more importantly, the power of a few well chosen words in the bar.

After Christmas, I had only five syllabus trips left at Linton before my Final Handling Test. But even at this late stage there was no guarantee I'd pass the course, while the winter weather meant even these few sorties could take weeks to complete. So we planned our move to Finningley for the third week of January.

Just as well, because I didn't fly the first outstanding exercise until Thursday 8th January 1981. Once I'd started though, it was all over in three days. A dual and a solo general handling trip on both the Thursday and Friday, then the pre-ride and the test itself on the Monday.

I'd like to say I remember the content of the Final Handling Test and my performance with laser-like clarity, but such was the tension of the occasion that I've forgotten many of the details. I know from my log book that the Test lasted one hour and five minutes and was flown with OC 3 Squadron. Compared to many testing officers at Linton, he was quite an avuncular figure, well practised at putting nervous students at ease. But with the many months of hard slog all leading to this point, I'd have found Father Christmas intimidating.

Allowing for the weather of the day, the squadron

commander would have asked me to plan a sortie including steep turns; a selection of stalls, probably including an incipient stall, a fully developed clean stall and a stall in the approach configuration; at least one full and one incipient spin; aerobatics, ideally linking at least the basic five manoeuvres – loop, barrel roll, stall turn, slow roll and roll off the top – into a sequence; and a normal, glide, low level and flapless circuit, either at the beginning of the sortie or at the end, depending on how busy the circuit at Linton was.

He could have decided to include any of the other disciplines I'd learnt over the last year or so, but he chose to test my greatest weakness. My log book indicates ten minutes of simulated instrument flying – under the hood – during which I completed a runway approach.

He'd also have engineered a number of emergencies to test my ability to cope with the unexpected. At least one would have been a major engine problem leading to a practice forced landing, perhaps at an airfield other than Linton.

Throughout, he'd have expected a good level of handling skill, sound airmanship and good decision making. Whether I produced the goods with any degree of consistency, I can't remember. But he saw enough to grant me a pass.

After 13½ months, including an enforced break for an operation and a change of course, I'd finally completed my basic flying training.

At times, it had seemed as if I lacked what it took to make it into the next week, never mind the end. And often, when the mental effort had seemed too much to sustain, I'd been tempted to call it a day. But the fear of throwing in the towel had always been greater than the fear of carrying on. So I continued, even if it meant making life a misery for myself, and those around me, especially Geraldine.

It would be wrong to say that I wasn't pleased to have passed a major milestone in the quest for my wings. But as with many such things, once it was behind me, basic flying training seemed less a giant leap that a tiny step. I was beginning to learn that in the military you couldn't afford to bask in the golden glow of any success. You had to focus on the next challenge.

For me, Rob and Bill, that was the Multi-Engine Training Squadron course at Finningley, universally known as METS. The course began in nine days time.

Chapter 20: METS

During those nine days, Geraldine and I completed the first of the 15 house moves we'd make over the next 25 years.

We'd really enjoyed our few months in the York area, falling in love with the City and its surrounding countryside, so much so that it remained top of the retirement list we kept in our heads for many years. Added to the general air of sadness at leaving was uncertainty about the future, not least what we'd make of Doncaster. We'd rarely heard anything good about the town, and some seemed very sniffy about it. But we've always tended to wait and make up our own minds, and Doncaster was a place with a bad press that we came to like.

We'd also loved 7 Linton Place, our first married quarter. And we knew we weren't going to be allocated anything as modern, light and airy at Finningley, if ever. It was, in fact, another 18 years before we lived in a comparable house, our 13th. But as it turned out, 10 Birch Avenue was particularly shabby.

A 1940s red brick, three bedroom, semi, it was set in the far corner of the far end of the quarters estate, in an area used to house the families of officers on the various courses at Finningley. It was what we've always called a back-to-front house. That is, its kitchen overlooked the road, while at the rear, the lounge looked out over a long garden that backed onto a wood, one of the few features we liked.

Small, metal-framed windows made the interior dark and claustrophobic, despite the psychedelic carpets and curtains. The kitchen was especially dated, with large, clunky, wooden cupboards and drawers coated with so many layers of white gloss that few of them closed. The kitchens of our next four quarters were exactly the same in this regard.

That said, much of this criticism is with the benefit of hindsight. If we hadn't been spoilt by 7 Linton Place, we'd have known no better. 10 Birch Avenue was twice as big as my parent's council house, it was fully furnished and the rent was very reasonable. We were glad to have it.

This was the first of many occasions when Geraldine left a job she enjoyed to follow me to another part of the country. And of course, she had no idea whether she'd find employment at the next location. The fact that prospective employers knew she and other Service wives might have to move on at short notice made it especially difficult. This time, it would be a maximum of six months, less if I failed the Finningley course.

At least we didn't have much in the way of possessions to move. All the Queen had to pay for was a small van to transport our newly-acquired washing machine and a few wedding presents we added to make the expense seem more worthwhile. Everything else fitted in our car. The move went well. After all, the distance was small – just 60 miles - and there was precious little for the removal firm to lose or break.

I don't have a receipt for this move, but the one from Finningley to Lyneham in Wiltshire seven months later was £161. It was one of the more unusual moves, our few possessions being loaded into a large removal van at Finningley, only to arrive at Lyneham crammed into a camper van, the top foot or so of our rubber plant sticking out of one of the rear windows!

Over the years, as we acquired our own furniture, appliances, home ware and ornaments, vans turned into lorries that had to be loaded one day and unloaded the next, and both the stress, and the expense to be borne by the defence budget grew accordingly. We could have added to the cost and saved ourselves hassle by having the removal firm do the packing and unpacking. But we learnt that they tended to do so reluctantly, and unsympathetically, heightening the risk of damage and loss. Partly for this reason, but also because we liked to prepare well before the day, we – that is, mainly Geraldine - spent weeks wrapping and packing things into boxes I'd scrounged from various Supply sections.

The moving day itself would be chaos, the removal men stamping about, grumbling at the weight of some of our boxes, and stopping for frequent cups of industrial strength tea. We soon learnt that the last thing to be packed and the first to be unpacked had to be the kettle. If the supply of tea had ever dried up, I dread to think of the consequences.

And yet, despite our best efforts to keep the movers onside, when we unpacked at the other end, we'd usually discover that a few things had been damaged in transit, while on a very few occasions something was missing. The damage and the losses usually involved items of practical or sentimental rather than monetary value, not enough to warrant a complaint, but enough to rankle.

Our measure of success for any move was to have everything unpacked and the car in the garage within 48 hours. And although some of our moves were real shockers, we never failed to make this benchmark.

We always loved moving to new areas, but the physical act of putting your life into a van and unpacking it at the other end became more and more of a chore, especially when children became part of the mix.

The Linton move was also the first time we'd had to clean a quarter ready for the march out.

I'd spent six years as an airman polishing and dusting my accommodation for regular bull nights, but I soon discovered that Geraldine's standards were at least as high as any NCO inspecting a property with white gloves. When not packing, she'd be cleaning. Over the years, the cleanliness of the various houses we vacated invariably raised favourable comment. But it took a great deal of sweat and elbow grease, especially to clean the cooker.

I once did a march out as a proxy for a friend who couldn't be there on the day. As we walked round his empty quarter, I became more and more embarrassed at the state of the place, dirt and dust everywhere. And when the Families' Officer opened the cooker, I found myself apologising for the grease and grime coating it. I also found it impossible to argue against a fine of £25, slapped on my friend for failing to bring his quarter up to an acceptable standard for march out.

I never did another proxy march out, but this one had highlighted that Geraldine could avoid hours of cleaning and scrubbing if we were prepared to put up with the disapproval of the Families' Officer and pay a £25 fine. It was tempting, but needless to say, such a solution wasn't for us. On all but two occasions when circumstances made it impossible and we turned to a cleaning firm, Geraldine continued to clean our quarters for March Outs.

It probably won't surprise you to hear that the stress of frequent moves and the poor quality of much MOD housing, especially since they were sold off to a private firm, are big negative factors for Service families. Successive governments promise to improve things, but nothing ever happens. As a result, many servicemen and women buy their own homes and contend with weekly separation. But many others choose to leave the Service.

On 21st January 1981, Rob, Bill Edward and I joined seven other members of No 16 Advanced Flying Training Course at No 6 Flying Training School, RAF Finningley.

Six were graduates of basic flying training at either Church Fenton or Cranwell. Five of these were totally new to me, having also done their officer training at Cranwell, but one, Darryl, had been one of the young school-leavers on my flight at Henlow. The seventh was Rich Hobbs. He'd somehow slipped onto a later multi-engine course than his fellow 43 Course members, Bawb and Dick Winterton.

Perhaps the delay had been lucky. Both Bawb and Dick had been chopped.

The aircraft on which the ten of us were to learn our new trade was the Handley Page Jetstream T1, a red and white military variant of a 16-seat regional airliner, powered by two turboprop engines - jet engines driving a propeller –

one on each wing. Before we could get anywhere near it though, we had to complete more than two months of groundschool.

The aim of ground studies at Linton had been to learn about the JP and the basics of military aviation. On METS, we'd learn about the technical aspects of the Jetstream and its systems, but also prepare for a future flying larger aircraft that could carry heavier loads and maybe passengers over longer distances, way beyond the borders of UK airspace.

Several subjects - Aerodynamics, Aircraft Systems, Aircraft Tech, Flight Instruments, Avionics, Aircraft Operations, Meteorology and Combat Survival – were familiar, but there were plenty of new ones, including Propellers, Aircraft Performance, Flight Planning and Aircraft Loading.

In the lessons and self study guides on propellers, we learnt about the design of these small aerofoils; their aerodynamics; the reasons for their different shapes; how and why the profile of the swiftly rotating blades changes from root to tip; and how they transform the power of the engine into forward motion.

We also studied the mechanical, electrical and hydraulic systems that, in the Jetstream, controlled the speed and pitch of the blades in answer to throttle movements. And finally, we learnt what could go wrong, what the consequences could be and what could be done about it; for instance, feathering the propeller blades – turning them face on to the airflow after an engine failure to reduce both further damage to the engine and drag.

And engine failures now included a whole new aerodynamic dimension.

When the single Viper engine buried within the fuselage of a JP failed, there were no forces to make the aircraft swing. But when an aircraft with engines offset from its centreline suffers an engine failure, an array of asymmetric forces come into play.

Let's say an engine on the left wing fails. That wing slows because of the loss of power and the drag of the propeller, while the right wing continues to surge forward. As a result, the aircraft swings to the left. But as the left wing slows it also produces less lift than the right wing, and the aircraft rolls to the left. If unchecked, this swing and roll can be self-perpetuating, leading to a spiral into the ground, if the aircraft doesn't break up before impact because of the forces at play.

A pilot who reacts quickly to counter both swing and roll with opposite rudder and aileron, while also feathering the relevant propeller and adjusting power on the live engine to aid control, might leave his passengers feeling no more than a slight jolt, their gin and tonics unspilt. But a tardy or incorrect response could lead to more than spilt gin, especially if the engine failure happens at low speed close to the ground, when the flying controls have less authority to counter the asymmetric forces.

Engine failures on multi-engine aircraft are one of those instances where the skill of the pilot can be the deciding factor between life and death.

Unfortunately, there can also be a point during take off where an engine failure is always going to be catastrophic, because the combination of asymmetric forces and poor control authority due to low speed make the aircraft uncontrollable. We were to learn more about this in the next subject, Aircraft Performance.

Aircraft Performance could be mind-boggling. In essence it's the study of how you can expect your aircraft to perform throughout its flight, from take off to landing, and what limitations different factors can impose.

Using the Jetstream as our template, we were taught how to work our way through sets of tables and graphs in a performance manual, overlaying factors such as aircraft weight and power with forecast atmospheric conditions to ascertain the expected climb profile, cruising height and speed, the descent profile, and how much fuel you'd expect to burn over the course of the flight.

Perhaps the most important calculations are those for take off and landing performance. Factors to be considered again include aircraft weight and power and forecast atmospheric conditions, but also runway length, surface - tarmac or grass - and whether it's wet or dry or covered in ice. If there's lying water, how much of the runway is covered and how deep is it? And if the runway is under snow, again, how deep is it, but also is it wet or dry snow, and is it sitting on ice?

Ploughing through yet more tables and graphs, we learnt to work out whether you could take off from and land safely on any particular runway; or, looking at it another way, what your maximum take off or landing weight should be for a given runway.

Separate publications gave details of the location and height of any natural or man-made obstacles within the take off and landing zones of specific runways, and again performance tables and graphs could be used to ensure that you could avoid them.

Other calculations for take off included the speeds for raising the aircraft nose – called rotate – and for getting airborne. But we also had to calculate other speeds: V1, the speed above which the take off would have to be continued if an engine failed because there'd be insufficient runway to brake to a halt; and V2, the take off safety speed, that is, the speed below which the aircraft would be unable to climb in the event of an engine failure.

As we'd learnt when studying asymmetric effects, there can be a significant time between V1 and V2, and if you have an engine failure during this period, you know you can neither stop in the available runway length, nor climb. You'll have to crash straight ahead wings level in an airman-like manner. Not a comfortable position to be in, especially in a large aircraft that may be carrying passengers in addition to you and the rest of your crew.

You'll be pleased to know that modern passenger aircraft are rarely if ever caught in this position, but it was – and probably still is - very much a reality of military aviation.

During Flight Planning lessons we learnt about the rules and procedures for different classes of airspace and different countries, but perhaps more importantly, where we could find such information from among a bewildering array of maps, charts and publications. One of the primary goals was to enable us to file a flight plan, a means of giving air traffic control authorities between departure and destination airfields information on an aircraft's proposed routing, heights and timings, as well as other things such as its fuel load and the number of persons on board.

Most military pilots spend the vast majority of their time avoiding having to file a flight plan. But some of the larger military aircraft spend much of their time flying in airspace for which one is mandatory. I'd have to submit a flight plan for several of my flights on the Jetstream, and submitting them would be one of my major duties as a co-pilot if I made it as far as a Hercules cockpit.

Aircraft Loading involves not only working out what can be loaded into an aircraft so as not to exceed the maximum weight dictated by aircraft performance calculations, but also where each item should be placed to ensure the aircraft stays within its centre of gravity limits, not only at the start of a flight, but also as fuel is burned from the various tanks.

On some aircraft, like the Jetstream, the pilot was responsible for load calculations, while on others, another crew member could be. On the Hercules, it was the loadmaster. But in every case, the captain, generally a pilot, has to check and sign the load sheet. As a result, we had to be on top of the subject.

But even when the aircraft load sheet was correct, there

was scope for mishaps.

During the Falklands War, I was the co-pilot on a Hercules that delivered a mixed load of passengers and freight to Ascension Island. It was one of many visits I made to this tiny volcanic outcrop five degrees south of the Equator midway between Africa and South America. It was the staging post for the War and so many aircraft were parked on its small pan of volcanic clinker that we were expected to depart as soon as our cargo was unloaded to make room for the next aircraft in a constant stream flying to the Island.

After landing, we left the movements staff to unload and disappeared briefly to update the weather and anything else that could affect our return journey. Walking out of the flight planning tent a few minutes later, we were flabbergasted to see our Hercules sitting back on its tail, the nosewheel and passenger steps several feet off the ground.

It seemed the passengers and much of their luggage had been taken out of the front door while a heavy pallet remained at the very rear of the aircraft waiting to be unloaded. As one of the final passengers disembarked, the aircraft tipped back.

In their haste to unload the passengers, the movements staff had failed to place a stabilising strut known as an Elephant's Foot under the rear ramp. We retreated to a safe distance to watch them scratch their heads. Eventually, through the simple expedient of throwing some bags back in through the front door and pulling down on the steps, they managed to right the aircraft long enough to fit the Elephants Foot and unload the offending pallet.

Luckily for all concerned, the damage to the rear loading ramp was only superficial and we were able to return to Lyneham via Dakar without further mishap.

In METS groundschool in 1981 and during my time on the Hercules, all the performance and loading calculations were taken from books, while the flight plans were all handwritten. I'm sure it's all done on computers now, and

260

probably has been for many years.

Many of our lessons were shared with a course of baby navigators. We lived next door to one on the married patch. Neither Geraldine nor I remember much about him, but Geraldine remembers his wife.

We often used to hear the sound of a vacuum cleaner, sometimes when we were lying in bed late at night or early in the morning. On a visit with some of the other wives for tea and cake, Geraldine discovered that the navigator's wife was indeed obsessively tidy. She positively hovered over them as they drank and ate, ready to deal with any spillages. And their cups and plates were whisked away as soon as they'd finished. They were hardly out of the door before they heard the sound of the Hoover sucking up any stray crumbs, real or imaginary.

She'd have had a fit if she'd seen our kitchen after our fellow course member, Rob, returned from a visit to Scotland with the gift of a haggis. We'd admitted it was a delicacy we'd never tasted – or cooked – and here it was. Geraldine steamed it, and I attacked it with a knife. At the first touch of the blade on its skin, it exploded, pebble dashing me and the kitchen in steaming hot offal.

So poorly decorated was our married quarter that I'm tempted to say it was an improvement, but it took us hours to track down and wipe up every last trace. We enjoyed the few bits that had stayed in the skin though!

Now Geraldine has always taken an interest in my work and supported me where she can. But our evening conversations have tended to be about the principles of what I was doing rather than the detail. Not the navigator's wife. She talked as if she was doing the course with her husband, and began dropping in regularly for cups of tea, pinning Geraldine against the fridge and bombarding her with acronyms and terms that meant nothing to her.

'He went for a div in the sim yesterday. They were meant to do an NDB to PAR, but they ended up doing a radar to ILS. And on the missed approach, they gave him *another* PD!'

Geraldine just used to nod and try and shuffle the woman out of the house when enough time had elapsed not to seem rude. She only escaped these visitations when she began working at a travel agent in Doncaster a few weeks after our arrival. She remained in the job until we moved on again seven months later.

A week after Bill, Rob and I began groundschool we heard that fellow 44 Course member, Paul Bishop, had been killed.

Approaching the end of their fast jet lead-in, the Course had detached from Linton to RAF Leuchars in Scotland to complete their outstanding navigation sorties. Paul, flying solo, had taken off and climbed through scattered cloud at 700 feet and into total cover at 1,000 feet. Shortly after transferring to a new radio frequency, he asked for a change of heading. Nothing more was heard from him and his JP dived from the cloud and smashed into the ground four miles from the airfield. It seems he'd become disorientated.

I'd known Paul only a few months, but I remember him as tall and youthful, with a ready smile, more studious and less boisterous than some of the others. A really nice young man.

A fortnight later, Rob and his wife, Bill Edward, Geraldine and I attended the 44 Course graduation lunch at Linton. It should have been a memorable occasion, but I struggle to recall any details. I suspect this is partly because 44 had never felt like my Course, but also because Paul's death made the lunch a subdued affair. Most, including Rob, had known him much longer than me.

Back at Finningley, even the familiar groundschool subjects had added dimensions. For instance, Meteorology had expanded to include more about the global climate and the weather phenomena we could expect to encounter in different parts of the world.

These included the Inter-Tropical Convergence Zone, a band of giant thunderstorms that straddle West Central Africa and the Atlantic just to the north of the Equator. In less than two years, I'd be threading through its spectacular pillars of cloud on numerous Hercules flights to and from Ascension Island. The lightning displays were never less than stunning, especially at night, but the storms themselves were downright dangerous and we often weaved hundreds of miles out of our way to avoid them.

Aircraft Tech and Systems lessons covered a lot of ground, not only because the Jetstream's airframe and engines were so much larger and more complex than the JP's, but also because there were simply more systems to learn about, such as pressurisation and de-icing.

Lessons included visits to the METS hangar to see the guts of the aircraft as they were being serviced, and I spent a fair amount of time chatting to the tradesmen. Inevitably we discussed the differences between working on the Jetstream and the Vulcan. For instance, back at Scampton, we could change one of the V bomber's massive Olympus engines and ground run it in about ten hours, whereas, although the Astazou engines fitted in the Jetstream were tiny in comparison, such was their complexity, and the added complications of harmonization with the propeller, that a similar operation could take four times as long.

The Jetstream also carried many more flight instruments and radios than the JP. They were much more modern and, supposedly, user friendly; for instance, the artificial horizons had become attitude indicators, with coloured displays that helped distinguish sky from ground. And the gyro compass had become a horizontal situation indicator, capable not only of displaying information from a wide range of radio beacons and airfield approach aids, but also of giving the pilot an indication of which direction to fly to intercept and follow their beams.

This should have made things easier, but I was to find

that there were so many switch and display options and combinations that I struggled to get to grips with them. Put simply, when the pressure was on, usually when instrument flying, if there was a choice of more than one switch or display, there was a fair chance I'd select the wrong one.

Combat Survival also took on a different flavour. The emphasis was now on how to co-operate and survive as a crew rather than as an individual. And dinghy drills also had an added dimension as we learnt to cope with nine-man rather than single-man dinghies.

Once again, I did well in my ground studies, but the groundschool prize would go to someone else, which, given my experience to date, seemed no bad thing.

Over the period in groundschool, the ten of us had melded into a tight-knit group, including one who seemed to set himself on fire with alarming regularity. Perhaps a little explanation is required.

As usual, a lot of our social interaction revolved around the bar. At the time one of the popular rituals for the more boisterous later in the night was to drink flaming Drambuie, a whisky-based liqueur, the fumes from which, when lit, burnt with a near-transparent blue flame. The trick was to throw the flaming liquid into your mouth without it or the glass touching your lips. The flames were extinguished as it slid down your throat.

But whenever he attempted the feat, Paddy invariably seemed to throw the flaming liqueur over his lips and moustache, setting both alight.

We came up with a new emergency drill: the face fire. As Paddy lifted his glass of flaming Drambuie, we'd stand round him with pints of beer, ready to dowse the flames, an intervention that proved necessary on more than one occasion.

The flying phase of the METS Course seemed to pass in a blur. My first flight was on 13th April and the last, Exercise 30, the Instrument Rating Test, less than 3 months later.

Many exercises were one hour thirty minutes in duration, and an instructor often took two students into the air, one sitting in the back and watching before moving forward to complete the same lesson. So we were often airborne for a whole morning or afternoon.

During the same timescale, I also completed 14 simulator sorties of similar length. During these, I learned procedures and techniques in preparation for key points in the flying syllabus, and how to deal with a range of complex emergencies more easily practised on the ground than in the air.

The instructors came from a range of multi-engine backgrounds, from transport to air-to-air refuelling to maritime patrol. On average, they seemed a little older than their JP counterparts, mainly in their mid to late 30s or early 40s.

The syllabus followed the same pattern as that at Linton, only with more crammed into every sortie. The early exercises especially whizzed past. After all, we'd already learnt the basics of effects of controls, straight and level, climbing, descending, turning and stalling. We just needed to hoist aboard the nuances of these things on the Jetstream.

The biggest difference of course was in complexity, and nowhere was this more apparent than in engine and propeller handling. Two engines meant many more knobs, levers and gauges than the JP, plus a wider range of potential problems and the complications of flying on one engine should the worst happen.

For understandable reasons, we only shut down a serviceable engine and re-started it in the air once. Sitting there watching the propeller of a perfectly good engine wind to a stop seemed a little surreal, but it had to be experienced, partly because it just wasn't the same doing it in the simulator. And in the air, it was a test of character as well as technique.

Otherwise, we spent a fair amount of time flying around with one engine throttled back, pretending it had failed.

This became more frequent as we moved into the circuit, when we had to prove we could land successfully in the event of an engine failure. Even the early exercises included plenty of circuit flying; for instance, on Exercise 4, my instructor and I completed 17 landings, with ten to 14 landings being common on later sorties.

Exercise 9 was the multi-engine equivalent of first solo, which meant flying in the left hand seat as aircraft captain, with one of your fellow students in the right hand seat as co-pilot.

My first experience of Exercise 9 was as co-pilot to Rich Hobbs, my old 43 Course colleague. It lasted one hour and Rich completed 11 landings. I remember no dramas. My own opportunity came just a day later on May 6th, when Bill Edward sat alongside me as I completed 13 landings during my first hour as captain of a multi-engine aircraft.

Again, as far as I can remember, there were no great dramas, with all of my landings being safe, if lacking in finesse. But it did give me a very real insight into a major difference between multi-crew and single seat flying: responsibility for other people's lives as well as your own.

The point was brought home with added force a week or so later when, on my second trip as captain, I did my best to kill myself and my co-pilot, Rich Hobbs. At a recent 43 Course reunion, Rich said he had no recollection of the event. Well that's as may be, but it's etched on my mind to this day, 37 years later.

As I close my eyes, I can see us at 50 feet on short finals to Runway 21 at Finningley. To our front right waiting at the holding point to enter the runway and take off is another red and white Jetstream, captained by Darryl, my erstwhile Henlow colleague. Whether there was much of a crosswind or any other factor to mitigate what happened next I'm not sure, but as we approach the runway, we begin to drift right toward the waiting Jetstream. I correct back to the centreline as I pass abeam him, too busy to wave. But as I close the throttle for the roundout, I begin to drift again.

While struggling to correct this, we drop onto the runway from far too high with a lot of sideways component. Surprisingly, we don't bounce, but do weave about a fair amount until I regain control and open the throttle for the next circuit.

I'd given the undercarriage and my brittle confidence a severe test.

We obviously survived to continue the sortie and the syllabus, and given Rich's indifference to the episode, perhaps I've over-played it. But one thing it did at the time was bring home the responsibility of having other people rely on your skill or, as in this case, lack of skill as a pilot. To kill yourself is one thing, to kill some other mother's son/daughter/husband/wife, quite another.

I flew another four Jetstream sorties as captain, and all passed without major incident as far as I can recall. The final one, Exercise 25, was flown with Rob. This must have been just before he was chopped and went off to train as a navigator. We'd both struggled at Linton, and with elements of the Jetstream course, but we'd done our best to support one another and it was sad to see him go.

The next time we met was on the clinker pan at Ascension during the Falklands War. Like most Victor aircrew at the time, he looked drawn and tired, closer to 45 than 25 years of age. It was the cumulative pressure of flying long sorties over the South Atlantic to refuel other aircraft, including the Vulcans that mounted the Black Buck raids on Port Stanley airfield. The Victors sometimes returned to Ascension on little more than fumes, having given as much fuel as they dared - and more - to other aircraft.

As the syllabus progressed, I coped with most things, and I continued to enjoy disciplines such as navigation, especially the one sortie we completed at low level; and formation flying, although I think only one syllabus sortie was devoted to this. I still couldn't afford to fly with a cold, but I suffered none of the extreme nasal symptoms that had plagued me on the JP – no excessively running or blocked nose. So perhaps I really was allergic to something in aircraft oxygen systems or masks.

But once again, instrument flying tested my skill and capacity to the limit. Compared to the JP, the Jetstream had more instruments of every sort to monitor, more radios and more complex calls to make, including increasingly long and complicated air traffic control clearances that had to be repeated back verbatim. There were also more navigation and approach aids to switch between and interpret and more switches, levers and controls to manipulate.

My log book reveals only one repeated sortie, Exercise 21, the Amber Instrument Rating test. It must have been a particularly sticky moment, but I know my performance on other instrument sorties was often below par. Most memorably, I persisted in failing to update the frequencies on my nav aids, leaving me to try and perform instrument approaches with the nav kit still dialled in to navigation and airways beacons I'd been using earlier in the sortie.

It was a sign of my limited capacity. Thankfully, I don't remember us having to recover from unusual positions on limited panel, and if we did, the set-ups were nowhere near as violent or extreme as on the JP. If they had been, I think I'd have been toast.

Despite all this, on 3rd July 1981, I passed the final flight on the syllabus, a combined test of my general handling and a White Procedural Instrument Rating, involving flight planning to join and fly along airways for a runway approach at a civilian airfield, followed by airfield and/or runway approaches at a military airfield or airfields. The flight lasted two hours 25 minutes and was the only instrument flying test I passed first time during my entire flying training.

This should have been the high spot of the course, but it wasn't. That honour went to our overseas trip to Berlin.

From 1949 to 1990, when Germany was reunited, Berlin, 100 miles from the West German border, became an enclave wholly surrounded by the Soviet-controlled state of East Germany. The city was divided into sectors, the Soviets controlling the eastern half, which became the capital of East Germany, the west controlled by France, the US and the UK. The two halves were generally referred to as East and West Berlin, especially after 1961, when the Soviets built a wall to fully enclose their sector and stop escapes to the West.

Berlin could be reached from the west only through a limited number of road, rail, water and air corridors. There were three air corridors which radiated out to West Germany from a central air traffic control zone with a radius of 20 miles around the centre of Berlin. The northern corridor led north-west toward Hamburg, the southern south-west toward Frankfurt and the central corridor westward to Hanover. Unarmed military aircraft of the three western powers and certain airlines had the right to use the corridors.

This was still the situation for my visit on 24th/25th June 1981.

The corridors and the zone around Berlin were controlled by the Berlin Air Safety Centre staffed by personnel from the four controlling nations, but the airspace outside the corridors was solely under East German, or in practice, Soviet control.

As we prepared for our flights in or out along the central corridor, the instructors ratcheted up the tension with tales of what would happen if we strayed outside the protected airspace. At best, they said, you'll be intercepted by Mig fighters and forced to land at an East German airfield. At worst, you'll be shot down. In either case, we could be the cause of a major international incident, if not a nuclear confrontation.

No pressure then!

As it turned out, I was to fly the return leg, so for the flight into West Berlin I sat back and watched a fellow course member fly through the corridor and land at RAF Gatow in the south-western district of Spandau. I'd never taken such a keen interest in someone else's navigation, or scanned the airspace around a Jetstream so meticulously. But we managed to pass along the corridor without a Mig appearing on our wing, a bit of a disappointment given the hype.

By this time, only eight of the ten that had started our METS Course remained, so in the end, four Jetstreams, each bearing two students and an instructor, sat on the pan at Gatow. We were to spend one night - I still have a Mess Bill for extra messing of two Deutschmarks 50 Pfennigs - and we were determined to see as much as we could in the time available.

Our instructors made it plain that we were on our own. We had the strong impression that they knew exactly where they were headed, and they didn't want either to babysit, or to have witnesses to whatever they had planned. So the eight of us set off to find the first on our list of things to see, the Berlin Wall at Checkpoint Charlie, the most famous crossing point into the East

To get there we had to use the West Berlin metro system, the U-Bahn. Even this seemed fraught with traps for the unwary. Chief among these was to find yourself inadvertently trundling into East Berlin on one of the two lines that still crossed under the Wall. It was made plain that nothing would please the Soviets more than to have eight young RAF officers to dangle over the battlements.

I'm pretty sure it would have been impossible for us to have ended up in this position without bypassing or ignoring a raft of checks and balances, but so successful had our instructors been in ramping up the potential for catastrophe, that when we bought our Umsteigers – tickets costing 1DM 50 – and set off, we checked the U-Bahn map every few seconds and viewed everyone around us as a potential spy.

All three occasions on which I've seen the Wall near Checkpoint Charlie have been powerful experiences in their own right. On the second occasion, I even passed through the Checkpoint and spent a morning in the East. But it's still this first visit that made the strongest impression.

It was partly because of the weather. Berlin was in the middle of a typical continental high pressure system. This meant soaring daytime temperatures, light winds and haze so thick it was akin to fog. In the late evening when we walked up the steps of a viewing platform to peer over the Wall, it was already feeling a little chilly, the sort of night on which men in homburgs and dark overcoats would be turning up their collars as they hid in the shadows lighting a cigarette.

Perhaps my mind has elaborated some of the details over the years, but the scene seemed no less sinister than any in a le Carré novel or film. Interrupted only by the enclosed strip of road and buildings that made up the Checkpoint itself, the Wall and its supporting paraphernalia stretched left and right into the haze. Beneath us were tens of yards of floodlit earth or raked sand – said to be mined – dotted with spiky tank obstacles, like the beaches of Normandy in 1944.

Beyond the sand, coiled barbed wire barriers ran parallel to the Wall in front of line after line of bullet-marked tenement blocks and warehouses. In the shadow of these, pairs of guards ambled up and down with rifles slung over their shoulders – ready to shoot not only civilian escapees, but also their partners if they tried to escape.

Every 100 yards or so were thick concrete pillars topped with observation posts like mini air traffic control towers. Each was tall enough to allow a view over the wall and contained a couple of guards. On cue, the two guards in the tower opposite our viewpoint each raised a pair of binoculars and peered at us.

I had to pinch myself. Having thought as I grew up in

Shropshire that I might never leave that county, here I was at one of the most iconic places on the planet. Over the years, I've been tremendously lucky to have had many more *pinch me* moments at various iconic locations, but this was the first. And rarely has any place had such a profound effect.

Even as I'd been preparing Vulcans to launch on Station exercises at Scampton, the Cold War had seemed a fairly distant, abstract, thing. But here, it came to life. The floodlights battling the haze added to the atmospherics, but the regime on the other side really did seem sinister, if not downright evil. After all, the whole set up was to keep the East Germans in, to stop them seeing or experiencing what was available to me in the west.

A regime that would put so much effort into achieving that end seemed capable of anything.

We walked around the wall toward the Brandenburg Gate, looking over into the East wherever we could. By the time we reached our objective, our spirits were dipping lower with every step. Since the fall of the Wall, the Brandenburg Gate has become a symbol of freedom. That evening, with its four horses drawing their chariot eastward into the gloom, it represented repression.

We needed something to cheer us up, and being young men, we set out for a meal, a drink and, given the City's reputation, a club. An hour or so later, having successfully achieved the first two objectives, we turned to the third. The trouble was we had no idea how to find the area in which we'd been told most clubs were situated.

Never mind, Darryl spoke German and he set about asking everyone we met... Well, we weren't quite sure what he was asking. Many of his victims seemed to have difficulty interpreting his words – but surely it would lead to a club sometime.

It did, but only because we bumped into a tout enticing people into one. It transpired that Darryl had been asking for *the place that men liked*, so we felt extremely lucky not to have ended up in a gay bar, not a good place for young RAF officers to be seen in that era, not least because the odds of someone adding notes to our dossiers seemed much greater than they did in York or Doncaster!

The club was called the Mon Cherie and its claim to fame was a bubble bath into which its mainly south-east Asian dancers would jump after cavorting on stage for a while. There was very little stripping in preparation for their dip, as they tended to be wearing little more than a g-string to start with.

Early on it became apparent that drinks were prohibitively expensive, and that audience participation was expected. The first didn't bother me, as I was flying the next day and had already drunk enough, but the second would have had me out of the door in a shot. Luckily however, there was a rowdy group of soldiers in front of us, and they proved only too keen to shed their clothes and jump into the bath with the dancers.

It was an educative experience for a Shropshire lad, but having achieved all we'd set out to do, I wasn't at all disappointed when we decided to call it a night, leaving the place to the Army.

The next morning, I flew out of Berlin along the central corridor without mishap, and we returned to Finningley.

Having said that 3rd July was not the highlight of my time at Finningley, it was a pretty good day - and night. A few hours after I'd passed my final test of the METS Course, Geraldine and I went to the Officers' Mess Summer Ball.

With the theme of European capital cities, it ran from 9pm, when the seafood bar opened, until 6am, when the champagne breakfast finished, although carriages – buses to the car park for those that had driven - were from 3am. I can't remember how much the Ball cost, but drinks, champagne included, were part of the deal.

I suspect Geraldine and I had a good night, tinged with sadness that we'd soon be leaving Doncaster, where she'd enjoyed her job and we'd had some good nights, usually including a visit to Toto's Pizza Restaurant.

My graduation was a week later.

Chapter 21 – Wings

On Thursday 10th July 1981, I dressed in my Number 1 uniform and stroked my hand over a tiny piece of Velcro sewn by Geraldine above the left breast pocket of the jacket. My brother Brian had driven my parents from Ludlow and they'd spent the night. They joined us for breakfast, and after taking some photographs in the garden, we set out for the graduation ceremony.

A short while later, I was sitting on a gold-framed upright chair with a red velvet seat cushion alongside the seven other surviving members of No 16 Advanced Flying Training Course. Each had a similar rectangle of black Velcro sewn above their left breast pocket, as did the 11 baby navigators - seven RAF and four Italian Air Force - sitting on the opposite side of an aisle. Our friends and relatives sat in the rows behind us, and VIP visitors, Station senior officers and their ladies occupied the rows ahead.

After a brief welcoming address from the Station Commander, we were each called onto a dais, where, to loud applause, Air Vice-Marshal F D G Clark CBE BA RAF, the Commandant of the National Defence College, presented us with our Royal Air Force flying badges.

The term flying badge is rarely used. It appears among the wording on a stamp in my log book and on a certificate marking my award, but otherwise the badges tend to be known as brevets, or in the case of pilots, simply *wings*.

Richly embroidered on a black background, my badge comprises a small circle of brown laurel leaves encasing the white letters, RAF, above which is a white queen's crown. Stretching out one and a half inches to either side of this central motif are shining white wings, embroidered with a feathered effect.

Other aircrew specialisations wear a flying badge with a single wing and the relevant letters within the laurel leaves, such as N for navigator or E for engineer. We'd soon be issued with several sets to be sewn on the left breast of all our uniforms and flying suits, but for now, we just had the one.

It wouldn't be long before I found a mirror in which to admire my new look. But until then, I could see the effect only by looking at the uniforms of my peers. Even so, it was a magical moment, the culmination of a long journey.

There'd been any number of reasons why it had seemed improbable while growing up in Ludlow, not least my abysmal academic performance following years of truancy. And although my attendance record and exam results improved dramatically when I joined the RAF as an apprentice, a commission had still seemed a remote prospect, while securing a place in flying training had been pretty much unthinkable.

And yet, even when I'd achieved both these objectives, the greatest challenge was still ahead of me.

The 15 months at Linton had tested me to my limits. I rarely seemed able to turn the hours of hard work on the ground into success in the air, and some days I was so wracked with nerves that I couldn't eat, while at night sleep eluded me as I went over and over what I needed to do when the sun came up.

The frustration at not being able to perform to the required standard had been mortifying. But as others fell by the wayside, somehow, I'd struggled on to the end, gaining the opportunity to have a crack at the next hurdle.

And although I don't remember the METS Course driving me so close to mental collapse, I know there were dark days when my performance was unacceptable and suspension seemed a foregone conclusion. But once again, I'd made it.

So as I walked off the dais, I could hardly believe it. At the age of 26¼, almost eight years after I'd joined, and two years since gaining my commission, I was a pilot in the Royal Air Force.

Whenever I perform the first of my three talks on my 32

years in the RAF, I hold up the wings presented by the air marshal that morning and try to explain their significance.

In essence, although my own journey through flying training had been more fraught than many, anyone wearing an RAF flying badge will have put in a prodigious amount of effort to win it. No pain no gain, they say. And on this measure, all our brevets are precious, priceless even.

My wings are certainly precious to me. I don't sleep with them under my pillow, but they are a prized possession, and the award of them is very much a high point in my life.

What few of the people watching that morning knew, and something we tried to put from our minds, was that if we failed to become combat ready on the aircraft types to which we'd been posted, the precious badges could be taken from us.

I certainly tried not to think about it as we tucked into the graduation lunch in the Officers' Mess. During the speeches, I smiled at the sight of an instructor on the other side of the wide table feeding my father glasses of port from a decanter he'd secreted under his chair. Just over a decade later, his daughter would be a student on the first University Air Squadron I commanded.

Sitting at that table among family and friends, I felt doubly lucky. I'd been role disposed to my chosen aircraft type, the Lockheed C-130, Hercules. Four others were also heading that way, including Rich Hobbs, Darryl and the incendiary Paddy.

If I could master the Hercules, another step up in size and complexity, I could fulfil another lifelong dream and travel the world.

Bill Edward had been the star of the Course and had secured a place on the Canberra, sometimes a stepping stone into a fast jet cockpit. This was Bill's hope, if his airsickness remained dormant. Sadly, his crash in Gibraltar meant he never had the chance to be considered worthy of the move.

The other three Course members were less happy. They were destined for what was seen as one of the least glamorous roles in the RAF, flying Victors. These large former V bombers were now used in the air-to-air refuelling role, spending long hours flying up and down the North Sea dispensing fuel to all-comers, and then landing back in Norfolk. Those that flew the Victor were known as Tanker Trash.

My friends couldn't know that in less than a year the Argentinean invasion of the Falkland Islands would erase that nickname - for a while at least – and the Victors would become arguably the most valuable asset in the RAF. Without them the Islands could not have been regained so swiftly, if at all.

And of course, I couldn't know that the Falklands invasion was to be the defining event of my time on the Hercules, but that's a story for the next volume of this memoir.

Epilogue

As you can imagine from the foregoing, I found coming to grips with the Hercules far from easy, but after an Operational Conversion full of incident and humour, I made it onto a front line squadron - just as the Falklands War began. As a result, much of the next few years was spent in the South Atlantic, but I also travelled much of the world, from Las Vegas in the western United States to Auckland in New Zealand and many points in between, including Ethiopia during the Band Aid period. Full of adventure, these three and a half years are the subject of the next volume of this memoir.

Author's Note

I originally planned to name all my instructors as a way of saying thank you for their efforts. But the response to early emails threw up some unease at my criticism of the flying training system. So reluctantly, because I felt the criticism had to remain, I changed the name of one instructor and used only the first names of all the rest bar Dingdong and Croucho, who gave their express permission. I think it's a shame, but I don't want to make anyone feel embarrassed or uncomfortable. If I've still caused such feelings, I apologise.

Once again, special thanks for the cover design go to Martin Butler. For their help with incidents and areas of detail and fact, my thanks go out to the members of 43 Course, and especially Bawb Alston and Keith Whittaker, and to Clive Crouch and John Dignan, two of our instructors. My heartfelt thanks go to an old RAF mate, Steve Phelps, who was particularly helpful in commenting on and correcting my drafts, as were the members of my writing group, The Tiny Writers of Penarth. Thanks also to anyone I've missed.

Future volumes of Shropshire Blue will follow me through flying C130s world-wide, including the South Atlantic during and after the Falklands War; several years as a flying instructor and instructor of instructors; calling in the flypast for the Queen Mother's 90th Birthday celebration on Horse Guards Parade and audiences in Buckingham Palace; command of two University Air Squadrons; responsibility for the careers of all the RAF's junior officer pilots; command of a Harrier detachment flying operations over the Balkans from southern Italy; two fascinating posts in the Ministry of Defence; commanding the Officers and Aircrew Selection Centre, the organisation that twice turned me away when I was a teenager; and my final post running the first stage of flying training for the British Army, Royal Navy and RAF, the dream job that turned sour and led to my early retirement.

You can find out more about me and my other books – Wings Over Summer, Wings Over Malta and Volume 1 of this memoir, Preparation For Flight - from my website: http://www.ronpowell.co.uk.

Glossary and Abbreviations

BFTS: Basic Flying Training School – in the late 1970s and early 80s: RAF Church Fenton, RAF Cranwell and RAF Linton-on-Ouse.

CFS: The Central Flying School, the oldest flying school in the world, responsible for the training of the RAF's instructors, and the examination of flying units to ensure they maintain the highest standards.

CO: Commanding Officer.

Echelon: Each successive wingman sits alongside the tailplane of the aircraft in front, so the formation flows diagonally from the leader.

Flaps: Surfaces on the inboard rear of each wing, lowered on final approach to increase lift, allowing a lower nose attitude and a higher stalling speed.

FRCs: Flight Reference Cards – cards bearing list of checks, such as the Starting, Take Off or Landing checks; and others to help with emergencies, such as Engine Fires or Forced Landings.

FSS: Flying Selection Squadron, the Chipmunk unit that aimed to winkle out those unlikely to succeed in basic flying training.

g: the effect of gravity on pilots in a manoeuvre, making them feel heavier or lighter. Pulling 3g makes them feel three times their normal weight and drags blood from their brains, while pushing to 0g makes them feel weightless.

Line Astern: a formation in which aircraft fly one behind the other, generally no more than a few yards apart.

METS: Multi-Engine Training Squadron.

OASC: Officers and Aircrew Selection Centre.

OCU: Operational Conversion Unit.

Pair: Formation of two aircraft flying a couple of hundred yards apart, each pilot looking primarily inward to quarter the airspace around the other.

PIO: Pilot Induced Oscillation – a problem caused by a pilot's actions being out of synch with his thoughts to produce ever-larger deviations from the required flight path, typically on landing or when flying in formation with another aircraft.

RLG: Relief Landing Ground – base, such as RAF Elvington, used to relieve some of the congestion at a major flying station

SOPs: Standard Operating Procedures.

UP: Unusual Position – when instrument flying, an extreme attitude on the artificial horizon that hasn't been selected by the pilot, necessitating a set recovery action.

Vic: a formation like an arrowhead with wingmen fanning back either side of the leader, each sitting to the side of the tailplane of the aircraft ahead.

Printed in Great Britain
by Amazon